CW01507232

J. E. LLOYD AN
OF WEL!

J. E. Lloyd and the Creation of Welsh History
Renewing a Nation's Past

Huw Pryce

UNIVERSITY OF WALES PRESS
CARDIFF
2011

www.uwp.co.uk

British Library CIP Data
A catalogue record for this book is available from the British Library.

ISBN 978-0-7083-2388-5 (hardback)
      978-0-7083-2389-2 (paperback)
e-ISBN 978-0-7083-2390-8

Typeset in Wales by Eira Fenn Gaunt, Cardiff
Printed by CPI Antony Rowe, Chippenham, Wiltshire

Er cof am fy nhad
Gwyndaf Pryce
1926–2008

I first encountered John Edward Lloyd's *A History of Wales from the Earliest Times to the Edwardian Conquest* in Cardiff Central Library during a vacation in the late 1970s when I read parts of the work after James Campbell, my tutor for several medieval papers at Oxford, had recommended it after I asked what I might read about medieval Welsh history. A few years later I acquired a copy of the third edition, bearing the inscription of the Irish scholar Séamus Pender, and over the last three decades or so this has been an indispensable companion in my own research on medieval Wales, especially during the years I was editing the documents of native Welsh rulers, when constant recourse to its precisely referenced political narrative finally put paid to the spine of volume II. While the present study is intended as an intellectual biography which tries to set Lloyd in the context of his own time, rather than to assess his strengths and weaknesses in the light of subsequent scholarship, the fact that he remains essential reading for historians of medieval Wales obviously helps to explain why I have written it. In addition, by the beginning of this century I had long been living under Lloyd's shadow at Bangor, where colleagues related stories they had heard about him and where he became a familiar face thanks to the portrait by Gertrude Coventry held by our department. However, while I had vaguely thought for some time that it would be interesting to look at Lloyd from a historiographical perspective, it was an invitation from Geraint H. Jenkins and the late Rees Davies to contribute an essay to a Festschrift for Kenneth O. Morgan and Ralph A. Griffiths that provided the catalyst which first turned this notion into something tangible, and I am grateful to the editors of that volume for having inadvertently set me on the fascinating path towards the completion of this book. Writing that essay made me aware of the wealth of material available in

Lloyd's papers deposited at Bangor, and led in turn to a successful application to the (now regrettably defunct) University of Wales Board of Celtic Studies to fund a research project on Lloyd; I wish to thank the board for its support as well as to its researcher Matthew Pearson for laying the foundations of this book by annotating and securing copies of relevant archival and printed material in Bangor, Aberystwyth, Manchester, Oxford and Reading in 2003–4.

In preparing and writing the book I have incurred numerous other debts which it is a pleasure to acknowledge, without of course wishing to implicate those named in its remaining defects. Mary Dodd, J. Gwynn Williams and the late Enid P. Roberts and Jean Ware generously shared their recollections of the elderly Lloyd, while Avril Jones of Hirnant near Pen-y-bont-fawr provided valuable guidance on his family roots in Montgomeryshire. Warm thanks are due to the archivists and librarians who have replied to queries and otherwise facilitated my research, including David Fitzpatrick, Aberystwyth University Archives (who kindly transcribed some of the college's council minutes); Alma Jenner, Mansfield College Library, Oxford; Andrew Mussell, Lincoln College Archives, Oxford; Alan Tadiello, Balliol College Library, Oxford; and Paul Webster, Liverpool Record Office. I am particularly grateful to Einion Thomas, Archivist and Welsh Librarian at Bangor University, for his support during my work on this project and, together with his colleagues Ann Hughes and Elen Wyn Simpson, for making the Bangor archives such a conducive environment for consulting Lloyd's papers and related materials. At Amgueddfa Cymru – National Museum Wales John Kenyon and Beth Thomas gave me access to a copy of the 1937 film introduced by Lloyd, and Nicholas Thornton discussed and showed me Evan Walters's portrait of Lloyd, painted in a some-what disconcerting 'double vision' style at the end of 1936. For bibliographical guidance and other help with sources I am grateful to Bill Jones, Euros Wyn Jones, Densil Morgan and Paul O'Leary. I have also benefited from discussion with Thomas Charles-Edwards, whose interest in the progress of this book is but the latest expression of long-standing friendship and support, and who gave me the opportunity to present a paper that eventually grew into chapter 2, as well as a version of chapter 7, to the Celtic Seminar at Jesus College, Oxford. Some of the latter chapter originated in my Sir Thomas

Parry-Williams Memorial Lecture at Aberystwyth (published as
Hynafiaid: Hil, Cenedl a Gwreiddiau'r Cymru (Aberystwyth, 2007)),
and various papers related to it were subsequently given at seminars
in Aberystwyth University, Bangor University, the University of
Leicester's Centre for English Local History and Trinity Hall History
Society, Cambridge. I am grateful for the invitations to speak on
those occasions as well as for the questions and comments of those
present.

Neil Evans has not only provided stimulus in discussions of
Welsh historiography over the past few years but generously read
a draft of the book, as has Peter Lambert: I am greatly indebted to
both of them for their valuable comments and suggestions. I was
able to devote the whole of the 2009–10 academic year to completing
the book thanks to an award by the Arts and Humanities Research
Council (AHRC) under its Research Leave Scheme, and I am very
grateful to the AHRC for its support, to Bangor University for grant-
ing me matching institutional leave and to departmental colleagues
who shouldered additional responsibilities during my absence. My
thanks go to the University of Wales Press, and especially to its
commissioning editor Sarah Lewis for responding so enthusiastically
and expeditiously to my original proposal and for her help thereafter, as well as to HEFCW for awarding a grant towards the costs
of publication. I am also grateful to Iestyn Pryce for the lively interest
he has taken in the progress of this project. My greatest debt is to
Nancy Edwards, who has not merely endured my preoccupation with
Lloyd over the past few years but, through her advice and encouragement in countless conversations, played an essential part in the book's
completion.

CONTENTS

ILLUSTRATIONS

1 Bryndifyr, Penygarnedd (August 2007).
Photo: Huw Pryce.

2 Isis Society, Lincoln College, Oxford, 1884.
Archives and Special Collections, Bangor University,
J. E. Lloyd Papers 356.

3 J. E. Lloyd acting in *Monsieur Hercules*, University
College of Wales, Aberystwyth, 20 December 1888.
Archives and Special Collections, Bangor University,
Bangor MS 21063.

4 The Senate of the University College of North Wales,
Bangor, 1 November 1923.
Archives and Special Collections, Bangor University,
Bangor MS 21079.

5 The Cambrian Archaeological Association,
Riversdale, Ramsey, Isle of Man, 4 September 1929.
Archives and Special Collections, Bangor University,
Bangor MS 21071.

6 Portrait of J. E. Lloyd by Elliott & Fry, 14 October 1932.
National Portrait Gallery, London.

Acad. Bd Minutes	University of Wales, *Minutes of the Academic Board*
Arch. Camb.	*Archaeologia Cambrensis*
BCS	Board of Celtic Studies
BU	Bangor University
Davies, 'Lloyd'	R. R. Davies, 'Lloyd, Sir John Edward (1861–1947)', *ODNB*
DNB	Leslie Stephen and Sidney Lee (eds), *Dictionary of National Biography*, 63 vols (London, 1885–1901)
DWB	John Edward Lloyd and R. T. Jenkins (eds), *The Dictionary of Welsh Biography down to 1940* (London, 1959)
Edwards, 'Lloyd'	J. G. Edwards, 'Sir John Edward Lloyd 1861–1947', *Proceedings of the British Academy*, 41 (1955), 319–27
Edwards, *Wales*	Owen M. Edwards, *Wales* (London, 1901)
EHR	*English Historical Review*
Ellis, *UCW*	E. L. Ellis, *The University College of Wales, Aberystwyth, 1872–1972* (Cardiff, 1972)
Evans, 'Men and mountains'	Neil Evans, '"When men and mountains meet": historians' explanations of the history of Wales, 1890–1970', *WHR*, 22 (2004–5), 222–51
HBC	Gweirydd ap Rhys, *Hanes y Brytaniaid a'r Cymry*, 2 vols (London, 1872–4)
History (1930)	J. E. Lloyd, *A History of Wales*, Benn's Sixpenny Library, no. 119 (London, 1930)

HW	John Edward Lloyd, *A History of Wales from the Earliest Times to the Edwardian Conquest*, 2 vols (London, 1911). *Note*: The addition of (1939) after the abbreviation denotes the third edition (London, 1939), in which the pagination of the preliminary matter (in roman numerals) differs from that of *HW*; however, the pagination of the main text is identical, as is the content apart from minor amendments and corrections.
Jenkins, 'Lloyd'	R. T. Jenkins, 'Syr John Edward Lloyd', *Y Llenor*, 25 (1947), 77–87
'List'	'A list of the published writings of the late Sir John Edward Lloyd', *Bulletin of the Board of Celtic Studies*, 12 (1946–8), 96–105
Lloyd, *Ail Lyfr*	John Edward Lloyd, *Ail Lyfr Hanes* (Caernarfon, 1896)
Lloyd, 'History of Wales'	J. E. Lloyd, 'History of Wales', *Transactions of the Royal National Eisteddfod of Wales, Liverpool, 1884* (Liverpool, 1885), pp. 341–408
Lloyd, *Llyfr Cyntaf*	John Edward Lloyd, *Llyfr Cyntaf Hanes* (Caernarfon, 1893)
Lloyd, *OG*	J. E. Lloyd, *Owen Glendower: Owen Glyn Dŵr* (Oxford, 1931)
Lloyd, *Trydydd Llyfr*	John Edward Lloyd, *Trydydd Llyfr Hanes (Hanes Cymru o 1066 hyd 1282.)* (Caernarfon, 1900)
LP	Archives and Special Collections, Bangor University, The Papers of Sir John Edward Lloyd
Morgan, *WBP*	Kenneth O. Morgan, *Wales in British Politics, 1868–1922* (paperback edn, Cardiff, 1991)
NLW	The National Library of Wales, Aberystwyth
NLWJ	*National Library of Wales Journal*

ODNB	H. C. G. Matthew and Brian Harrison (eds), *Oxford Dictionary of National Biography* (Oxford, 2004); references to online edition, accessed at *www. oxforddnb. com*
OU Cal.	*Oxford University Calendar*
Price, *Hanes Cymru*	Thomas Price (Carnhuanawc), *Hanes Cymru* (Crickhowell, 1842)
Stubbs, *CH*	William Stubbs, *The Constitutional History of England*, 3 vols (library edn, Oxford, 1880)
TCHS	*Transactions of the Caernarvonshire Historical Society*
THSC	*Transactions of the Honourable Society of Cymmrodorion*
TNA	The National Archives, London
TLWNS	*Transactions of the Liverpool Welsh National Society*
Tout Papers	The John Rylands University Library, Manchester, T. F. Tout Papers
UCNW Cal.	*University College of North Wales Calendar*
UCNW Mag.	*The Magazine of the University College of North Wales*
UCW Cal.	*The Calendar of the University College of Wales, Aberystwyth*
UCW Mag.	*The University College of Wales Magazine*
Univ. Ct Minutes	University of Wales, *Minutes of the University Court*
UW Cal.	*The Calendar of the University of Wales*
WHR	*The Welsh History Review*
Williams, *History of Wales*	Jane Williams, *A History of Wales* (London, 1869)
Williams, *UCNW*	J. Gwynn Williams, *The University College of North Wales: Foundations 1884–1927* (Cardiff, 1985)
Williams, *Univ. Wales*	J. Gwynn Williams, *The University of Wales 1893–1939* (Cardiff, 1997)

Introduction

In May 1940 John Edward Lloyd, now entering his eightieth year, received a letter from Robert Richards (1884–1954), Liberal Member of Parliament for Wrexham, congratulating him on his life's achievement:

> You and Lloyd George in two very different ways have managed to put Wales on the map. Every student in every country in Europe knows now that the History of Wales is not a mere echo of the History of England and in this matter I always couple your name in my mind with the name of Pirenne the Belgian Historian.[1]

While the flattering comparisons with David Lloyd George (1863–1945) and Henri Pirenne (1862–1935) reflected the sender's personal predilections, these sentiments encapsulate a view of Lloyd as a seminal historian of Wales that was widely held during his lifetime and has continued to hold sway ever since.[2] This book concurs with that view, and starts from the premise that Lloyd was a key figure in the writing of Welsh history whose work merits serious attention. However, it differs from previous assessments by exploring Lloyd's life and work in greater depth than before in order to try to offer a richer and more complex understanding of their significance. This is not to claim that its coverage is comprehensive: readers seeking detailed discussion, say, of Lloyd's religious activities and ideas or of his duties as registrar at Bangor will be disappointed. Rather, it concentrates mainly on the interaction of two related but by no means identical impulses, both implicit in the passage just quoted – namely, attempts to promote and legitimize, on the one hand, a distinctive Welsh identity and, on the other, the specific mode of inquiry into the past constituted by the scholarly discipline of 'scientific' history. Accordingly, a central objective of the present study is to elucidate why and especially how Lloyd sought to establish the history of Wales as an academic subject in its own right. (Thus it should be stressed at the outset that it does not seek to assess how far his interpretations were correct: my concern is to situate Lloyd in his own time and intellectual milieu.[3])

In order to answer these questions the book adopts a twofold approach designed to set Lloyd's work in its multiple contexts. Part One provides an account of his life, with particular emphasis on his upbringing, education and subsequent career as a historian, viewed against the background both of efforts to give expression to Welsh nationhood through educational institutions and of wider developments in the professionalization of historical scholarship in Britain. In Part Two the focus shifts from the biographical to the thematic and examines why Lloyd privileged the early and medieval Welsh past and how he depicted this in his most important work, *A History of Wales from the Earliest Times to the Edwardian Conquest*, first published in 1911. These chapters investigate key themes in Lloyd's interpretation with reference not only to previous accounts of Welsh history but also to the broader intellectual and scholarly context of his own time. Finally, the conclusion assesses Lloyd's significance in the light of the preceding discussion and considers how justified he was in believing that he had 'created Welsh history'.[4]

The suggestion that he was the Welsh Pirenne invites us to locate Lloyd in a European context. Although a comprehensive comparison with other European historians of his time lies beyond the scope of the present study, a brief comparison with Pirenne will serve to point up some general considerations that inform the following discussion. While his written output was considerable, Lloyd's reputation rested primarily on one great work: a two-volume history of his native land down to the late thirteenth century. By contrast,

Pirenne was far more prolific and his range and influence were much greater. His history of Belgium (1899–1932) occupied seven volumes and extended from ancient times to 1914; besides that, he produced not only monographs and critical editions of sources relating to various aspects of Belgian history but also major studies of medieval European social and economic history, and held a dominant position in the historical profession that was recognized well beyond his own country, a status reflected in his presiding over the International Congress of Historical Sciences at Brussels which Lloyd attended in 1923.[5] Yet, if the Welsh historian seems to suffer by comparison with his Belgian contemporary, the contrasts between them also help to pinpoint factors crucial to appreciating the former's significance. For example, Pirenne's achievement owed much to opportunities not available to Lloyd in late nineteenth-century Britain, notably professional historical training, focused on rigorous criticism of primary sources, first at the Belgian university of Liège, then in Paris, Leipzig and Berlin.[6] This meant that, from his student years onwards (1879–85), Pirenne belonged to a community of western European historians steeped in canons of historical scholarship disseminated through much of continental Europe (and extending also to the United States), thanks in large measure to the influence of Leopold von Ranke's seminar in Berlin.

At the same time, though, this community was by no means uniformly committed to the political history of the nation-state favoured by Ranke and, more particularly, his disciples. Indeed, Pirenne was drawn to a dissident from this paradigm, Karl Lamprecht (1856–1915), whose history of Germany assimilated aspects of the social sciences and focused on society and economy, an approach that provided Pirenne with a vital unifying principle for his history of Belgium as 'a "microcosm" of western Europe', a commercial crossroads where both German and Latin culture converged and different ethnic groups coexisted – a principle very different from the emphasis on a single ethnicity favoured by Lloyd (as well as by both previous and subsequent Belgian historians).[7] These differences of approach reflected the differing historical experiences of the two countries in question. Pirenne's 'Belgian people' transcended the deep-rooted divisions between Flemish and French speakers, its history culminating in the independent kingdom established by revolution in 1830, whereas, despite the hegemonic ambitions of some of its medieval princes, Wales had never achieved statehood coterminous with its geographical borders and had been united with England since the sixteenth century; hence the 'Welsh people' of Lloyd's narrative was defined above all in terms of a common ethnic identity. It should be added, though, that Pirenne's vision of a unitary nation provoked a reaction that led in turn to competing interpretations of Belgian national history designed to legitimize the respective identities of its two main ethnic groups, the Flamingants and Walloons.[8] Nor was Belgium unique in witnessing the construction of alternative national histories along cultural and ethnic fault lines; the same was also true, for example, of Ireland, Scotland, Bohemia and Finland.[9] On the other hand, in writing the history of Wales Lloyd was unencumbered by such alternatives: he inherited – and promoted – a historiographical tradition united in its focus on only one ethnic group, the Welsh people.

These contrasts in turn illustrate a more general point: that, while the writing of national history was a widespread phenomenon with many common characteristics, its precise character varied according both to the specific historical experience of each nation, including its sense of national identity, and to the intellectual and academic formation of its historians.[10] Comparison can help to achieve a balance between the general and the particular by identifying questions – about, say, historical training or ideas of nationhood – which, because they are widely applicable, may be particularly illuminating in assessing the significance of individual cases. Viewed in a European perspective, then, J. E. Lloyd is one of many variations on a common historiographical theme. Yet, to change metaphors, the threads he wove into this highly variegated pattern were coloured by very specific contexts that require close attention in any attempt to appraise his contribution as a historian.

Many early reviewers highlighted two aspects of the *History*: its roots in a renewed sense of Welsh nationality in the late nineteenth and early twentieth centuries and its 'scientific' – that is, critical and impartial – approach.[11] The latter aspect is discussed in chapter 6. However, the assessment of the work as 'an abiding expression of an awakened national consciousness' calls for some preliminary comment, as it forms an essential backdrop both to Lloyd's life and to the kind of history he wrote.[12] As the Swiss Celtic scholar Rudolf Thurneysen perceptively observed, a new sense of Welsh nationality emerged in the late nineteenth century as the result of a twofold process, namely the democratization of the Church through the growth of protestant Nonconformity coupled with a wider democratization of society, which created the largely Welsh-speaking 'people of Wales'.[13] These changes occurred in a context of massive demographic growth fuelled by rapid industrialization and, consequently, were most apparent in the industrial towns and ports of the south: over the fifty years between Lloyd's birth in 1861 and the publication of his *History* the population of Wales almost doubled from nearly 1,300,000 to just over 2,400,000.[14] However, the 'people of Wales' was an ideological construct fashioned in the mid-nineteenth century by Nonconformist leaders seeking to challenge the dominance of a largely anglicized, Anglican landed elite and secure recognition of Wales as a distinctive nation rather than as merely a geographical extension of the neighbouring world power of England. A major catalyst was the furious and widespread reaction, promoted through the columns of a vigorous Welsh-language periodical press, to a government report on the state of Welsh education in 1847 which castigated the Welsh as not only ignorant but immoral, and blamed their perceived faults on two key markers of their national identity: the Welsh language and Nonconformist religion.[15] Popularly condemned as *Brad y Llyfrau Gleision* ('The Treachery of the Blue Books'), the report provided a glaring source of grievance which Welsh Nonconformist leaders, in particular, were able to seize upon over the following two decades to mobilize Welsh opinion in support of a reforming agenda designed to secure recognition of Wales's particular needs, and thus contributed significantly to the growing alliance between Welsh Nonconformity and the Liberal Party. However, despite the formation of short-lived home-rule movements within Welsh Liberalism (1886–96), 'the supreme object of these Welsh national leaders was essentially equality within the United Kingdom and an expanding empire, not severance from it'.[16] Indeed, the imperial dimension was celebrated as a source of national pride, and even intrudes onto the pages of Lloyd's *History*, which describes the uplands of Glamorgan as 'now among the busiest seats of industry in the Empire', in contrast to their pastoral simplicity in the early Middle Ages.[17] The 'national awakening' promoted by Welsh Nonconformist Liberals thus concentrated on achieving improvements in education, culture and religion, priorities symbolized by the establishment of a new system of intermediate or secondary schools (1889), a national university (1893), a national library and national museum (both 1907) and the disestablishment of the Church of England (1920).[18]

At the same time, though, reaction to the Blue Books controversy exposed contradictory tendencies that continued to resonate into Lloyd's day.[19] The report's declaration that the Welshman suffered because 'his language keeps him under the hatches' may have provoked much indignation, but during the 1850s and 1860s the assumption that English was the language of progress found increasing favour among a Welsh people eager to confute their detractors and get on in the world by parading their credentials as paragons of Victorian respectability.[20] Two decades after the report's appearance this assumption received weighty intellectual endorsement from Matthew Arnold's lectures 'On the study of Celtic literature', delivered at Oxford in 1865–6 and strongly influenced by the Celticism of Ernest Renan.[21] However, the lectures could support different interpretations. On the one hand, Arnold declared that the advance of English was 'a necessity of . . . modern civilisation', and looked forward to the rapid disappearance of the Welsh language 'as an instrument of the practical, political, social life of Wales';[22] at the same time, his racial stereotyping of the Welsh as imaginative but impractical and sentimental seemed to disqualify them from full participation in the modern world unless guided by their more level-headed neighbours in England, whom they should in turn help to civilize by ceasing to compose literature in their native language and instead expressing their genius in English. Conversely, though, Arnold was markedly more sympathetic than the education commissioners towards Wales and its native language. Thus he commended the medieval literature of Wales as a refreshing antidote to the alleged philistinism of England, claimed that the greatness of English literature owed much to its infusion with a Celtic spirit and urged that Oxford University should establish a chair of Celtic; this last prescription was followed in 1877 and enhanced the prestige of Celtic studies, including Welsh language and literature. One result was that many Welsh intellectuals found in Arnold an authoritative affirmation of their culture and variously assimilated his ideas to their patriotic aims: a good illustration of how significant elements in Welsh 'national thought' had English parentage.[23]

Arnold's book famously begins with his recollection of how, on a visit to the National Eisteddfod at the coastal resort of Llandudno in 1864, he had turned his gaze westwards towards 'Wales, where the past still lives . . . and where the people, the genuine people, still knows this past . . . while, alas, the prosperous Saxon . . . has long ago forgotten his'.[24] As we shall see, Lloyd, who bought a copy of Arnold's lectures while a student, agreed that a defining characteristic of the Welsh people was its keen sense of the past.[25] True, the contrast with England is misleading; indeed, engagement with the past arguably intensified not only there but elsewhere in nineteenth- and early twentieth-century Europe in response to economic, social and political changes that were unprecedented in their scale and rapidity.[26] However, it is clear that the Welsh displayed considerable interest and pride in their past in the nineteenth century – quite possibly in part because they, too, were catapulted into modernity as a result of massive industrial and demographic growth, an experience mediated for many through a sharpened awareness of cultural difference. After all, such was the popularity of 'Hen Wlad fy Nhadau' ('The Old Land of My Fathers'), with its praise of past heroes and hopes for 'the old language', that the song rapidly achieved the status of a national anthem over the three decades from its composition in 1856.[27] The publication in the periodical press and elsewhere of historical romances, ultimately inspired by Walter Scott, together with poems, plays and other accounts of Welsh heroes and tales drawn from folklore confirm this fascination with the Welsh past and also reflect a concern that it was not sufficiently well known compared with that of England, which dominated the history taught in Welsh schools.[28] This concern prompted Lloyd's contemporary O. M. Edwards (1858– 1920) to give considerable coverage to Welsh history in the periodicals he established from the 1890s onwards as part of a wider project of Welsh cultural renewal.[29] Edwards drew on and strongly promoted a view of the Welsh past that sought to connect the Nonconformist 'people of Wales' with both its own religious tradition and a more remote history; hence a celebration, on the one hand, of leading figures of Protestantism and Nonconformity, not least through memoirs of individual ministers, and, on the other, of early saints and medieval princes.[30]

There were also attempts to sustain an interest in the Welsh past through more substantial works of historical writing. Several new histories appeared in the nineteenth century, including two in Welsh written, respectively, by Thomas Price (Carnhuanawc) (1842) and R. J. Pryse (Gweirydd ap Rhys) (1869–72). Broadly speaking, these histories largely continued to follow trajectories set in the early modern period. The work with the most durable influence was David Powel's *Historie of Cambria* (1584), which continued to be published in various editions until 1832. Drawing extensively on the medieval Welsh chronicles, this focused mainly on the period down to Edward I's conquest of Wales in 1282–4.[31] Another strand consisted of works presenting legendary origins for the Welsh that starred ancient Britons, druids and other distant ancestors. Its prime representative was Theophilus Evans's *Drych y Prif Oesoedd* ('A Mirror of the First Ages'), first published in 1716, which endowed the Welsh with biblical origins by tracing their ancestry back to Gomer, son of Japhet. This ran into twenty editions by 1900 and was the most popular history book in Victorian Wales, tapping into a thirst for consoling visions of past greatness which also lapped up further Celticist brews from the Romantic period, notwithstanding the critical voices raised in some quarters.[32]

By the time J. E. Lloyd began to compose his *History of Wales* at the beginning of the twentieth century those voices had become more numerous and voluble, being epitomized by John Rhys and David Brynmor-Jones in their volume *The Welsh People* (1900). The following year O. M. Edwards published a popular account of Welsh history, which likewise adopted a critical stance with respect to legendary origins and also marked a fresh departure in terms of its chronological coverage.[33] Lloyd participated, then, in wider attempts to provide more critical narratives of the Welsh past, consonant with notions of an 'enlightened' Welsh nation promoted by patriotic scholars and intellectuals, attempts necessarily defined in relation to previous interpretations, which therefore form an important backdrop to the history he set out to create.[34] However, essential though it is to locate Lloyd in the twin contexts of national revival and 'scientific' scholarship, his work as a historian was also, of course, the product of an individual life – a life that began, not in Wales, but in mid-Victorian Liverpool.

PART ONE

A HISTORIAN'S LIFE

1

Welsh Liverpool, 1861–1877

The earliest surviving history written by J. E. Lloyd focused not on the early and medieval Welsh past but on his own life as a member of an ethnic minority in Victorian Liverpool, then a major European seaport and commercial hub of the British Empire. That, at least, is one way of viewing the diary entries he made throughout 1876 and the early months of 1877. Although these were not explicitly presented as history or even as autobiography, the 14-year-old Lloyd embarked on the enterprise with an eye to the future, prefacing his first diary with the declaration:

> To keep a daily account of all that takes place in one's circle of life, is, if done carefully, not only a very useful and beneficial way of spending one's leisure, but also extremely valuable for future reference and instruction. Moreover many journals have been of public utility, and although it would be extreme audacity for me to suppose that my humble efforts should be so honoured, yet I cannot but hope that <u>some</u> good will accrue to myself and others, from them. This then is my Apology.[1]

The persona he chose to reveal in the following entries throws vivid light on the world Lloyd inhabited in his early years, and thus on the key question of how his upbringing helped to forge the convictions and intellectual capacity that underpinned the decision, by his early twenties, to be a historian of Wales. That world was dominated by a middle class which, though clearly a product of its English urban environment, had a distinctive cultural identity sustained above all by the institutions and values of Welsh Nonconformity. Indeed, this Nonconformist culture not only encouraged the self-reflection evident in the diaries but also elicited Lloyd's first known historical work in the strict sense, and also his first work in the Welsh language, namely a competitive essay on ten famous Welshmen which ranged chronologically from the Puritan John Penry (1563–93) to the sculptor John Gibson (1790–1866).[2] An understanding of this bicultural background is crucial, then, to any assessment of the young Lloyd's opportunities, experience and outlook before he commenced his studies at the University College of Wales, Aberystwyth in October 1877.

By the time Lloyd was born in Liverpool on 5 May 1861, the town had over 440,000 inhabitants, among them a substantial minority of migrants, especially from Ireland but also from Scotland and Wales. His parents, Edward Lloyd (1837–1917) and Margaret Lloyd (née Jones; 1834–1921), had married in Chester Street Wesleyan Methodist chapel on 6 August 1860, shortly after their arrival in Liverpool from northern Montgomeryshire, where their families had deep roots and, indeed, were related, as we shall see.[3] This was but one instance of a continuing influx from Wales whose scale appears to have been fairly constant throughout the second half of the nineteenth century, as about 20,000 Welsh-born people are recorded in Liverpool for each decade from 1851 (when they accounted for about 5.4 per cent of the borough's population). Moreover, this core was augmented by those, like Lloyd himself, who were born in the town to Welsh parents and brought up to speak Welsh and participate in Welsh religious and cultural activities: by 1900, this wider Welsh community may have comprised as many as 70,000 individuals (indeed, the city's lord mayor claimed it was as high as 100,000).[4] Though socially and occupationally diverse, the Liverpool Welsh included a substantial middle-class component, involved especially in the building trades but also in timber yards, cotton warehouses and other retailing.[5]

Edward Lloyd conformed to this pattern, and his position in Liverpool illustrates how both previous occupational experience and kinship ties helped to determine the pattern of migration.[6] He was brought up by his paternal grandmother on her remote hillside farm of Tynyfedw in the Hirnant valley near Pen-y-bont-fawr in Montgomeryshire, and retained a lifelong liking for the countryside and agricultural pursuits. He evidently received some schooling, and this helped to prepare him for the world of business, which he entered in the mid-1850s when he began work as an apprentice at London House, a general store in Llanfyllin, the nearest market town, situated some 6 miles south-east of his home, an establishment founded by the brothers Edward, John and Thomas Jones (although John soon returned to set up his own business in Liverpool, where he and Thomas had previously been apprentices to cloth and linen retailers). Significantly, the brothers were related to Edward Lloyd, being grandsons of his great-grandfather, Edward Lloyd of Pen-ygarnedd Fach (1754–1825). Moreover, their sister Margaret Jones kept house for them, and quite possibly it was while working in Llanfyllin that Edward Lloyd first became acquainted with his future wife; such a combination of commercial and familial connections often paved the way for marriages at this period.[7] Eventually, he followed the example of her brother John Jones and sought new opportunities in England. After a brief spell in Manchester, Edward Lloyd became an apprentice in a draper's shop in Berry Street, Liverpool, before establishing his own linen draper's shop in 1860 about half a mile away in his home at 184 Falkner Street, a business that continued until the Second World War.[8]

The rapid commercial growth from *c*.1850 to the early 1870s made this a propitious time for such an enterprise, and the Lloyd family – expanded by the birth of John Edward's two younger siblings, Margaret (Maggie) Alice (1864–1940) and Thomas Arthur (1866–1917) – seems to have prospered.[9] Mrs Lloyd ran her home with the help of two Welsh-speaking servants from her native Montgomeryshire, and by May 1876 the business was doing well enough for the family to move from accommodation above the shop, on the fringe of the city centre, to a new house at 16 Overton Street, Edge Hill, just over half a mile away to the north-east.[10] It took several months for the house to be got ready to the family's satisfaction, and the young J. E. Lloyd was impressed by the result: 'The walnut-graining in the dining-room is superb!'[11] The property also boasted a breakfast room that looked out on a garden planted with holly, privet and rhododendrons purchased from a nursery in Walton, and Lloyd himself took pleasure in tending the garden.[12] Yet there were limits to comfort, too: in winter his own room could be unbearably cold.[13]

The residential environment of Lloyd's upbringing in Falkner Street and Overton Street were typical of the Liverpool middle class, and the same was true of many of his activities and attitudes. There is nothing to suggest that he or his parents exhibited 'the rampant snobbery' all too prevalent in some Welsh Nonconformist circles in Liverpool;[14] however, Lloyd was clearly conscious of belonging to a class defined by a certain level of wealth and, crucially, by respectability. Thus, in recounting a visit to the resort of New Brighton in September 1876, he complained that 'the shore is very crowded and not very select in its frequenters', while the 'street-boys' who pelted him and his fellow pupils with snowballs appear to have been viewed as a nuisance rightly sent packing by a police officer.[15] This is not to imply that the young Lloyd was averse to snowball fights in the right company; he also enjoyed fireworks, cricket, shinty ('A good healthy game'), bagatelle and charades.[16] However, these and other recreations, notably playing the piano and harmonium, formed part of an essentially middle-class culture and outlook.[17] So too was the commitment to Liberalism he shared with his parents. As well as supporting the distinctively Welsh Liberal goal of disestablishing the Church of England in Wales, the young Lloyd also showed sympathy for broader Liberal causes, notably through the strongly anti-Turkish sentiments he expressed in 1876, which were evidently indebted to the agitation, especially marked in northern England, condemning atrocities against the Bulgarians who had joined a wider Balkan uprising against Ottoman rule, and he attended a Liberal public meeting at Hope Hall in Liverpool in March of the following year.[18]

Another important consequence of Edward Lloyd's commercial success was that it allowed him to provide his eldest son with a private education that laid the foundations for the latter's scholarly career. Admittedly, this education was relatively modest, even in the context of Liverpool. However, by 1870 he was paying £1 10s. per quarter for the instruction of 'Master Lloyd' at Chatham Institute, a small private school in Chatham Street – and thus close to the shop on Falkner Street – run by James Veitch, a graduate of Edinburgh University, and John Edward remained there until the summer of 1877.[19] This investment paid off, as Lloyd succeeded in his Oxford

Local Examinations, his subjects including Latin, French and German as well as geography, English literature and history.[20] He also enjoyed physics and chemistry, but was less comfortable with mathematics, especially trigonometry.[21] Besides its academic benefits, the school helped to extend Lloyd's social experience beyond the Welsh environment of family and chapel by facilitating friendships with some of his English fellow pupils.[22] Above all, as his early diaries amply attest, this schooling gave him a command of English prose, and probably also helped to instil the notion – widespread among Welsh literati in this period – that English was the language of education and scholarship. By paying for an academic education, first in Liverpool and later at Aberystwyth and Oxford, Edward Lloyd evidently sought to give his eldest son an opportunity he had never had, an ambition that implied high expectations. However, his father also believed that John Edward should acquire some business experience through helping with the draper's shop – for example, by spending time there in the afternoon when Edward Lloyd went for his tea; by calling on customers to try and recover debts; and by assisting with the accounts, a task not always to Lloyd's liking: 'Did some of the Ledger for Papa. Stock-taking all ev[e]n[ing]. A very miserable sort of day.'[23] Whether his father hoped that John Edward would follow him into the business is unclear; eventually, it was his younger brother Thomas Arthur who took this path.[24] Be that as it may, it is tempting to speculate that these early spells of bookkeeping helped to hone the precise habits of mind that would characterize Lloyd's work as both scholar and administrator.

Important though the shop was in establishing the economic and social foundations of Lloyd's early life as well as in providing practical experience, its educational and cultural influence could not rival that of the chapel. For the middle-class Welsh population of Victorian Liverpool the town's Welsh Nonconformist churches were crucial both to defining social status and to maintaining a distinctive ethnic identity, and Lloyd's family was no exception. Admittedly, the family was unusual in that the husband and wife belonged to different denominations and attended different chapels. Lloyd's mother Margaret was a Wesleyan Methodist, his father a Welsh Independent or Congregationalist, and, while he followed his father, remaining a deeply committed Congregationalist throughout his life, Lloyd also attended services and other church events with his mother – who in turn was equally hospitable to both Congregationalist and Wesleyan ministers in her home.[25] Although the differences between the two denominations were not huge, this early experience of religious tolerance may well have contributed to Lloyd's generally liberal outlook.[26] The chapel to which Lloyd's father belonged had originally been established in 1853 by William Rees (Gwilym Hiraethog, 1802–83) as Salem, Brownlow Hill, but moved to a spacious new, mock-Italianate Romanesque building on Grove Street in 1867.[27] Though not as grand as the Calvinist Methodists' Princes Road chapel, built to accommodate over 1,200 worshippers,[28] Grove Street bore witness to a confidence typical of the town's Welsh Nonconformist congregations at that time; moreover, the chapel enjoyed considerable renown thanks to its founding minister, whose preaching, prolific literary endeavours and politically committed journalism had made him a major figure in Welsh public life, and by the later 1870s its congregation numbered over 300 members. Among these, Edward Lloyd enjoyed considerable standing as a deacon since 1869 and one of the most generous contributors, giving over £20 a year.[29] He played a leading role in the difficult negotiations to find a successor to William Rees following the latter's retirement in 1875, negotiations which eventually resulted in a successful call to William Nicholson, who served as minister from the end of 1876 to his death, attributed to overwork, at the age of forty-one in 1885.[30] While Edward Lloyd's prominence, further enhanced by his appointment as the church's treasurer in 1877, was doubtless related in part to his wealth and, quite possibly, the skill and tact for which he was praised in his business dealings, his commitment to the Congregationalist cause was deep and went back to his upbringing in Montgomeryshire.[31] (It was entirely consistent with his position in Grove Street that he was one of the Liverpool-Welsh elite which established the town's Welsh National Society in 1885, serving on its council from the following year, and he later achieved civic recognition from the town's Liberal administration through his appointment as a Justice of the Peace.[32])

Lloyd became a member of Grove Street on 7 November 1875.[33] There is nothing to suggest that he shared the dissatisfaction of some other contemporaries, stemming in significant part from their weak grasp of the Welsh language, with the Welsh Nonconformist churches of Liverpool which their parents obliged them to attend.[34] Quite the contrary: he responded enthusiastically to sermons and prayer meetings that inspired him. For example, after Rowland Williams (Hwfa Môn, 1823–1905) preached at Grove Street on 8 September 1876, Lloyd wrote: 'I am myself very fond of his graphic delineations, and touching episodes; so much so that I could listen for a very long time without feeling at all wearied or fatigued.'[35] Even his critical comments suggest disappointment at a failure to meet higher standards rather than dismissal of the religious tradition in which he was raised.[36] His upbringing certainly ensured that Lloyd was deeply immersed in Welsh Nonconformist culture. In addition to his regular attendance at services and other meetings in Grove Street and elsewhere he came into personal contact with a host of ministers who stayed at his home while on preaching engagements. Some of these early experiences left an abiding impression: he retained vivid memories of Gwilym Hiraethog in the years after his retirement in 1875, while a few weeks before his death Lloyd recalled meeting as a child an elderly minister who could remember the famous Methodist hymn writer William Williams, Pantycelyn (1717–91).[37]

Above all, the chapel was the principal forum for the expression and practice of the Christian faith which was a fundamental aspect of Lloyd's life. Though conventional, his declaration at the beginning of 1877 sounds sincere: 'May I do more for the cause of Christ this year than ever I have done yet, and may his grace keep me "unspotted from the world".'[38] The quotation from James 1:7 is but one illustration of the profoundly scriptural emphasis of the Nonconformist culture to which Lloyd subscribed. Admittedly, while not yet espousing the higher criticism and its associated theological liberalism, by his mid-teens he believed, following Gwilym Hiraethog, that Christian faith could accommodate aspects of secular culture and learning, provided these did not conflict fundamentally with biblically revealed truth (a viewpoint that put Darwinian evolution beyond the pale).[39] That Lloyd was no rigid literalist is clear from a paper he read to Grove Street's literary society on the 'Agreement of Geology and Scripture' in December 1875. This defended the compatibility of the creation story in Genesis with the findings of nineteenth-century geology by offering an interpretation of the biblical account, which, while claiming to adhere accurately to the original Hebrew, offered a metaphorical understanding of the period of time signified by the seven days of creation, being indebted to the work of the Evangelical Scots journalist Hugh Miller (1802–56), 'the leading popular expounder of geology in the 1840s and 1850s', whose views on this question had also been welcomed by Hiraethog.[40] Science and religion met again in April 1877, when Lloyd read another paper to the chapel's literary society on 'The atmosphere', which appeared later in the year as its author's first substantial published article.[41] Nor did Lloyd see any fundamental conflict between his faith and the enjoyment of literature. Commenting on a story he found 'interesting and "adeiladol" [edifying]', he wrote in his diary:

> I differ very much from those who condemn all fiction as weakening the intellect and disturbing the mind by unnatural ideas . . . if every work is selected with due caution as to its moral and religious tone and the reputation of its writer, great benefit is derived from the perusal of fiction.[42]

True, the story appeared in *The Quiver*, a weekly paper that claimed to be 'Designed for the Defence of Biblical Truth, And the Advancement of Religion in the Homes of the People'. However, the paper's religious tone had relaxed considerably by the 1870s, and Lloyd's qualified approval of fiction extended to a wide range of literature, including English classics such as Shakespeare and Dickens as well as a particular penchant for the recently published novels of Jules Verne, whose *Twenty Thousand Leagues under the Sea* was, he declared, 'a book of the most thrilling interest, yet absolutely harmless'; indeed, it inspired Lloyd to submit a translation for a competitive meeting at Park Road chapel under the pseudonym of 'Nemo', the novel's principal character![43]

The chapel also helped to shape Lloyd's life by providing a weekly routine. Nonconformity's strong commitment to constant self-improving activity, which reflected wider Victorian middle-class values, was nowhere more apparent than in the round of meetings organized by its chapels.[44] In addition to two services and Sunday school on Sundays, Grove Street Chapel held a Society (*Seiat*) on

Monday evenings and Young Men's meeting (later referred to as the Literary Society) on Fridays, not to mention various prayer meetings, additional services such as those held during special preaching weeks and, from January 1877 onwards, meetings of the Good Templar temperance lodge on Tuesdays.[45] By the time he was fifteen Lloyd also appears to have taken an active organizational role, helping to put together the programme of the Literary Society, making arrangements for a competitive meeting in May 1877 and acting as secretary for both that society and the Good Templars' lodge. These last responsibilities prompted the following comments, which, though they may strike us as the precocious musings of a young man who took himself a little too seriously, are worth quoting for the insight they provide into the mind of a future university registrar and meticulously careful scholar:

> I always endeavour to keep the Minutes of both the societies to which I have the honour to be Secretary, with the most scrupulous care, and attention to details. For although it may seem apparently of little or no consequence, serious complications have often arisen from negligence or slovenliness in this work. 'Whatsoever thy hand findeth to do, do it with all thy might.'[46]

Participation in chapel activities also, of course, had an important social dimension. Lloyd's younger contemporary, the Celtic scholar J. Glyn Davies (1870–1953), wrote of his youth in late Victorian Liverpool that '[e]ach chapel was a small world in itself, and decided to a large extent the circle of friends'.[47] The same was true for Lloyd. By 1876, his best friend was Edwin Morris, whose father, Thomas, was closely associated with Edward Lloyd as a fellow deacon at Grove Street, and also its secretary.[48] The two youngsters seem to have spent time together most days when they were in Liverpool – attending the multifarious activities of their chapel and the wider Welsh Nonconformist community, planning the programme of the Young Men's society, going on walks, lending each other books and discussing a wide range of topics including the Church of England, the Welsh colony in Patagonia, the Welsh language and the 'Negro Question'.[49] However, although illustrating the dominant role of the chapel in framing social ties and activities, the friendship, for all its closeness, also points up differences within such congregations, as Edwin worked at Edward Lloyd's shop (an instance of the common tendency for the well-to-do in chapels to provide employment for their fellow members) and thus lacked the educational opportunities enjoyed by his employer's son.[50] Indeed, Edwin seems to have felt a sense of deprivation, for he sought to improve himself by subscribing to *The Popular Educator* and following its plan of study, 'as he feels himself rather deficient in the more liberal branches of knowledge, especially natural science'.[51]

It was his family, though, which provided the most important social ties for the young Lloyd. As was usual for someone of his middle-class background in this period, he saw much less of his father, who was occupied for long hours in the shop, than his mother, who had no paid employment and whose principal role, greatly prized by Nonconformists, was to oversee the running of the home and ensure her family's well-being.[52] Apart from fulfilling these domestic responsibilities, Margaret Lloyd had a significant influence on her children's upbringing through her strong commitment to Wales and its native language and culture. She ensured that Welsh was spoken at home, something not always easily achieved among the second-generation Liverpool-Welsh families, and helped to foster Lloyd's sense of Welsh nationality.[53] Lloyd also appears to have been close to his father, while at the same time being keenly aware of his parent's status in Grove Street Chapel and the wider Welsh Nonconformist community in the town.[54] Thus, as head of the family, Edward Lloyd remained at some remove from the daily activities of his wife and their children. John Edward spent much time with his younger siblings: in his teens he accompanied his mother and sister on various visits and not only played with his brother Thomas Arthur but also sometimes gave him lessons.[55] In addition, there was frequent contact with Margaret Lloyd's brother John Lloyd Jones – who, as we have seen, had preceded the Lloyds to Liverpool in the mid-1850s – and his wife Selina (Lena) (née Spriggs) together with their daughter 'little Lena', a reminder of the family connections that helped to sustain the Liverpool-Welsh, just as they did other middle-class communities in Victorian Britain.[56] True, by the time he was fifteen Lloyd occasionally found some of his younger relatives rather trying, as they called to drag him out on long walks and thus prevented him from getting on with reading and writing, and, when Thomas Arthur and a friend 'made a terrific disturbance all the afternoon and evening with their usual noisy games', Lloyd wondered '[h]ow strange it is that children cannot enjoy themselves quietly and like rational beings'![57]

In addition, the family retained close links with relatives in the Tanat valley in northern Montgomeryshire, the area from which Lloyd's parents had originated – a connection expressed in the Powysian dialect of Welsh that Lloyd spoke throughout his life.[58] In terms of its demography, economy and society, this largely agricultural, sparsely settled and overwhelmingly Welsh-speaking environment was a world away from the cosmopolitan metropolis on the Mersey, whose population of almost half a million in 1871 dwarfed that of the market town of Llanfyllin, then inhabited by fewer than 2,000 persons.[59] Nevertheless, as the migration of Lloyd's parents illustrates, the worlds were also closely connected, and were brought even closer by the expanding railway network of the mid-nineteenth century: a station was opened in Llanfyllin in 1863, and could be reached from Liverpool in a matter of hours.[60] Family ties were maintained in part by giving younger relatives from the Welsh countryside the opportunity to experience life in Liverpool. Thus, early in 1877, Lloyd's cousin Lizzie Williams arrived from Montgomeryshire and stayed with him for two months, just as another cousin, Maggie Ridge, had done the previous year.[61] However, connections with the family's roots were sustained above all by the annual summer holiday in Penygarnedd, where Lloyd's father later leased – and eventually bought – a house, Bryndifyr (fig. 1).[62] This return to Wales was a fairly common practice among the wealthier Liverpool-Welsh.[63] It certainly left a deep impression on Lloyd, who continued to spend some of the summer in Penygarnedd at least until his mid-fifties; he looked back on the area with great affection when he wrote of his parents as follows in the short family history he composed towards the end of his life:

> Their true home, a country dear to me to this day on account of a close connexion with its people and a host of early memories, was the Tanat Valley, where Montgomeryshire borders on Denbighshire. There was never a time in my life when I was not very much at

home in Penygarnedd and Pen-y-bont-fawr, and in Llanfyllin, their market town.[64]

He also recalled the 'wonders' he experienced on his frequent visits as a child to his uncles' shop in London House, Llanfyllin, with its sugar loaves, barrels of currants and iron bars.[65]

Lloyd wrote his fullest account of a summer holiday in Penygarnedd when he was fifteen, in his diary for 1876.[66] The stay, which lasted just over six weeks, was marked by fine weather; indeed, the heat occasionally proved intolerable. Days revolved around visits to relatives, especially 'Uncle Ridge' at Pen-y-bont-fawr, whose harmonium gave Lloyd much pleasure, and excursions, often by trap, to Llanfyllin and various spots in the neighbouring country-side such as Mynydd Llys, Pistyll Rhaeadr and Llyn Moelfre.[67] True, despite all this company, Lloyd felt the lack of a friend of his own age, a situation alleviated only briefly by a short visit from Edwin Morris. On the whole, though, he seems to have managed by keeping himself characteristically busy. In part, life at Penygarnedd was a continuation of activities in Liverpool – reading, preparing for the Young Men's meetings at Grove Street, working on a large map of Wales, helping to look after Thomas Arthur (for whom Lloyd constructed and painted a toy cottage) and, of course, regular attendance at chapel. However, Lloyd also took pleasure in his rural surroundings, observing haymaking and making notes on the remote upper reaches of the Tanat valley and its medieval church of Pennant Melangell, which he visited with his uncle: 'I think I shall publish in some form or other, the result of my observations in this much neglected district.'[68]

By 1876, then, Lloyd had developed a keen interest in Welsh culture and history, and regarded this as providing an essential element in his life over and above both his English education at school and the routine activities of chapel: as he put it in October of that year, 'I am really in need of something (Welsh) to do'.[69] He obtained a knowledge of current affairs in Wales through reading Welsh-language newspapers and periodicals and became familiar with a number of historical works, including *Hanes Cymru* ('History of Wales', 1842) by Thomas Price (Carnhuanawc) and, especially, *Hanes y Brytaniaid a'r Cymry* ('The History of the Britons and the Welsh', 1872–4) by Robert Pryse (Gweirydd ap Rhys). He also discussed the proposal to erect a monument to Prince Llywelyn ap Gruffudd (d.1282), commenting perspicaciously, 'I fear it wont [*sic*] take with the ministers'.[70] It would be rash to conclude, however, that Lloyd was already firmly committed to becoming a historian. He later claimed that the emphasis on rote learning of dates had destroyed the interest of history at school, an observation consistent with the praise lavished on the apparently exceptional efforts of a supply teacher in February 1876 who gave 'a very good history lesson, for he will let us ask any questions of any sort whatever'.[71] It seems, rather, that an interest in Welsh history was part of a broader interest in Wales and its culture, reflected also in the reading of Welsh literature, upon which he expressed some strong views, notably a marked preference for poetry in free verse rather than 'childish' *cynghanedd* in the strict metres.[72]

In part, this engagement with Wales stemmed from family influence and personal predilection, but it also reflected the articulation of a strong sense of national identity by the affluent and fully bilingual Welsh middle class in the second city of England – an identity underpinned by the twin imperatives of countering charges of inferiority to the English while asserting a certain superiority among the Welsh.[73] In other words, his upbringing in Liverpool was crucial to forging the young Lloyd's sense of Welshness. At the same time, though, the formation of this Welshness in a major metropolis of the British Empire reinforced the incentives for it to encompass many aspects of Victorian culture, including a strong identification with progress and modernity, and helped to encourage a broad range of interests. The different strands of this experience are exemplified by the newspapers and magazines Lloyd read in his father's shop and at home, which included *The Australian News*, *Y Beirniad* ('The Critic'), *Y Darlunydd* ('The Illustrator'), *The Graphic*, *The Liverpool Mercury*, *Yr Herald Cymraeg* ('The Welsh Herald'), and, in February 1877, the newly launched *Y Genedl Gymreig* ('The Welsh Nation').[74] Just as the shop itself depended on wider economic ties that supported a middle-class life with its own distinctive ethnic and linguistic inflection, so too was the print culture which Lloyd consumed there and elsewhere the product of general commercial and technological developments that not only facilitated an engagement with the world at large but also helped to promote a sense of Welsh identity.[75] Nor was this varied experience restricted to the printed word, for Lloyd also heard news and ideas through his attendance of lectures on topics as diverse as temperance, phrenology, Oliver Cromwell and David Livingstone, as well as public meetings, including an address in May 1877 at St George's Hall by the former American president, General Ulysses S. Grant; while on a walk with Edwin Morris he gained further insights into recent history from a veteran of the Crimean War who 'related us some adventures in his experience, which were very interesting'.[76]

In conclusion, during his early years in Liverpool Lloyd developed several attributes that would serve him well in the future. Two characteristics come across particularly clearly in the diary entries he wrote in his mid-teens: almost constant activity and a confidence in his opinions. Not only did Lloyd devote himself assiduously to his studies at school, where he benefited from an English education that included essential linguistic skills, but he extended his knowledge and skills through participating enthusiastically in the Welsh-language culture centred on, though not exclusive to, the chapel. His capacity for work was enhanced by a critical intelligence: to judge by the diaries in particular, Lloyd was ready to comment and reflect on what he had read and experienced, rather than merely to record and describe. Yet, if the person we encounter in his early writings can strike us as disconcertingly mature and serious for one so young, they also reveal a lighter side in the enjoyment of music, games and other amusements as well as warm affection for family and friends. Although the departure for the University College of Wales, Aberystwyth in October 1877 opened a new phase of his life, it did not mark a dramatic rupture, for Lloyd would return regularly to the city that continued to influence his outlook over the following years.

2

Expanding Horizons: Aberystwyth and Oxford, 1877–1885

The eight years Lloyd spent in completing his formal education, first at Aberystwyth and then at Oxford, were crucial in equipping him to become a historian and in confirming the strong commitment to Wales that determined the main focus of his historical writing. True, compared with that of his contemporaries in Germany, France or the United States, his historical training was limited in scope, as he studied history for only two years on an undergraduate degree course designed to provide a liberal education rather than the technical skills required to undertake historical research.[1] Of course, this reflected the opportunities available in late Victorian Britain, where history was in a transitional phase from being essentially a branch of literature pursued by amateurs to a fully fledged academic discipline with its own professional qualifications and career path. Thus Lloyd's research training, if such it may be termed, consisted of prolonged study of ancient and modern languages followed, in the School of Modern History at Oxford, by the inculcation of skills of critical analysis and argument applied both to broad questions and to particular problems and sources. By contrast, his engagement with Welsh history was a matter of extracurricular endeavour, highlighting how his student years also facilitated his development as a scholar by giving him valuable time to pursue his interests in Wales.

Aberystwyth

The move from the bustling metropolis of Liverpool to the small seaside town of Aberystwyth in west Wales might seem to represent a drastic narrowing of horizons.[2] The college Lloyd entered in October 1877 had been open only five years and its future remained highly uncertain, as its financial position was precarious due to a lack of government funding, which in turn reflected doubts in some influential quarters about its viability as an institution.[3] Moreover, while at first sight the provision of ten staff for just over sixty students looked generous, the very varying abilities of the latter required a proliferation of classes across a wide range of subjects in both the arts and sciences that stretched their teachers and called into question the institution's claim to be a university college.[4] Indeed, for some of its detractors, the college was no more than a 'high class grammar school', a contention given some weight by the age profile of its students: Lloyd was by no means the only 16-year-old who arrived there, and by October 1879, when detailed figures become available, the ages of over one-third of the fifty-nine students ranged from fifteen to eighteen. On the other hand, a slightly higher proportion were significantly older, being aged between twenty-four and twenty-nine inclusive, and Lloyd later recalled that all benefited from the presence of these older men, mainly training for the Nonconformist ministry, who brought 'a wide outlook, a philosophy of life and a power of criticism which made for real university culture'.[5]

Nevertheless, despite – indeed, partly because of – its various difficulties, the self-styled University College of Wales had a significance out of all proportion to its size. As its name indicated, it claimed to provide a university institution specifically for Wales, and thus symbolized the aspirations of Welsh patriots who believed that their country had been neglected with respect to educational opportunities and consequently lagged behind the other countries of the United Kingdom. (In a speech to the House of Commons in 1879 Hussey Vivian, Liberal MP for Glamorgan, estimated that, whereas 1 in 840 of the population of Scotland and 1 in 3,121 of that of Ireland were university students, the proportion in Wales was only 1 in 8,000.[6]) Support for Aberystwyth had been strong among the Welsh of Liverpool, and Lloyd's father knew the college's first principal, Thomas Charles Edwards (1837–1900), who had served as a Calvinist Methodist minister in the town before taking up his new responsibilities in 1872.[7] The decision to go to Aberystwyth was, then, a vote of confidence on the part of Lloyd and his parents in the college and the aspirations it represented.[8]

That the college was intended to serve the needs of Wales did not mean that the education it provided had a distinctively Welsh character. Quite the contrary: the main aim was to replicate the kind of higher education available in England and, in the case of the most gifted students, enable them to obtain degrees awarded by the University of London or facilitate their entry to Oxford or Cambridge. This was in keeping with the outlook of the largely London-based Welsh professionals and businessmen who had pushed for the college's creation, not least the indefatigable educationalist and modernizer Hugh Owen (1804–81), men who continued to exert influence through their membership of its governing council.[9] Crucially, it also reflected the attitude of T. C. Edwards, instilled in him by his father, Lewis Edwards (1809–87), the Edinburgh-educated principal of Bala Calvinist Methodist College, and implanted deeper by four years spent as a scholar at Lincoln College, Oxford, where he obtained a first in Literae Humaniores or Greats (Classics and philosophy) in 1866 and won the esteem of the college's rector, Mark Pattison, as well as of Benjamin Jowett, the influential master of Balliol; both of these men later encouraged Edwards to accept the principalship.[10] This background helps to explain why T. C. Edwards believed that English culture and learning were essential components of the modern Welsh heritage. As he wrote in the first issue of the college *Magazine* in November 1878:

> All that is best in our literature, our religion, and our daily life is thoroughly saturated with English influence; and the College will not cease to be patriotic by striving to take possession of all that is best in English culture, any more than England ceases to be national by striving to be cosmopolitan.[11]

Thus it was that, shortly after his arrival in Aberystwyth, Lloyd and his fellow students were summoned to an address on English literature by Mark Pattison, by then a member of the college council, who urged them 'to acquire the habit of regarding literature as a portion of history, of the facts of the past'.[12] Thus, too, each volume of the college's annual *Calendar* invoked a wider agenda of university reform in Britain by quoting a passage from Matthew Arnold's *Schools and Universities on the Continent* (1868) that stressed the need to take 'superior instruction' to the students, although this was somewhat disingenuous inasmuch as, after the words quoted, the passage went on to advocate creating new universities 'in the eight or ten principal seats of population', a description that hardly fitted Aberystwyth![13] Furthermore, English language and literature were compulsory elements in the college's syllabus for its qualification of 'Associate', with no provision for Welsh until the final examination (though it was an examinable subject for entrance scholarships).[14]

Nevertheless, instruction was available in Welsh, following the appointment in 1875 of the eminent literary scholar and lexicographer Daniel Silvan Evans (1818–1903) to a chair in the subject.[15] The college also advertised its Welsh credentials by including in its (admittedly monolingual English) *Calendar* an almanac that recorded the birth or death of Welsh notables only, ranging from medieval princes to the recently deceased journalist – and member of the college council – John Griffith ('Y Gohebydd') (1821–77).[16] Moreover, at the end of Lloyd's first year, the Revd H. N. Grimley, the Cambridge-educated professor of mathematics and natural philosophy, urged the students to put their vacation to patriotic use by exploring the Welsh landscape and sites associated with 'heroes of your own nationality'.[17] It would be anachronistic to dismiss these explicit nods towards Wales as empty gestures belied by an overwhelmingly anglicizing agenda, for the antithesis implied would have been alien to T. C. Edwards and other leading figures of the college. Rather, Edwards believed that his goal was unequivocally patriotic: to provide young people in Wales with new educational opportunities equal to those available elsewhere in Britain. Like other advocates of university education in Wales at this period, his rationale for the college at Aberystwyth was framed in national terms. This was not simply a matter of seeking recognition of the distinctive cultural and linguistic complexion of Wales, but entailed forging a vision of the nation as an entity that could subsume disabling political and especially religious differences whose effect the 'exceptionally liberal-minded Calvinist Methodist' principal of Aberystwyth knew all too well from bitter personal experience.[18] Referring, early in 1880, to the government inquiry into Welsh higher education chaired by Lord Aberdare, he wrote:

> We do not base our argument for a Welsh University and Welsh Colleges on the distance by rail from Aberdaron to Oxford, but on the nation's wish. For this wish represents the national life, the national *solidarité*. A Welsh University in Wales would bring the best and highest culture of the age to bear immediately on the Welsh people; and it would become the expression of the nation's consciousness of an intellectual life and power . . . If this is given us, we shall have found at last what Wales has so long yearned for in vain, the one uniting power that will be strong to counteract the evil influences of our unhappy divisions, and render our differences the harmony of diversity in unity.[19]

Such, then, were the views that set the parameters of Lloyd's education at Aberystwyth and influenced his outlook thereafter. Although a full picture of what he studied at the college defies reconstruction, some elements are clear. On arrival in 1877 he sat the scholarship examination and was placed among the runners-up ranked *proxime accesserunt*. This in turn meant that he was able to proceed immediately to the second examination for associate, which he passed with flying colours at the end of his first year, coming top of the first division and winning first prize. Further success followed, as he was awarded a scholarship in modern languages and literature and proceeded to pass the matriculation examination for London University in June 1879, coming twenty-fourth in the honours division and qualifying for a prize.[20] Thereafter, however, he does not appear to have proceeded to sit either the third examination for associate in his own college or examinations for the London degree. Instead, his sights were set on Oxford – indeed, he had announced his intention of 'going up for the Oxford' as early as January 1878.[21] On the advice of T. C. Edwards, he subsequently applied in 1881 to Edwards's old college, Lincoln. Presumably, then, Lloyd spent much of the rest of his time at Aberystwyth in preparing for Oxford, and especially in improving his knowledge of the classical languages whose mastery was prized so highly at that ancient university.[22] Careful preparation was particularly necessary since, while at school in Liverpool, Lloyd had studied Latin but no Greek. Admittedly, how much Greek he learnt is uncertain, as he later claimed to have left Aberystwyth with very little; yet he must have gained a reasonable grounding in the language to have been able to pass Responsions, the preliminary examination that tested knowledge of Greek, Latin and mathematics, at the end of his first term in Oxford.[23] The need to focus on Classics during his final two years at Aberystwyth was probably all the greater because, to judge by the designation of the scholarship he held, Lloyd had until then shown most aptitude for modern languages. His associate examination in the early summer of 1878 had contained three compulsory papers, one on English language, one on English literature (covering selected authors from Chaucer to Milton) and a third on either French or German (there is some evidence to suggest that Lloyd sat the latter).[24] In addition, candidates could choose two other papers from a wide range of other subjects, including English history, although only some of these – in Greek, Latin, mathematics and the sciences – were set in 1878; which of these he took is unknown.

However, Lloyd also took the opportunity to study subjects for their own sake, without the incentive of examination. In his first two years he studied Sanskrit, attending lectures by Hermann Ethé, an idiosyncratic, beer-loving, radical German emigré whose teaching encompassed not only French and German but a wide array of oriental languages.[25] In addition, Lloyd read Zeuss's *Grammatica Celtica* (1853) and was among the small group who attended D. Silvan Evans's lectures on Welsh grammar and literature.[26] Moreover, as in his school days, Lloyd pursued his Welsh interests outside the curriculum and during holidays: for example, in September 1878 he won the prize for a 'Welsh Dictionary of Scientific and Philosophic Terms' at the National Eisteddfod in Birkenhead.[27] The following term saw the launch of a new college *Magazine*, which, together with denominational periodicals, provided Lloyd with a further outlet for literary activity. Several of the essays he wrote while at Aberystwyth focused on Welsh writing of the eighteenth and nineteenth centuries, including the development of periodicals and the work of Ellis Wynne and Theophilus Evans;[28] indeed, he believed that the nineteenth century was a golden age in Welsh literature.[29] By contrast, he had little time for the 'artificial, monotonous verse' of the poets of the princes, though he was far warmer in his appreciation of medieval Welsh prose tales.[30] He also wrote about the connections between the Welsh and the ancient Celts, and stressed the need to trace the history of the Welsh language, drawing a contemporary analogy with the efforts of Baker and Livingstone to trace the source of the Nile, in an essay that opened by claiming that the Welsh were distinguished as a nation by their love of antiquities.[31]

Even so, Lloyd's eyes were firmly fixed on the future. His patriotic hopes for Wales received further stimulus from the company of like-minded students such as Tom Ellis (1859–99), the future Liberal MP and leader of the Cymru Fydd (Young Wales) movement, for whom Aberystwyth, with its panoramic views across Cardigan Bay from St Davids Head in the south to Bardsey Island in the north, literally opened new vistas of Welsh unity.[32] The college's role in fostering cultural nationalism through bringing together young men from different places and backgrounds was noticed by contemporaries, who later commented on both the academic brilliance and patriotic fervour of the small band of Welsh students to which Lloyd belonged in the late 1870s.[33] Lloyd's own heightened sense of Welsh identity is revealed by the scheme he drew up, in Welsh, for a Cymdeithas Lenyddol Gymreig (Welsh Literary Society), membership of which required passing exams in a variety of subjects including Welsh literature and history, as well as by his keeping a diary in Welsh, now lost, in 1879.[34] However, as in Liverpool, chapel provided his most regular formal exposure to Welsh-language culture. In accordance with advice given by the minister of Grove Street, Lloyd regularly attended Aberystwyth's Welsh Congregationalist chapel in Baker Street, making notes of the sermons given by its minister, Job Miles, as well as by others, including the principal, T. C. Edwards, whose preaching was renowned.[35] Indeed, by January 1878, still aged only sixteen, Lloyd caused his parents much consternation by declaring that he himself intended to enter the ministry.[36] However, although a year later he delivered his first sermon, in the familiar home surroundings of Grove Street, and continued as a lay preacher for almost four decades, Lloyd was never ordained; more mature consideration persuaded him that his vocation lay elsewhere.[37]

Nor was his public speaking restricted to the pulpit. In February 1879 Lloyd joined a deputation, led by Tom Ellis, protesting against the standard of food in the college (where, like a substantial minority of the students, Lloyd was resident, as recommended by the principal), and the following June was one of five representatives who met an external examiner appointed by the College Council to inform him that the students refused to be examined, as they had been given too little notice to prepare.[38] Admittedly, such activism was exceptional. Lloyd found more frequent opportunities to exercise his rhetorical skills in the officially sanctioned forum of the college's Debating Society, of which he was president in 1879–1880, participating in debates on contemporary issues such as spiritualism, the war in Afghanistan, female suffrage, vegetarianism, capital punishment and cremation, as well as occasional historical topics: for instance, Lloyd spoke against a motion that the execution of Mary, Queen of Scots had been justified.[39] A striking feature of these debates is how few of them focused on specifically Welsh issues, a further illustration of the college's ethos of engagement with a wider British world, although in October 1878 Lloyd read a paper responding affirmatively to the motion, 'Ought the Welsh to be preserved as a spoken language?', and in subsequent years chaired a debate on whether Wales needed a university and seconded a motion that Wales required only one university college.[40] Lloyd also took part in the Debating Society's 'entertainments', on one occasion performing in a quartet who sang 'Three Merry Chafers', and his interest in music, already developed in Liverpool, is further revealed by his attendance of a performance of the opera *Blodwen* in a farewell concert for Joseph Parry (1841–1903), the work's composer and erstwhile professor of music at Aberystwyth, whom Lloyd greatly admired, later considering the closure of the music department that prompted Parry's resignation 'a serious mistake'.[41]

Oxford

On his arrival at Lincoln College, Oxford, in October 1881 Lloyd entered an environment that was markedly different from any he had experienced before. During the previous four years he had studied at a small, struggling institution still in its first decade, most of whose students were Welsh Nonconformists; now he found himself in a college over halfway through its fifth century, belonging to a university that was not only the oldest in Britain but steadily expanding, with over 2,000 undergraduates, the vast majority of whom were Anglicans, and over half from English public schools.[42] Admittedly, the contrast was less stark than this brief characterization suggests. For one thing, at Aberystwyth Lloyd had already been imbued to some extent with the ethos of Oxbridge, including living in college. In addition, though significantly more expensive than Aberystwyth, compared with most other Oxford colleges Lincoln was small, poor and socially diverse.[43] It had just over fifty undergraduates in residence and, by the mid-1890s at least, drew only a minority from public schools, a feature it shared with only four other colleges or societies, in contrast, say, to Balliol, New or Christ Church, which consistently recruited over 70 per cent of their students from such schools.[44] Moreover, a sizeable proportion of Lincoln undergraduates were, like Lloyd, from commercial backgrounds, part of an increasing middle-class presence at Oxford at this time facilitated in part by the incentives to Nonconformists provided by the abolition of the Anglican religious tests for MAs in 1871.[45]

The new arrival adapted well to his new surroundings, participating in college customs such as breakfasting rowing crews during Torpids and Eights Week, the transition eased by the friendship of W. Silvanus Jones, from Corris, in the year above, whom Lloyd also accompanied to watch cricket matches in the University Parks – an interest that went back to boyhood days in Liverpool.[46] Concerts provided further familiar diversion.[47] Although, given his upbringing in England, his spoken English probably lacked the marked Welsh intonation of his compatriot Tom Ellis, Lloyd may have felt obliged to adopt the distinctive English accent, diffused from the public schools, that was increasingly becoming the norm among undergraduates at this period – over fifty years later, he was described as someone whose 'speech and thoughts accuse him of having been nourished in the atmosphere of Oxford'.[48] On the other hand, his strong Nonconformist principles and commitment to temperance may help to explain his apparent avoidance of the kinds of rowdy behaviour that disfigured university life in the eyes of some contemporary observers.[49]

Be that as it may, the influence of his new environment was certainly far from all encompassing, for in significant respects Lloyd's experience of Oxford was coloured by the attachments and attitudes he had formed earlier in his life. As at Aberystwyth, he returned home for vacations, attending chapel and also accompanying his family to Montgomeryshire; indeed, he spent the Lent term of 1884 in Liverpool, attending public meetings as well as sitting on committees preparing for the city's National Eisteddfod, held the following September, one of whose competitions allowed him to make a prize-winning debut as a historian of early Wales.[50] He also continued to take an interest in his old college in Wales and to contribute to its *Magazine* as well as to attempt more ambitious pieces of extracurricular writing.[51] While this is most evident in the eisteddfod essay on Welsh history, two years earlier the prospect of an eisteddfod prize at Cardiff had inspired him to embark on a history of Welsh literature, 1300–1650, which, though not submitted, seems to have provided material for an article in Welsh on traditions concerning the early Brittonic poet Taliesin.[52]

In addition, connections established at Aberystwyth helped to ensure that his social life in Oxford had a pronounced Welsh complexion. Looking back on his time there in a radio broadcast delivered almost sixty years later, Lloyd noted that his Welsh friends at Oxford fell into two consecutive groups. During the first two years he associated mainly with other Welsh students, also formerly at Aberystwyth, who had established the short-lived Aberystwyth College Club (or ACC) – men including Tom Ellis, Thomas Francis Roberts (1860–1919), who became the first professor of Greek at Cardiff and subsequently, in 1891, the second principal of Aberystwyth, and, in Lincoln, W. Silvanus Jones. In his third and fourth years, however, he made a broader circle of acquaintance, mainly in his own college, partly because the ACC had collapsed through a lack of new blood. However, he still had like-minded

Welsh friends, notably O. M. Edwards and J. Puleston Jones, both of whom arrived at Balliol in October 1884 after spending a year at Glasgow, and he also formed a close friendship with John Arthur Price – whose background and views, as a high Anglican, non-Welsh-speaking Tory from Shrewsbury, were very different from Lloyd's.[53]

Price later recalled:

> It was from Professor Lloyd, while he was under the spell of Welsh Liverpool, that I learned my first lesson in modern Welsh Nationalism, as we took many a walk together in the country roads round Oxford, and passed scenes immortalized by men like Newman and Matthew Arnold in modern times and 'Fair Rosamond' and Amy Robsart in the days that are far away. Lloyd explained to me that Welsh Nationalism was not a memory of the ages that were past but a real power in the hearts of modern Welshmen. And from him I learned that Welsh Nonconformists were really interested in the past of Wales and proud of it.[54]

It is clear that Lloyd arrived at Oxford with a strong commitment, originating in his upbringing in Liverpool and nurtured during his years at Aberystwyth, to the promotion of Wales and Welsh culture. His strong sense of Welsh identity and connections with other Welsh students were a crucial aspect of his Oxford experience, providing an emotional and intellectual hinterland that helped to set him apart from the vast majority of undergraduates. Thus meetings of the ACC, of which Lloyd became secretary in Trinity term 1882, included a debate on the motion 'That the state of Welsh Periodical Literature is a healthy indication of the Literary activity of the Principality', and a paper by Lloyd – known as the 'Honourable Member for Liverpool' – on 'The Fine Arts in Wales'. Not that the meetings of the club were entirely taken up with matters of high seriousness. Its prime purpose was social: in 1882 there was a St David's Day 'spread', and one meeting was given over to acting charades, in which Lloyd participated.[55] Although the ACC no longer functioned during his last two years, Lloyd was able to share his strong interest in things Welsh during walks not only with J. A. Price but also with O. M. Edwards.

Nevertheless, although he later seemed to regret that he had not followed Tom Ellis's example and mixed more widely in Oxford, Lloyd was by no means detached from the broader life of the university.[56] One constant interest was religion. He occasionally attended university sermons at St Mary's, although he had a low opinion of these by the end of his third year, citing with approval the 'rooted dislike' for these expressed by William Stubbs in his farewell lecture as regius professor of modern history in May 1884![57] He doubtless felt more at home with fellow Nonconformists, who were estimated to be no more than one to two hundred in number, roughly 5 to 10 per cent of Oxford undergraduates at this time.[58] In accordance with his mixed denominational background, on the first Sunday of his first term he divided his devotions between the Congregational chapel on George Street in the morning and the Wesleyan chapel in New Inn Hall Street in the evening, to whose recently arrived minister, the renowned Welsh preacher and vigorous evangelical revivalist Hugh Price Hughes (1847–1902), Lloyd, in common with many other students, became strongly attracted.[59] In addition, like Tom Ellis and several other Welsh contemporaries, Lloyd joined the university's Nonconformists' Union, established in May 1881 by the Congregationalist R. F. Horton, a fellow of New College (where he was Ellis's history tutor), to cater for the growing number of Nonconformist students who would otherwise have had to rely on Evangelical Anglican clergy for pastoral care; according to another Welsh student at this time, Horton had 'done a great deal to consolidate and elevate Nonconformity in the University'.[60] Among Lloyd's contributions to the group's meetings were papers on disestablishment and 'The impression made on contemporaries by the man Christ Jesus', the latter revealing his critical approach to scripture in its insistence on the need 'to be sufficiently endued with the historical spirit to read what we find there [in the Gospels] simply, without dogmatic or other bias'.[61]

However, Lloyd's engagement with contemporary concerns was not restricted to the religious sphere. His time at Oxford coincided with currents of liberal reform, notably the arguments of the Idealist philosopher T. H. Green (1836–82) insisting on the ethical imperative to work for the common good which influenced, among others, Tom Ellis and Arnold Toynbee; Lloyd heard the latter's lecture criticizing Henry George's *Progress and Poverty* (1880) in December 1882.[62] Lloyd also attended some of John Ruskin's last lectures following his reappointment as Slade professor of fine art in March 1883.[63] Lloyd found more regular opportunities to indulge his keen interest in culture and current affairs as a member both of Lincoln College's Isis Society (fig. 2) and of the Oxford Union.[64] The Isis Society discussed issues, such as the rights of women and cremation, already familiar to him from the Debating Society at Aberystwyth, while at the Oxford Union he attended debates on Egyptian policy, Home Rule and the place of bishops in the House of Lords as well as vivisection and other topics dealt with by Convocation, the university's supreme governing body.[65] These included the 'Examination of Women', which the union debated on 8 May 1884 in response to a vote in Convocation the previous week to admit women to certain honours examinations (though not degrees), a vote Lloyd warmly welcomed:

> To the average intelligence the innovation does not seem very violent
> . . . but in Oxford, where every stone that falls is replaced next day
> by another of exactly the same size and contour, it amounted to a
> revolution . . . The result was exceedingly gratifying to all who believe
> in the educational future of women, and not less so those who would
> fain believe in the intellectual progress of Oxford.

Characteristically, he went on to note that the only first in moral science in the Cambridge Tripos had been awarded to a Welsh woman.[66]

For all his extracurricular activities, though, the 'honourable member for Liverpool' clearly worked hard at his studies. The first two years were spent studying classical moderations (Mods), in which Lloyd obtained a first in July 1883. His college had elected him to an exhibition of £20 in his second year, which suggests that, while unsuccessful in the entrance scholarship examination, he had made rapid progress.[67] Thus, although a friend remarked that the result in Mods was all the more impressive since Lloyd seemed to have done so little work compared to others, appearances were doubtless deceptive; despite his preparation at Aberystwyth, he must have had to apply himself very hard in order to catch up with the majority of undergraduates who had already been drilled for years in both ancient languages at English public schools.[68] The course certainly demanded a high level of linguistic competence in Greek and Latin, with all candidates being required to translate previously unseen passages in both languages, to compose Latin prose (a transferable skill in the case of one fellow student who wrote in Latin to congratulate Lloyd on his first)[69] and to answer questions on at least five authors, including Homer, Demosthenes, Virgil and Cicero. (In practice, the norm seems to have been to prepare eight, and Lloyd evoked further admiration for having offered only seven.) In addition, candidates were expected to offer a variable number of further papers from a choice of Greek prose composition, both Latin and Greek verse composition, comparative philology with special reference to Greek and Latin inflexions, the history of Greek drama or Roman poetry and deductive logic.[70]

It is uncertain whether his original intention was to complete the Classics and philosophy course by proceeding to Greats (Literae Humaniores) for his final honour school but, in any event, by the summer of 1883 Lloyd had decided to read modern history, a decision that caused some regret to his Classics tutor at Lincoln, W. Warde Fowler.[71] Since 1872 it had been possible to read for modern history as a final honours school on successful completion of classical moderations, and the subject attracted some seventy to one hundred students a year by the mid-1880s.[72] In two years, the student was expected to prepare for ten examination papers in six subjects, the main focus being on 'The continuous history of England' in both its constitutional and its more general political, religious and social aspects (four papers), supplemented by a period of general or 'Foreign' history (two papers), a special subject (two papers) – Lloyd seems to have chosen 'The Age of Louis XI and Charles VIII', focusing on the later fifteenth century – and political economy and geography (one paper each).[73] In 1886, the year after Lloyd graduated, C. R. L. Fletcher wrote a paper emphasizing that modern history was no soft option compared with Greats and setting out how best to complete the course requirements.[74] Undergraduates should begin to prepare for the constitutional history papers by reading Stubbs, Freeman and Green in the long vacation immediately after finishing Mods. The first year would then be spent mostly on English constitutional and political history, although students were expected to make a start on their reading for the period of general history in the third term. After revision and preparatory reading over the long vacation, the Michaelmas term of the second year would complete the general history as well as political science and political economy. The special subject, 'the most interesting part of the work, but . . . one in which the Student must rely chiefly on himself', had to be mastered in the Lent term and Easter vacation. The last term was left for revision.[75]

Preparation for this demanding course of study took three forms: attendance at lectures (where registers were kept) in the mornings, reading and essay writing. Teaching was undertaken by the college history tutors, who cooperated in an inter-collegiate association that organized lectures and largely controlled the curriculum.[76] Cherishing their role as professional teachers, the tutors tried, by and large successfully at this period, to keep the professors at arm's length, so that these had little personal contact with undergraduates. One of the tutors' tasks was to make the reading required for the course more manageable and memorable by providing outlines and summaries in lectures, some of which were printed as 'handouts'. Despite the central place accorded in the curriculum to his *Constitutional History* and *Select Charters*, Stubbs attracted very few to his lectures on constitutional history, whereas the classes by the tutors A. L. Smith and Arthur Johnson expounding his work – the 'Steps to Stubbs' – were packed.[77] (Whether Lloyd ever met Stubbs or heard him speak is uncertain.)[78] Lloyd's own tutor was Richard Lodge (1855–1936) of Brasenose, who later held chairs at Glasgow and then Edinburgh, and it was to Lodge, therefore, that he will have turned for advice on organizing his time and which lectures to attend, and for whom he will have written a weekly essay. Unfortunately, Lloyd has left no detailed account of his tutorials, although he did recall that Lodge had the disconcerting habit of brandishing a poker, which fortunately he eventually put back on the fireplace when provoked by a student who wrote a long essay on the Anglo-Saxon constitution but had no idea what the fyrd (royal army) was![79] This peril aside, it is to be hoped that the tutorials were more satisfactory than the one given by Reginald Lane Poole (1857–1939), then a lecturer in history at Jesus College, described in January 1888 by his student John Arthur Jones in a somewhat desperate letter seeking Lloyd's assistance with how to manage Stubbs's *Constitutional History*:

> Poole is a very learned man but a poor tutor. On Monday morning, for instance, I went to him with a paper on Edw[ard] I and the Church. He opened with a gay remark as to the odd way in which his continental friends address him, one going so far as to address him as reverend. From this he passed to the reflection that he had a large collection of foreign stamps. These he showed me one by one. Half an hour is now gone. We begin the paper. A pope is incidentally mentioned. Mr Poole must see if he can recall the names of the Popes of the whole reign. He manages, missing out two. He then accounts for his omissions. Three quarters of an hour gone. I then hastily blurt out my paper. I have half a mind to go to a coach. May I have your advice, and that quickly.[80]

In theory, at least, the history course required a prodigious amount of reading and memorizing. Irrespective of his dependence on lectures or handouts Lloyd must have read widely. His 1884 diary contains a list of works by historians such as Green, Freeman, Stubbs, Froude, Gardiner, Ranke, Macaulay and Lecky, together with constitutional histories by Stubbs, Hallam and Erskine May. That he prepared thoroughly is also indicated by Richard Lodge's assertion in a testimonial of 1891 that Lloyd 'never neglected the necessary work for his examination'. Moreover, his examination performance demonstrated that he had mastered the skills of relevance and compression that were valued so highly. To quote Lodge again: 'Some of his papers, especially those on Constitutional History, were models of what examination papers should be – terse, full of information, and always to the point.'[81] In addition, he will have been inculcated in key assumptions about what history entailed as an academic discipline, assumptions that came to influence his own approach as a historian.[82] One of these, whose importance was emphasized by Stubbs and also upheld by Freeman, was the need to adopt a critical approach to sources, although, even in the special subject, this largely boiled down to digesting a pre-selected set of extracts and assessing how far these agreed with each other, rather then examining their underlying assumptions.[83] This was of a piece with the more general method, derived from the study of Classics in which both teachers and students had been steeped, of basing teaching on authoritative texts, be they published primary sources or secondary works: Stubbs's *Select Charters* (1870) and *Constitutional History* (1874–8) are prime examples. The mastery of these authorities in turn served to sustain an optimistic and moralizing interpretation of the past that emphasized the progressive continuity of English history and judged individual political leaders in terms of their contribution to that development.[84]

However, Lloyd's historical studies were not confined to preparing for the final examinations. In his last year he attended meetings of the Stubbs Society, previously called the Oxford Historical Seminar, now chaired by E. A. Freeman, the new regius professor of modern history.[85] On 2 March 1885 he read a paper there on Wales and the Marches in the reign of Stephen. This presumably drew on the prize-winning eisteddfod essay on Welsh history, the revised version of which he completed at the end of that month, and provides particularly striking testimony to his readiness to venture beyond the bounds of the curriculum.[86] The occasion was described as follows by O. M. Edwards:

> The point of interest was, what the chairman would say concerning so Celtic a subject as the doing of Gruffydd ap Llewelyn or Madoc ap Meredydd. Would he say that the time of the Society was wasted in recounting border frays between lawless marchers and Welsh savages? For there are three things Freeman hates, – Froude, hunting, and Celts. When the applause consequent on the reading of the paper was over, he began to inveigh against the method usually adapted by Eisteddfod writers in dealing with the history of Wales, and favourably compared with theirs the truly historical method taken by Mr Lloyd . . . The learned professor ended by saying it was the most pleasant evening he had spent for a long time.[87]

As Edwards explained, the History Society consisted mostly of professors and tutors, and 'aims at encouraging what is too rare in our over-grown boarding-school of a University, – original research'.[88] In fact, many history tutors felt little compulsion to undertake research, believing this to be the duty of the professors, nor did they seek to train undergraduates in the skills necessary for research. According to Paul Frédéricq, a Belgian professor sent to study the teaching of history at British universities in about April 1884, this encouraged superficiality. The 'vast extent' of the reading required at Oxford meant that 'the student cannot thoroughly grasp any part of it', while, on the other hand, there was far too little opportunity to study sources and original documents.[89] While he did not venture into the archives, in his eisteddfod essay – which offered an account of Welsh history from prehistory to 1194, being briefly extended in the published version to 1282 – Lloyd showed that he, at least, wished to obtain a thorough grasp of his subject through critical analysis of printed sources that he had discovered on his own account. This is consistent with Richard Lodge's assessment of him as someone who 'showed a very independent mind: refusing to accept second-hand conclusions, he was always anxious to work things out for himself'.[90]

Lloyd's contacts with Freeman were probably more a symptom than cause of his interest in research. The same is true of the most important professorial influence on him at Oxford, that of John Rhys, appointed first professor of Celtic at Jesus College in 1877, an appointment that helped to give legitimacy and prestige to the study of early Wales.[91] When the two men first met is uncertain. Lloyd bought a copy of Rhys's *Celtic Britain* shortly after its appearance in 1882 and drew on it in his eisteddfod essay, one of the adjudicators of which was none other than Rhys himself, who declared it to be 'the best historical production ever sent me by the Eisteddfod for adjudication'.[92] However, the earliest reference in Lloyd's diaries to a meeting is a Sunday lunch with the professor in November 1884, followed by breakfast in Jesus bursary the following week.[93] It may be, then, that it was the essay adjudicated in Liverpool the previous September that drew Lloyd to Rhys's attention. In any case, from 1884 onwards Lloyd kept Rhys's address on the Banbury Road in his diary, together with that of J. Gwenogvryn Evans, whose editions of Welsh texts, in collaboration with Rhys, were making key sources available for the study of medieval Welsh literature and history.[94] These extra-curricular connections at Oxford brought Lloyd into contact with scholarship that would be fundamental to his own work on the early Welsh past.

By the time he was dining with Rhys in November 1884 Lloyd had received a letter that would decide the next phase of his life: an invitation to return to his old college in Aberystwyth as a lecturer in both Welsh and history after completing his degree.[95] However, the certainty of future employment did not breed complacency, for Lloyd ended up with the best first of his year.[96] For a number of his contemporaries, his success was not merely personal but brought honour to the Welsh nation. Thus one correspondent writing to congratulate him in July 1885 referred to the 'large numbers of Welshmen who have with pride and joy watched your upward career and who look to you as one who will prove the world that the "Cymro" is in no sense behind in the great race of scholarship and learning'.[97] Of course, Lloyd was not unique in this respect: after all, O. M. Edwards enjoyed an even more brilliant undergraduate career at Oxford and went on to hold a fellowship at Lincoln College.[98] Lloyd belonged to an age in which, paradoxically perhaps, success at Oxford was valued as yet one more expression of Welsh renewal, and more specifically gave the lie to notions of Welsh inferiority vis-à-vis the English. Study at an ancient English university enhanced his authority as a historian of Wales. It also influenced his approach to history, as we shall see.

3

Towards A History of Wales, *1885–1911*

After his return to Aberystwyth in September 1885 Lloyd spent the rest of his life in Wales. Admittedly, to judge by two unsuccessful attempts at the All Souls fellowship examinations, Lloyd initially harboured hopes of returning to Oxford; thereafter, however, he was content to seek new opportunities within the principality.[1] His academic positions, first at Aberystwyth, then at Bangor from 1892, provided not only financial independence but also plenty of scope to put into practice his strong commitment to national renewal, especially in the field of education.[2] Above all, he was able to build on his undergraduate studies by training himself to become a professional historian and thus to write his greatest achievement, the *History of Wales* published in January 1911.

Aberystwyth

His new post took Lloyd to the front line of continuing efforts to advance Welsh education that were fundamental to the national revival of the 1880s led by the Liberal, Nonconformist middle class to which he belonged. As the first university college in Wales, Aberystwyth was a potent symbol not only of the aspiration to create a Welsh educational system but also of the fragility of this enterprise. True, since Lloyd had left for Oxford in 1881 the college had overcome the doubt on its future viability cast by Lord Aberdare's parliamentary committee on Welsh education (1880–1), for in 1884 Gladstone's administration agreed to fund Aberystwyth (which hitherto had relied on voluntary contributions), although less generously than the recently established colleges in Cardiff and Bangor.[3] Yet this improvement in fortunes was soon followed by another, potentially lethal, blow: the fire which extensively damaged the college building in July 1885, an event that precipitated a major two-year campaign to raise money for reconstruction during which Aberystwyth's principal, Thomas Charles Edwards, addressed over 500 public meetings and in which Lloyd also actively participated.[4] Thus, after a brief stint in chapel schoolrooms, Lloyd began his teaching in the nearby Queen's Hotel, rented as a temporary replacement for all classes except those in natural science.[5] This was hardly the most propitious start to an academic career. Admittedly, the college weathered the storm, which may even have appeared providential. After all, in August 1885 the new Conservative administration increased the government grant to £4,000 per annum, putting Aberystwyth on a par with the two other Welsh university colleges, and, despite fears of an exodus, students remained loyal – indeed, their numbers had more than doubled since 1881, with over 130 registered for Michaelmas term 1885.[6] Nevertheless, thereafter the pace of growth slowed, with the total number of students remaining below 150 during all but one of Lloyd's years on the staff.[7] Moreover, to judge by the recollections of one of his colleagues, although decline had been averted, a sense of crisis persisted in the later 1880s, owing to a perception that the college still had to justify its existence by emphasizing its particular contribution to west and mid Wales: 'This was a bracing belief, and the little band of professors and lecturers in those days worked the more strenuously because they had to "live dangerously".'[8]

In addition to contributing to Aberystwyth's recovery, Lloyd actively participated in initiatives to develop Welsh education at all levels, notably through his involvement in a major conference at Shrewsbury in January 1888 called to promote these initiatives, including the formation of a Welsh university, the securing of equal educational opportunities for girls and the creation of a comprehensive network of Welsh intermediate or secondary schools from which the university colleges might recruit students; the latter call resulted in the Welsh Intermediate Education Act of 1889 which established an institutional framework for setting up such schools.[9] Lloyd also belonged to the Society for Utilizing the Welsh Language, a relatively small lobby group that carried considerable influence due to its high-profile membership of Welsh education-alists and cultural patriots, which pressed for the greater use of Welsh in elementary (primary) schools.[10] His attendance of meetings in support of these various causes contributed to a highly peripatetic life that also included regular 'extension' (extramural) lectures on behalf of the college as well as preaching engagements.[11] (His sermons support his later recollection that while teaching at Aberystwyth he abandoned a literalist understanding of the Bible in favour of the critical approach to scriptural texts known as higher criticism, an approach entirely consistent with his scholarly instincts.)[12] These frequent journeys were a key characteristic of his years at Aberystwyth: as well as testifying to considerable commitment and stamina, they deepened Lloyd's familiarity with Wales and thus helped to foster the keen sense of topography that informs his historical writing.

By contrast, the history Lloyd taught at Aberystwyth had little to do with Wales, as the courses he offered were largely driven by the matriculation and degree examinations set by London University. Admittedly, not all students sat the London degree: some never graduated, while others went on to take degrees at other universities in England and elsewhere, as had Lloyd himself (indeed, his appointment raised hopes that he would be particularly well equipped to serve the needs of students wishing to read for the School of Modern History in Oxford).[13] Nevertheless, London set the agenda. Thus the new lecturer was expected to provide both broad surveys of English history, usually extending from Roman Britain to the seventeenth century, to satisfy requirements for matriculation and more specialized courses for degree examinations focusing on periods of early modern history – for example, 'The reign of Elizabeth' and 'English history from 1700 to 1740' – as well as constitutional history in the senior class.[14] Hence it was that one of his earliest students remembered Lloyd, not as an expert on medieval Wales, but as 'a young lecturer who knew a lot about

King Charles' Parliament'.[15] To judge by the examination papers, the emphasis throughout was on writing essays rather than analysing primary sources, as passages for comment excerpted from the latter are conspicuous by their absence.

Its status as a London degree subject ensured that English history was relatively popular, attracting seventy students in Lloyd's first term. By contrast, only fourteen took Welsh, a reflection of its absence as a preliminary degree subject in the London syllabus, and the disparity in numbers remained largely the same throughout Lloyd's years at Aberystwyth.[16] Yet, few though they were, the students choosing Welsh had to be taught across a broad spectrum of topics, including grammar and composition. In his first two years – following a plan he had outlined while still at Oxford – Lloyd sought to introduce a historical dimension by offering lectures on 'the History of the Welsh people', apparently with a strong early and medieval emphasis, as well as on the history of Welsh literature and the Welsh language, together with an 'Advanced Class' reading Middle Welsh prose tales.[17] However, the Welsh history course seems never to have been examined, and from 1887 it was abandoned, perhaps because of lack of demand, although the 'Old Welsh' reading class gave some consideration to the historical context of the texts studied.[18] Nevertheless, the linguistic and textual focus of his teaching was highly relevant to Lloyd's development as a historian of Wales, providing vital technical preparation.

It is telling that it was to these fields, too, that Lloyd turned in his research at Aberystwyth. As his teaching hours were fairly low, averaging about six hours a week (with, say, a further five hours of external lectures each term), he had considerable time for other work once initial preparation had been done.[19] In any event, the teaching did not prevent Lloyd from assiduously devoting himself to publication; indeed, several of his articles originated as lectures to students and others.[20] As well as continuing to make frequent contributions on a wide range of historical, literary and other topics to the college *Magazine* (which he also edited for three years from 1889), he sought to enhance his scholarly credentials by embarking on research in two areas that would inform his historical writing in the future: Welsh names and medieval Welsh law.[21] The immediate stimulus for the latter was a request to prepare for posthumous publication a substantial volume on the subject by the jurist Hubert Lewis (1825–84).[22] This editorial work compelled Lloyd to immerse himself in Welsh law: as he later recalled, 'I gave a great deal of time to it when I was at Aberystwyth and found that it had endless ramifications'.[23] He pursued these ramifications further over the following years, and relied heavily on the legal evidence in his depiction of medieval Welsh society.[24]

One consequence of the small size of Aberystwyth was that staff took a leading role in the college societies catering for students. Lloyd was no exception. As well as serving on the committee of the *Magazine*, he was closely involved with the Celtic Society, of which he was president, addressing its first meeting in May 1889 on the subject of modern Welsh poetry.[25] He also held offices in the Literary and Debating Society – to which he gave a paper on 'Welsh Princes and their Courts' – and, his commitment to temperance unabated, the Total Abstinence Society.[26] In addition, he found outlets for his long-standing love of music and drama through acting in several productions of the Dramatic Society – including 'Monsieur Hercules' in December 1888 (fig. 3) – and singing in the choir of the Musical Society.[27] However, owing to his recent departure for Bangor, in April 1892 he 'was missed among the basses' at the Musical Society's performance of Mendelssohn's oratorio *St Paul*, a work which in Lloyd's (characteristically serious-minded) view was ideally suited to the society's twin aim of 'the training of the voice and the formation of a correct musical taste'.[28] Term-time brought other diversions too: tea or dinner with colleagues, soirées and, in the summer, picnics and tennis.[29] Admittedly this was only one side to his personal life, as 'home' for Lloyd remained Liverpool and the Tanat valley, where he largely spent his vacations. However, it was at Aberystwyth that he found a new, life-long claim on his affections: Clementina (Tina) Miller, a former student who had come to the college from Aberdeen in 1887 and attended Lloyd's history classes. Although her tutor found fault in her examination performance ('Does not attempt enough'), he evidently came to appreciate her other qualities, for the couple were close by the end of 1891 and they married just over a year later.[30]

Bangor

By the time of his wedding Lloyd had left Aberystwyth. In the summer of 1891 he had applied to become the college's principal following the resignation in May of Thomas Charles Edwards, but, notwithstanding strong Congregationalist support, the application was unsuccessful, and another 30-year-old Oxford graduate, T. F. Roberts, professor of Greek at Cardiff, was appointed to the position.[31] However, feeling undervalued at Aberystwyth, Lloyd still looked out for fresh opportunities, and, after some fraught negotiations, in March 1892 he accepted an appointment as secretary and registrar of the University College of North Wales, Bangor, taking up his duties the following month. By then the college had also appointed him to the post of 'Permanent Lecturer in Welsh History', a clear recognition of his wish to continue historical research on Wales.[32] Bangor was already known to Lloyd through preaching and lecturing engagements, and he had first encountered Harry Reichel (1856–1931), principal of the university college, while an undergraduate at Oxford. Despite having a very different background from this Anglo-Irish Anglican, Lloyd shared his experience of study in Oxford – where both men had achieved firsts in modern history – that helped to inform a common outlook with respect to the development of Welsh higher education.[33] Nor did Bangor represent a radical change of environment. True, with a population of almost 10,000 it was somewhat larger than Aberystwyth, and, unlike the latter, boasted a cathedral and city status. Even so, it was a relatively small town, dwarfed by Lloyd's native Liverpool – whose Welsh population alone may have been seven times greater – as well as by Cardiff and Swansea in south Wales.[34] The college, which had been founded in 1884, was certainly small: when Lloyd arrived in 1892, it had 133 students, only slightly fewer than Aberystwyth, though the number increased significantly over the following years, peaking at 350 in 1909.[35] Yet if, in terms of both size and general ethos, the institution to which he had moved was broadly similar to that he had left, it posed fresh challenges and opportunities. In part, of course, this resulted from the change in duties: Lloyd's main responsibility was to provide administrative support to the principal, the college council and other committees. But it also resulted from changing contexts. In particular, the establishment in 1893 of a federal University of Wales, with degree-giving powers, not only brought with it new administrative structures but had a major impact on the teaching offered at the university colleges by creating a need to devise new schemes of study for the Welsh degree as alternatives to those of London University.[36] More specifically, the new dispensation allowed Welsh history – like Welsh language and literature – to become an examinable preliminary degree subject.

In addition to these new directions in Lloyd's professional life, the appointment at Bangor also led to a fundamental change in his personal circumstances that helped to shape his work as a historian. The post of registrar brought Lloyd a salary of £350 per year, very substantially more than the £200 he was receiving by the end of his time at Aberystwyth.[37] This made marriage a feasible prospect, and within a year of his arrival at Bangor he took a fortnight's leave to celebrate his wedding with Clementina Miller in Aberdeen on 16 February 1893 and spend a honeymoon in Cornwall.[38] (Prior to his departure he wrote to the editor of the college magazine that he could not possibly deliver an article he had promised, as he had to go away 'on very important business'!)[39] The couple began their married life at Caederwen Cottage, presumably on or near the later College Road in Upper Bangor, but moved in 1894 to another house in the vicinity, namely Tanllwyn on Holyhead Road, and their first child, Eluned (Lin) Clunes Lloyd, was born in November 1897.[40] Just over six years later they moved again, to Gwaen Deg, a spacious semi-detached house on Siliwen Road that could accommodate a larger family, and their second child, Edward Arthur, was born there in September 1904.[41] Initially leased, Gwaen Deg was bought for £800 in July 1913 and remained the home of Lloyd and his wife for the rest of their lives.[42]

Employing at least one maid and securing the regular services of a gardener, Lloyd ensured that his family enjoyed a comfortable middle-class existence similar to that in which he had been brought up: the scholarship of the *History of Wales* was facilitated by a favourable home environment sustained by a wife and domestic staff. The detailed household accounts Lloyd kept from the mid-1890s, a testimony in all likelihood to the lasting influence of his father's business background, reveal the minutiae of material existence – including velveteen for a dress and a blue cape listed under 'Clothes & Pin Money (Tina)' – as well as the precise mind that imposed order on the fragmented evidence for early Wales. The accounts also highlight continuities in Lloyd's outlook and activities: for instance, his membership of the Liverpool Welsh National Society and Bangor Liberal Club, his taking of the *Manchester Guardian* and, above all, his almost weekly preaching engagements, the profits from which were carefully noted. These amounted to over £36 in the twelve months up to the end of February 1895, almost enough to pay for the piano purchased that year, and well over double the annual wages paid to the couple's domestic servant.[43] Holiday expenses were likewise detailed. While summers were still punctuated by spells at Penygarnedd, the married Lloyd of these years also ventured farther afield to his wife's family in Scotland as well as to Yorkshire, the Isle of Man, Ireland and Switzerland.[44]

In addition, there were more regular escapes from the routines of work. Lloyd still enjoyed plays, concerts and tennis, and in his mid-forties took up golf.[45] Moreover, his interest in religious and cultural matters remained strong. As well as preaching, Lloyd was still actively involved in the temperance movement and also supported the students' Christian Union at Bangor.[46] Indeed, as in Aberystwyth, he was closely involved with a number of college societies and addressed several of these on historical, literary and other topics. From the late 1890s his long-standing interest in Welsh culture found a congenial outlet in the flourishing Cymric Society, of which he was president on several occasions and where he heard papers on the visual arts by the renowned Welsh sculptor W. Goscombe John and the artist J. 'Kelt' Edwards, on Welsh folk songs by his colleague J. Lloyd Williams and on 'The foreign element in the Welsh language' by the Celtic scholar Kuno Meyer from Liverpool University and, in October 1902, on the medieval poet-prince Hywel ab Owain Gwynedd. This last paper was delivered by T. Gwynn Jones, who was rapidly making a name for himself as one of Wales's leading poets, having just won the chair for his romantic strict-metre ode *Ymadawiad Arthur* ('The Departure of Arthur') at the Bangor National Eisteddfod the previous summer, and whose decision to devote himself to Welsh literature had in turn been inspired by hearing Lloyd lecture on the medieval Welsh court poets in 1896.[47] Nor were these the only expressions that year of a renewed interest in the Middle Ages, for at their eisteddfod in 1902 students at Bangor performed the premiere of the operetta *Cadifor*, set in twelfth-century Snowdonia, described by Lloyd as 'a most enjoyable evening, spent in watching a succession of charming scenes and listening to captivating music and hearty Welsh banter'.[48]

By then Lloyd had commenced the *History* that would offer a more prosaic but much fuller, more accurate and better-crafted depiction of medieval Wales (his recording of the precise date he began it, namely 26 January 1901, suggests a high estimation of the book's significance).[49] Why did he wait until his fortieth year before embarking on this magnum opus? After all, he appears to have expressed an intention of writing such a work since his days at Oxford, and it was eagerly anticipated from the late 1880s onwards.[50] The short answer is that, after his arrival in Bangor, he gave priority to other tasks before settling down to what he doubtless realized would be a lengthy and arduous project, tasks which in turn throw valuable light on both his broader outlook and, more specifically, his development as a historian. In terms of professional duties, it is worth emphasizing that, until he succeeded Reichel as professor of history in October 1899, he carried out the work of registrar single-handedly, thereafter being relieved of some of his administrative responsibilities by an assistant registrar.[51] In other words, by the time Lloyd started writing his *History* he was more fully employed as a historian than he had been for most of the 1890s.[52]

Although he had secured the position of lecturer in Welsh history on his arrival at Bangor in 1892, Lloyd did not offer to teach the subject to undergraduates until the 1895–6 session, perhaps spurred on by O. M. Edwards's complaint that none of the colleges of the new University of Wales had yet offered 'a course of lectures on Welsh history'.[53] Moreover, he provided only one 'special course', to third-year students, on the 'History of Wales up to 1600'.[54] To judge by the list of topics and suggested reading, the coverage was heavily tilted towards the period down to the Edwardian conquest in the late thirteenth century, prompting Edward Edwards, brother of O. M. Edwards and Lloyd's successor as professor of history at Aberystwyth, to wonder: 'Dont [*sic*] you think that your scheme emphasises the <u>early</u> part at the expense of the later Tudor part?'[55] Lloyd evidently saw no reason to change his mind, as the course remained on the history syllabus, with minor variations in nomenclature, until he retired.[56] However, from 1899 he spread his wings as a result of the additional obligations arising from his appointment as professor of history, and gave, in alternate years, two eighty-lecture courses on 'The history of Great Britain and Ireland in its connexion with the history of Western Europe', one covering 56 BC to AD 1485, the other continuing thereafter to 1815. In addition, he taught a 'junior course' on English history to 1688 and an 'honours course' on 'The Age of the Renaissance' (1453–1527).[57] This pattern continued for a decade, being modified only from 1910–11 following the appointment of J. F. Rees as assistant lecturer in history.[58] Among the changes introduced was a survey course on western Europe 1000–1815 and the inclusion, in the first-year course, of a weekly lecture on a 'special period of Welsh history' – initially the age of Owain Glyndŵr, then the age of Giraldus Cambrensis – alongside lectures on England and Wales 1485–1815.[59] To judge by the recollections of one of his early students at Bangor, Lloyd's sober, dignified style of lecturing engendered respect rather than enthusiasm; and students who fell short of his exacting standards were greeted with 'a deadly atmosphere of cold courtesy' that made his disapproval painfully clear.[60]

The advanced course on Welsh history continued, and involved reading selected passages from printed primary sources in Latin and Welsh, some of which were set for translation and comment in the examination together with essay questions. 'The Age of the Renaissance' likewise required the study of 'original authorities'.[61] Lloyd placed great weight on these specialized courses, 'as I think them a valuable introduction to the study of the real history'.[62] The emphasis on primary sources may simply indicate deference to the example of Oxford, where some history papers in Lloyd's undergraduate days had contained passages for comment; certainly, he thought that this model justified another aspect of the Bangor examinations, namely the choice of questions given candidates, observing to the external examiner, O. M. Edwards, then a fellow of Lincoln College, 'it is the Oxford practice, is it not?'[63] Yet Oxford history was predominantly centred on the essay and, though he no doubt shared Reichel's conviction of the need for the new University of Wales degree to maintain the stringent standards of Oxford and Cambridge, Lloyd was probably also responding to new developments in the professionalization of history in Britain, and especially to calls for more rigorous training in historical methods and sources.[64] In June 1902 he heard F. York Powell, regius professor of modern history at Oxford, declare that history was a branch of science whose undergraduate syllabus should include research.[65] Four years later a far more effective advocate of this approach, T. F. Tout, delivered his famous lecture at Cambridge urging the creation of 'Schools of history'. This struck a chord with Lloyd, who claimed that, in his special course on Wales, he was trying to achieve exactly what Tout recommended with respect to such specialized final-year courses, although lack of space had prevented him from holding seminars in a room equipped for this purpose, a deficiency he intended to rectify in the projected new college building.[66] How far Lloyd was able to go further and foster postgraduate research in history during these early years in Bangor is, however, unclear.[67]

The special course he offered on Wales must have helped Lloyd to extend his familiarity with the terrain he came to traverse so thoroughly in his *History*. So too did two other enterprises he undertook in the 1890s. In August 1892 he was asked by Daniel Lleufer Thomas (1863–1940), a barrister with a strong interest in history, to take on some of the Welsh entries for the *Dictionary of National Biography* (*DNB*) 'as a sort of recreation for the holidays'.[68] Lloyd readily complied, and between 1893 and 1900 published over one hundred entries.[69] A substantial number of these dealt with medieval figures: for instance, the first article to appear was on Madog ap Maredudd (d.1160), ruler of Powys. However, over half the people covered dated from the sixteenth to nineteenth centuries, and included individuals with whom Lloyd had been personally acquainted, such as the brothers John Thomas (1821–92) and Owen Thomas (1812–91), both ministers in Liverpool;

he also sought personal recollections of the editor and author David Owen (Brutus, 1795–1866).[70] The care he took to ensure the accuracy of his entries was characteristic of his historical scholarship, but their chronological breadth was arguably no less significant.

His second major writing project at this time comprised three short bilingual textbooks for elementary (primary) schoolchildren, outlining the history of Wales from the Stone Age to the death of Llywelyn ap Gruffudd in 1282.[71] Lloyd later said that his work for these had helped to lay the foundations for the much more substantial *History*.[72] However, that was neither their immediate nor their most important purpose. Nor is it likely that he was mainly motivated by the additional income they – like the *DNB* articles – provided, in contrast to Tout, who gave priority to producing textbooks before embarking on a major, more time-consuming work whose financial rewards would necessarily be delayed.[73] Rather, Lloyd's decision to devote time to producing these books – published successively in 1893, 1896 and 1900 – was probably determined above all by his broader commitment to the advancement of Welsh education at all levels, and their bilingual format was explicitly tailored to the new provision in 1893, linked to the adoption of Welsh as a class subject in elementary schools, that 'the instruction may generally be bilingual'.[74] These changes had been a key objective of the Society for Utilizing the Welsh Language, which Lloyd had supported from its inception in 1885; indeed, it was at the society's request that he had written the books, whose bilingual format reflected an attempt to put into action the method – which he later wryly admitted was probably flawed – advocated by the society of teaching English to Welsh-speaking children through using their mother tongue.[75] The Welsh texts also adhered to the new standard orthography approved by the society (including Lloyd, who had sat on the relevant committee), an orthography devised by his Bangor colleague John Morris Jones, who also checked the volumes, incidentally voicing strong disapproval of their author's allegedly 'Roman Catholic' treatment of the early Christian writer Pelagius, 'a very fine fellow'![76] Nor did his commitment to school education cease with the appearance of the third textbook, for from 1903 onwards Lloyd regularly gave lectures on the history of Wales to the annual summer schools for schoolteachers held by the recently reconstituted Cymdeithas yr Iaith Gymraeg or Welsh Language Society (as it was renamed in English).[77]

Further evidence of Lloyd's sense of obligation to foster the new educational opportunities in Wales – as well as of his continuing interest in Welsh literature – in his early years at Bangor is found in his work for the University of Wales's Guild of Graduates, established in 1894. Its second warden, Tom Ellis, stressed that the guild had a special responsibility to ensure the preservation and dissemination of the literature and records of Wales. Lloyd agreed, and was impatient to get things done: he recommended creating committees on dialects, folklore and place-names to gather material from all over Wales, 'bearing upon Welsh history and philology' as well as natural history.[78] Moreover, he put his principles into practice as secretary of its literature section in 1897–9, undertaking a voluminous correspondence and attending numerous meetings in order to ensure the appearance of a series of classic texts of Welsh literature for the use of university students.[79] This service to the guild – fittingly recognized by Lloyd's election as warden in succession to Tom Ellis following the latter's death in 1899 – reflected an enduring conviction that, in order to be effective, research on Wales needed to be coordinated in an organizational framework.[80] Nor was his commitment to educating his compatriots confined to the formal structures of school and university. As at Aberystwyth, he also responded to the demand for talks on Welsh history from various societies in Wales and England – for example, by giving a lecture on Giraldus Cambrensis illustrated by twenty-six lantern slides, which he prudently tried out before their first public showing in March 1897.[81] Occasionally, too, his learning was sought by those in government: shortly after Lloyd's arrival in Bangor, Tom Ellis urgently requested corrections of the spelling of Welsh place-names so that these could be forwarded to a parliamentary committee on the Ordnance Survey, and the following year he wrote from the Treasury asking to borrow a lecture on Llywelyn the Great.[82] Lloyd's close involvement with the Cambrian Archaeological Association, which he joined in 1896, and whose annual meetings he attended regularly from 1902, likewise illustrates his desire to disseminate knowledge of the Welsh past beyond the walls of school and university.[83]

His early years at Bangor serve to underline, then, that Lloyd's work as a historian of Wales developed in the broader contexts of fostering Welsh education and of making their past more accessible to the Welsh. Much of his lecturing and writing no doubt fed into the preparation for writing his magnum opus (a lengthy paper on eleventh-century Wales is a notable example [84]). However, it would be misleading to characterize these activities as mere preludes to the great work that emerged from the press in January 1911: Lloyd evidently believed that they were worth undertaking in their own right. Moreover, even when his *History* was under way, he continued to spread his wings much wider, writing short pieces on educational and cultural topics as well as a booklet in Welsh on the history of the Welsh Congregationalists and a volume on Caernarfonshire in the Cambridge County Geographies series.[85] The latter publication appeared in July 1911, six months after the *History*, and, even if the volume was begun when the magnum opus was largely finished, that he took it on at all is striking testimony to his dedication and stamina. Yet, while other writing commitments help to explain why the *History* took almost ten years to complete, the main explanation lies elsewhere. Most important was the sheer scale and difficulty of the challenge posed by the work and the thoroughness, amply attested by the detailed notebooks used to assemble material from primary and secondary sources, with which Lloyd addressed it. In addition, as registrar and professor of history, there were still other major demands on his time: he later claimed, albeit rather in jest, that he was 'lecturer in the morning, registrar in the afternoon, and researcher in the evening'.[86] Moreover, while teaching was restricted to term time, his duties as registrar continued throughout the year. In other words, Lloyd had frequently to break off his journey through the early centuries of Welsh history, as he introduced his students to medieval and modern British and Irish history or 'The Age of the Renaissance', continued to deliver lectures to audiences outside Bangor, corresponded with the Treasury concerning university finance and took minutes at college committees.[87]

Those committees included one established to raise funds for a new college building whose planning and construction coincided with the composition of Lloyd's magnum opus.[88] When the site for the building was accepted in April 1902 the *History*, too, was still in its very early stages, with Lloyd poised to step from the 'The Historic Dawn' into the Roman period.[89] Thereafter, however, the book progressed far more rapidly than the building: by the arrival of King Edward VII to lay the foundation stone on 11 July 1907 three-quarters of the text was completed, Lloyd being well into a survey of the political conditions revealed by an earlier visitor to Bangor, Giraldus Cambrensis, in the account of his journey round Wales in 1188.[90] In December 1909 Longmans agreed to publish the work, to the great delight of its author, who received the first proofs the following month and his first copies of the two volumes a year later, on 30 January 1911.[91] As Lloyd told T. F. Tout soon afterwards: 'You cannot imagine how relieved I am to get the book finally out of my hands, after ten years' work.'[92] Yet there was little time to relish his achievement, for from early February Lloyd was preoccupied with the move to the new college buildings, which 'are taking up nearly all my time'.[93] The buildings – embellished with statues of notable Welsh historical figures, including St David and Owain Glyndŵr – were officially opened on 14 July 1911 by King George V, who had been crowned three weeks earlier. The opening followed the royal investiture of the prince of Wales in Caernarfon the previous day, and formed part of an extensive tour to inaugurate the new reign that took in Ireland and Scotland and culminated in a spectacular durbar in Delhi five months later.[94] In their different ways, both the new buildings and the *History* expressed a modern sense of Welsh nationality that not only sought legitimacy in the depths of the past but also claimed a place in the sun at the high noon of empire.

4

Historian of Wales, 1911–1947

Shortly after his fiftieth birthday in May 1911 Lloyd received a letter from the historian A. G. Little (1863–1945), who had himself given popular lectures on medieval Wales a decade earlier at the university college in Cardiff, congratulating him on the appearance of his magnum opus and declaring: 'A grateful country should give you two years off to browse unhindered in the BM and P.R.O. and continue the history.'[1] It is unlikely that Lloyd had such expectations, and he continued to combine the twin roles of registrar and professor of history at Bangor until he stepped down from the former position in February 1920.[2] Nor does this redefinition of responsibilities seem to have created more time for research and writing, as over the following decade Lloyd faced the challenges of new administrative tasks resulting from the reorganization of the federal University of Wales in the wake of the Haldane Commission's report on Welsh higher education. Thus it was only after retiring in 1930, aged sixty-nine, that he was relieved of his teaching and departmental duties, although he continued to play an active part on university committees and also to attend what he considered his three main annual meetings of the Welsh Congregationalist Union, the National Eisteddfod and the Cambrian Archaeological Association (fig. 5).[3] There were new commitments, too, notably membership of the Royal Commission on Tithe Rent Charge in 1934–5.[4] Apart from increasing deafness in his final years, Lloyd enjoyed generally good health throughout this active retirement and his mental faculties remained undiminished.

Active though he was, Lloyd never again published anything as substantial and significant as the *History* which appeared in January 1911. In large part this was because he considered the work his defining achievement. As well as keeping copies of reviews – underlining particularly favourable comments in blue pencil – he kept track of sales and profits (the work sold well), continued to add material to the preparatory notebooks and listed corrections on points of detail received from others or spotted by him.[5] Yet, apart from incorporating those corrections and adding a new introduction designed to take cognizance of recent developments in prehistoric and Roman archaeology, Lloyd made no substantive changes to the third edition published in 1939, two-thirds of whose 750 copies were destroyed in the blitz on London, and there is little to indicate that he saw any reason radically to change the interpretation at which he had arrived over three decades earlier.[6] Nevertheless, his understandable satisfaction with the *History* is not sufficient to explain why this remained his only magnum opus, or, to put it differently, why his career from 1911 onwards followed the path it did. Two other considerations also need to be taken into account, one negative, the other positive: the difficulties of moving forwards into the later Middle Ages posed by the need to draw extensively on unpublished source material; and a commitment to creating favourable conditions for the long-term development of Welsh historical and other scholarship on modern 'scientific' lines. (Apart from the requirements of teaching, he never seems to have considered turning his attention to fields of historical inquiry beyond Wales.[7])

A. G. Little was not alone in hoping that the *History* would be continued into the later Middle Ages or even beyond.[8] However, the nearest Lloyd came to doing this was in his Ford Lectures on Owain Glyndŵr, delivered at Oxford in 1920. Significantly, it took him over ten years to rewrite these for publication – as long as he had spent on writing the far longer and more ambitious *History* of 1911.[9] At the root of this delay was the difficulty Lloyd encountered in finding new evidence from unpublished archival and manuscript sources, materials which he had hitherto found little occasion to consult and in which he had neither the time nor, perhaps, the inclination to immerse himself in detail; he once admitted that the *History* ended in 1282 because thereafter the apparatus was unmanageable.[10] That his engagement with later medieval Wales was limited does not mean, however, that the rest of his life should be viewed as an anti-climax. For one thing, he continued to write a great deal, including, besides the volume on Glyndŵr, numerous scholarly articles and a short survey of Welsh history down to 1930; he also initiated and contributed to two major collaborative works, a county history of Carmarthenshire and a dictionary of Welsh biography.[11]

Above all, the *History* cemented his scholarly reputation; he was given public recognition by, for example, the award of the Cymmrodorion Medal (1913), the conferring of doctorates by the universities of Oxford (1918), Wales (1922) and Manchester (1937), election as a fellow of the British Academy (1930) and – rather late in the day in Lloyd's view – a knighthood (1934).[12] Likewise, it was to him that *The Times* turned after Lloyd George's appointment in 1916 as the first Welsh prime minister for an article on Welsh statesmen in England.[13] (A student cartoonist at Bangor was rather less flattering in 1912, portraying Lloyd striding forth in a top hat with his nose in the air beside the caption 'Pomposo'![14]) Moreover, Lloyd's advice was sought by official bodies in Wales on a variety of subjects – ranging from the choice of individuals to be represented by 'statues of the most eminent Welshmen in the history of the Principality' in Cardiff City Hall to a suitable crest and motto for the Royal Air Force base at St Athan in Glamorgan – as well as by the organizers of historical pageants, although A. P. Graves, father of the author Robert Graves, was unable to persuade Lloyd to take part in the episode on Owain Glyndŵr he had apparently helped to devise for the 1922 pageant at Harlech when this was repeated seven years later![15] Even so, there was a sense in which, in later life, Lloyd himself became an iconic representative of Welsh history, being the subject of four portraits.[16] His standing was also further recognized by invitations to preside or speak at various public gatherings and by his appearance in a short film made in 1937 to help encourage Americans of Welsh descent to contribute funds to an extension of the National Museum in Cardiff.[17]

The reputation secured by the publication of the *History*, coupled with his administrative talents, meant that Lloyd was well placed to promote the development of Welsh history as an academic discipline and help create institutional frameworks that could sustain it in the future. These organizational efforts, then, provide the main focus of the following discussion. Its key contention will be that, while Lloyd both participated in and contributed to a wider process of professionalization of history in Britain, his attempts to foster historical studies continued to be conceived essentially within a context of national educational and scholarly advance distinctive to Wales.

Of course, Lloyd did not concentrate on fostering Welsh historical studies to the exclusion of all else. Many of the routines and interests of earlier years were maintained. Although he ceased to preach in 1917, Lloyd remained a committed Congregationalist, playing an active part in his church in Upper Bangor, and he took particular pride in his election as chairman of the Welsh Congregationalist Union in 1934–5.[18] Equally, though, he continued to indulge his fondness for the theatre, sometimes taking the opportunity offered by meetings in London to see productions in the West End.[19] During his retirement he also frequently participated in play readings in Bangor.[20] He also welcomed the new forms of entertainment offered by the radio, including broadcasts of concerts, as well as by the cinema, where he saw, for example, D. W. Griffith's *Intolerance*, *The Blue Angel* starring Marlene Dietrich and, apparently with his granddaughter, Walt Disney's *Snow White and the Seven Dwarfs*.[21] Further novel forms of recreation in these years were provided by whist drives and the acquisition of a dog, Crib (1926–40), to whom his master became greatly attached.[22] Apart from the war years, annual holidays remained a regular fixture, and in the 1920s Lloyd returned twice to Switzerland and also visited Belgium, Boulogne, Jersey and Northern Ireland; after his retirement, however, destinations were confined to England, Scotland and, for a last holiday in 1946, close to home at Cricieth.[23]

These holidays were taken with his wife, Tina, and sometimes their children. Both Eluned (1897–1979) and Edward (1904–64) followed in their father's footsteps to Oxford.[24] The latter pursued a career in business and in 1931 married Arabella Davies, who gave birth to a daughter, Anne Patricia Westbury Lloyd, in 1934. Anne's evacuation during the Second World War to Caernarfon, only about seven miles south-west of Bangor, ensured that she often visited her grandparents' home at Gwaen Deg, where, according to the later recollections of one of her companions, Lloyd was very good with the children and got them to play charades just as he had done in his own childhood in Liverpool – a legacy of his Victorian upbringing no less significant than the rather forbidding formality of his public persona.[25] (Anne would eventually marry an American, Robert Hess, and move to New Jersey, where the couple had three children.[26]) Eluned, by contrast, shared her father's academic interests and eventually obtained a position in Liverpool University; in 1923 she married William Garmon Jones (1884–1937), professor of history at the university and later also its librarian, and a scholar much respected by Lloyd. Sadly the marriage was cut short by Garmon Jones's untimely death in May 1937, leaving Eluned a widow aged only thirty-nine. Just over twenty years previously Lloyd's family had suffered another premature loss, as his younger brother, Thomas Arthur, died from typhoid in January 1917.[27] He was followed to the grave by their father, Edward Lloyd, two months later and by their mother, Margaret Lloyd, in December 1921.[28] This did not break the connection with Liverpool, however, as from 1923 not only did Lloyd regularly attend meetings for several years of the board of directors of his father's business but, more importantly, Eluned lived in neighbouring Birkenhead until she moved back to Bangor in 1945 (and her brother relocated to Liverpool later in the same year).[29] On the other hand, the death of Elizabeth Ridge (1869–1946), a cousin who had lived in the family home of Bryndifyr, finally severed the long-standing connection with Penygarnedd in northern Montgomeryshire which Lloyd recalled so warmly in his old age.[30] Perhaps it was in homage to his roots that he chose to be buried overlooking the Menai Strait on Ynys Tysilio (Church Island), Anglesey, as Tysilio had been the patron saint of the medieval kingdom of Powys which had included the later county of Montgomeryshire.[31] It was in this peaceful location, then, that Lloyd was laid to rest following his death in hospital in Bangor on 20 June 1947. His gravestone sums up how he wished to be remembered with eloquent economy: 'Hanesydd Cymru' ('Historian of Wales').[32]

Professional historian

How, then, did this self-styled 'Historian of Wales' influence the development of history, and especially Welsh history, during the years after the publication of his magnum opus in 1911? Let us begin by considering his role in teaching and postgraduate research. As we have seen, in 1906 Lloyd informed Tout that the new library at Bangor would contain a specially designated room to facilitate seminar teaching in history, and after the opening of the new college building in 1911 this history research room, intended for honours and MA students, became a favourite haunt of Lloyd's for the rest of his life: he was distressed to find the Tudor historian J. E. Neale holding a class in it during University College London's relocation to Bangor during the Second World War![33] Yet, although he identified with the calls by Tout, Firth and others to establish schools of history on the continental European model, Lloyd seems to have had only limited success in putting these precepts into practice. Lack of time and resources clearly militated against small-group teaching and the development of postgraduate training. Staff in the department of history remained very few, Lloyd being supported only by an assistant lecturer from 1909 to 1919, when a further post of lecturer in modern history was created, supplemented by the designation in 1920 of the college's librarian as reader in modern Welsh history. Small wonder that Tout, who with his colleague James Tait had developed a powerful school of history at Manchester, remarked to Lloyd in 1918 that 'your very solitary condition appeals to my sympathy very profoundly'.[34] Moreover, until 1920 Lloyd continued to shoulder the responsibilities of registrar, rendered even more onerous by the disruption of the First World War, when the number of students plummeted to 147 by 1917, and colleagues – including his own assistant lecturer, A. S. Turberville – were called away on military service; as Lloyd put it in June 1916, 'these are the days in which we are all trying to do twice as much work as we can manage (at any rate, it is in my own case)'.[35] Peace brought fresh challenges as student numbers at Bangor rapidly increased, reaching 672 in 1921 (a figure not exceeded until 1946), and, although this growth was most apparent in mathematics and the sciences, the numbers taking history recovered to their pre-war levels of around one hundred and reached 119 in 1920.[36]

The promotion of Turberville to the new lecturership in modern history in 1919 and his succession as assistant lecturer by A. H. Dodd (1891–1975) made possible the first major change to the undergraduate syllabus in history since 1911, and the revised syllabus remained virtually unchanged until Lloyd's retirement in 1930. The first-year 'intermediate course' was expanded by offering a choice between two surveys of England and Wales, one from 55 BC to AD 1485, the other from 1485 to 1815, previously available only in alternate years; the latter was accompanied by an additional 'special period' of Welsh history in 'the age of the Puritan Revolution (1625–1660)'. The provision of European history was also increased, with two courses respectively covering 1300–1815 and 1815–1901, and opportunities were given to study modern economic history, the history of imperial Rome and political philosophy through 'accessory courses' taught in other departments. Yet there were continuities, too, including Lloyd's two specialized honours courses on Wales to 1603 and on the age of the Renaissance.[37] Moreover, while Lloyd oversaw the provision of greater coverage and choice for undergraduate students of history at Bangor, this was not accompanied by any major innovations in the methods of teaching, which still relied heavily on lectures, essays and the mastery of prescribed texts, although Dodd managed to fit in some classes with small groups; in particular, there was no requirement to undertake original research on the lines of the compulsory thesis established at Manchester from 1909.[38]

Research, then, was reserved for postgraduate study. How far Lloyd promoted this is unclear. Since the 1890s the University of Wales had recognized two routes to an MA degree: a combination of examinations and a thesis on a prescribed topic arising from a special study, and a thesis presenting the fruits of original research.[39] Yet regulations for the first part of the former option do not appear in the Bangor *Calendar* until 1926, and there is no evidence that any Bangor student successfully completed one of the designated theses.[40] As in the other Welsh colleges, the preferred postgraduate route was the thesis by research. Nineteen such history theses from Bangor were accepted for the MA between 1911 and

1929, their coverage ranging chronologically from the Middle Ages to the early twentieth century. Just over half of these dealt specifically with Wales.[41] One was a study of 'Wales under the Propagation Act, 1650–3' (1914) by Thomas Richards, a former student whom Lloyd had encouraged to write an MA thesis in Welsh history a decade earlier; however, he dissuaded Richards from pursuing medieval topics, and the thesis was eventually completed above all thanks to the inspiration of Thomas Shankland, librarian at Bangor.[42] Indeed, during Lloyd's last twenty years in post only two MA theses on the history of medieval Wales were accepted from Bangor.[43] One was by Ruth Easterling, whom Lloyd saw frequently in 1913 while she completed her work on the friars in Wales, the fruits of which were soon published in an article which concluded by thanking both Lloyd and A. G. Little, by then well established as a distinguished historian of the Franciscans.[44] The other, accepted in 1924, was a study of the medieval lordship of Montgomery.[45] Of course, it is possible that Lloyd had given guidance to other students undertaking dissertations on medieval topics not primarily concerned with Wales, and he certainly encouraged work on Welsh history as a whole. Thus, from 1923, the entry for the history department in the college *Calendar* informed its readers:

> Special facilities are offered to graduates desiring to carry on research in the History of Wales. Full provision has been made in the Library for the needs of such students, and the Reader in Modern Welsh History is prepared to give such guidance and assistance as may be required.[46]

Nevertheless, given Lloyd's expertise, the paucity of research on the history of medieval Wales by Bangor graduates is striking, especially when compared with the far larger output of successful MA theses in this field at Aberystwyth – at least six by 1910, with no fewer than a further seventeen between 1911 and 1928.[47] This contrast was probably due above all to the fact that, in addition to its professor of history, Edward Edwards, Aberystwyth employed E. A. Lewis (1880–1942), initially as an assistant lecturer in Welsh history (1910–12), then as professor of economics and political science (1912–31). Lewis had worked extensively with archival sources in his research on the medieval boroughs of north Wales for a University of Wales MA dissertation (1902), subsequently expanded into a doctoral thesis at the London School of Economics, and had benefited from the instruction in advanced historical studies given there by Hubert Hall of the Public Record Office. Lewis went on to impart what he had learnt to students at Aberystwyth, where, among many other duties, he taught palaeography and diplomatic.[48] In this he differed significantly from Lloyd, who seems never to have provided such technical training. Indeed, it is doubtful whether Lloyd considered it essential: as we shall see, his priority as a historian was to try and impose coherence on the past through meticulous investigation of the published source material, and he made relatively little use of unpublished manuscripts and documents.[49] He may well have deemed a similar approach sufficient for postgraduate research. To judge by the article summarizing the findings of her thesis on the friars, his student Ruth Easterling certainly seems to have thought so, stressing that she made 'no claim to bring forward new, in the sense of hitherto unpublished, material', but had, rather, sought 'to clear the ground by bringing together and sifting information gathered from a variety of sources'.[50] However, the point should not be pressed too far: after all, a decade later Dora Ward used archival documents for her thesis on the medieval lordship of Montgomery.[51] Another constraint on developing postgraduate work on medieval Welsh history may, of course, simply have been Lloyd's mastery of the subject, especially down to the late thirteenth century: as with other groundbreaking studies, the very qualities of the 1911 *History* that inspired admiration may also have inhibited further research in the field it transformed.[52]

In addition to promoting postgraduate research at Bangor, albeit on a limited scale, Lloyd examined theses at other universities and served as external examiner in history at the National University of Ireland during the challenging years from 1916 to 1919.[53] He also played a part in other developments that contributed to the wider professionalization of history in Britain, which, because of the lack of specialized research institutes until 1921, was driven largely by the creation of 'invisible colleges' focused on a 'growing network of journals and associations'.[54] Thus, Lloyd was a life-long subscriber to the *English Historical Review* almost from its inception in 1886, became a fellow of the Royal Historical Society in 1911 and at about the same time started to attend meetings of the Historical Association, an organization for teachers of history in schools as well universities founded in 1906, and served on its council. In addition, he occasionally attended international historical conferences, namely the Anglo-American Conference of Historians in London (in 1921, 1931 and 1936) and the International Congress of Historical Sciences, first in London in 1913, then, ten years later, in Brussels, where reaction to the nationalist excesses of the First World War cast doubts on the validity of national history.[55] It was perhaps appropriate, then, that Lloyd's paper on Owain Glyndŵr and the bishopric of Bangor was overshadowed by the simultaneous attraction of Marc Bloch speaking on 'What is a fief?'[56] We can only guess whether Lloyd met Bloch at Brussels in April 1923. What is clear, though, is that they represented not only different generations but, much more importantly, different understandings of history, one focused on the nation, the other on themes and problems common to different societies.[57] More generally, such congresses gave Lloyd an opportunity to hear leading medievalists of the earlier twentieth century, such as Charles Homer Haskins, Felix Liebermann and Henri Pirenne in 1913.[58] However, it is difficult to tell how receptive he was to the various approaches they represented; his identification with an international community of historians does not appear to have significantly influenced his own historical work. On the other hand, the reputation he enjoyed as a historian of Wales resulted in a heavy correspondence, including enquiries on Welsh place-names, personal names and historical questions from scholars elsewhere in Wales, in England, Ireland, continental Europe and the United States. Thus he gave considerable help to Doris Stenton as she edited medieval English pipe rolls (royal financial accounts), corresponded with Edmund Curtis – who praised Lloyd's *History* as 'a model to Celtic historians of patriotic affection combined with thoroughness & impartiality' – concerning Welsh landholding near Dublin and assisted Adrian Morey with a decree of Pope Alexander III.[59]

Promoting Welsh scholarship

Yet, if Lloyd felt he belonged to a wider world of professional historians, his overriding commitment was to fostering historical and related studies in Wales. He had already tried to put his ideals into practice in the 1890s through his work for the University of Wales Guild of Graduates and had urged the need for greater cooperation to further research in Wales in a lecture to the Cymmrodorion in Carmarthen in 1911.[60] He repeated the call in November 1918 in an address to the Liverpool Welsh National Society in which he quoted verbatim from the earlier lecture. By then, however, he had the satisfaction of knowing that the University of Wales was about to establish a body that could realize his aspirations: the Board of Celtic Studies.[61] The formation of the board had been recommended by the Royal Commission on University Education in Wales, which met in 1916–17 under the chairmanship of Lord Haldane with the aim of reorganizing the University of Wales into a more effective federal organization, and was based on a 'Memorandum on Celtic Studies with Special Reference to the Language, Literature and History of Wales' submitted by J. H. Davies, then registrar at Aberystwyth.[62] Though its proposals differed in certain respects from those that Lloyd had presented earlier, they show that he was not alone in urging the need for adopting a coordinated approach, and the key recommendations were supported by Bangor as well as Aberystwyth. According to Davies's proposals, the board would be responsible to the university for directing research in Celtic, and more particularly Welsh, studies in the different colleges, though it would also have representatives of the National Library and National Museum of Wales, whose foundation in 1907 had marked important steps in the movement 'to shape a rib cage for nationality' in the late Victorian and Edwardian eras.[63] The intention, therefore, was not to create a centre for the advanced training of scholars, on the lines of the Institute for Historical Research established by the University of London in 1921,[64] but, rather, a supervisory body that would make more effective use of existing resources through drawing up plans for research and publication and supporting these with limited grants, yet without superseding the postgraduate and other research work of the individual colleges.[65]

In November 1918 the University of Wales approved the Haldane Commission's recommendation for the establishment of a Board of Celtic Studies, and the first meeting was held the following January. Lloyd was among the members nominated and from then on he played a crucial role, as he drew up a statement of the board's functions and in March 1919 was elected chairman, a post he held until 1940 without ever missing a meeting.[66] The commission had identified three principal aspects of 'Celtic Studies in Wales': language and literature; history; and archaeology and art (including music).[67] Lloyd expanded the second category to 'the history, laws and customs of the Celtic peoples', no doubt reflecting a desire to ensure the inclusion of legal studies that had been fundamental to his own work as a historian (although it should be added that 'Early Laws and Institutions of the Celtic Peoples' had already featured in J. H. Davies's memorandum).[68] His influence may also be seen in the expansion of the board's membership to include representatives of two learned societies in Wales – the Cambrian Archaeological Association and the Honourable Society of Cymmrodorion – as well as of the three constituent colleges, Jesus College, Oxford and the National Library and National Museum.[69] It appears that Lloyd sought to make the board even more representative of Welsh scholarly endeavour than had been originally envisaged, thereby linking it more directly with earlier scholarly efforts, in line with the proposals he had advanced with respect to historical and archaeological research in 1911, and occasionally his annual reports explicitly note that the board had cooperated with the Cambrian Archaeological Association in supporting excavations.[70]

Lloyd's resignation as chairman elicited the following tribute:

> No University Board was more fortunate in its Chairman, for he combined in his person all the main interests – historical, archaeological, linguistic, and literary – for the promotion of which the Board was established, while to the routine work of administration he brought unfailing tact, an intimate knowledge of Welsh life, and a rare maturity of judgment.[71]

Notwithstanding the predictable panegyric, the emphasis on Lloyd's broad interests was fair. He was very well informed about

Welsh language and literature – which he had of course taught at Aberystwyth – as well as archaeology, and had drawn extensively on these disciplines in writing his *History*; he therefore took for granted the close interrelatedness of the different branches of Celtic studies that fell under the board's remit. This abiding allegiance to interdisciplinarity was given eloquent expression in a lecture at the National Museum in Cardiff in 1932 which stressed the need to combine the findings of both archaeology and history in study-ing the Welsh past.[72] Nor was his familiarity with archaeology restricted to what he had read, for he had frequently visited archaeo-logical sites and monuments, especially during the annual summer meetings of the Cambrian Archaeological Association. In addition, Lloyd was actively involved in helping to preserve the material remains of the Welsh past as a member of the government's Advisory Board on Ancient Monuments in Wales, having oversight of the board's inspectors in the counties of Caernarfonshire and Denbigh-shire.[73] He was particularly anxious that the sites should not be damaged as a result of conditions during the First World War and successfully pressed for an inspector to be employed in 'keeping an eye on the vandals or those who think anything is justified in war time, in the interest of our irreplaceable antiquities'.[74] During his retirement he also served as a member of the Royal Commission on the Ancient and Historical Monuments of Wales, having been appointed in 1930 to succeed John Morris-Jones.[75]

Nevertheless, Lloyd saw himself as a historian above all. He often deferred to the linguistic and literary expertise of Ifor Williams (1881–1965), a colleague in the Welsh department at Bangor from 1907; likewise, late in life he once declined to offer an opinion on a matter of 'pure archaeology' which he felt fell outside his com-petence.[76] Accordingly, when the board began to publish a journal, the *Bulletin of the Board of Celtic Studies*, in 1921, Lloyd edited its history and law section, the language and literature and archaeo-logy and art sections being left to specialists in those fields. One main function of the *Bulletin* was to make available editions of primary sources, from both the Middle Ages and later periods, a task subsequently expanded from the late 1920s through the establish-ment of a 'History and Law Series', consisting of volumes providing calendars and texts of unpublished sources, especially documents held in the Public Record Office in London.[77] The Record Office's Hubert Hall had been co-opted as a member of the board and gave the credit for the series to Lloyd, whom he praised for his 'brave efforts to uphold the importance of publishing the materials for Welsh history in the English medieval or post-medieval archives'.[78] Yet, if his influential position on the board allowed Lloyd to promote work on the history of Wales, as in his earlier years he saw this as part of a wider scholarly enterprise: his primary objective was not to professionalize historical studies but to further research across a broad spectrum of studies pertaining specifically to Wales. The main concern of the board during Lloyd's chairmanship was supervising the compilation of an authoritative dictionary of the Welsh language; it also issued a revised version of the guide on Welsh orthography originally published by the Welsh Language Society (a reminder of the continuities of previous priorities), sought to record Welsh dialects and initiated abortive discussions on preparing a survey of Welsh place-names. In addition, grants were awarded towards the costs of archaeological excavations.[79]

Lloyd's work for the Board of Celtic Studies may be seen, then, as continuing a lifelong commitment to placing Welsh scholarship on a sound footing, not least by filling major gaps in provision. The same was true of two large-scale editorial projects that occupied much of his retirement: a history of Carmarthenshire from prehistory to 1900 and a substantial one-volume Welsh biographical dictionary. Both were attempts to break new ground. Lloyd had initiated the Carmarthenshire *History* in 1930 on the grounds that, though geographically the largest in Wales, the county lacked an authoritative account of its past. But in so doing he hoped to realize a larger ambition, namely to provide a model for other Welsh county histories through treating the county as a single entity rather than an agglomeration of parishes, as had tended to be the case with previous works of this kind.[80] (At the beginning of the century, an alternative model, combining thematic and detailed topographical coverage, was briefly in prospect as an abortive attempt was made to launch a Welsh counterpart to the *Victoria History of the Counties of England*.[81]) Bringing the Carmarthenshire project to fruition proved a slow and difficult enterprise, hampered by financial problems, and the publication of the second and final volume in 1939 brought great relief to its editor, who declared that he had had little idea when he embarked on the task that 'this would be my chief concern and cause of anxiety day and night for almost nine years'.[82] However, as soon as the work was off his hands, Lloyd, now well into his seventies, started on what would be the last major enterprise of his life: helping to edit the dictionary of Welsh biography commissioned by the Honourable Society of Cymmrodorion in 1937 and eventually published in 1953.[83] In close cooperation with his colleague R. T. Jenkins, appointed lecturer in Welsh history at Bangor in 1930, Lloyd played an important role in the formative stages of the dictionary by defining its scope and approach and by writing sixty-two articles.[84] Thus the scholar who had cut his historian's teeth on the *Dictionary of National Biography* in the 1890s ended his career half a century later by laying the foundations of a comparable, albeit much more compact, reference tool intended specifically for those interested in Welsh history.

Most of the articles he wrote for the *Dictionary* were on medieval subjects – saints, princes and churchmen – with which he had long been familiar. However, a few dealt with modern antiquarians and scholars, some of whom, such as the archaeologist J. Romilly Allen (1847–1907), he had known personally.[85] A willingness to draw on his memories was a further aspect of Lloyd's sensibility as a historian, which, while by no means new, gained in significance as advancing years heightened his awareness that he represented a vanishing generation.[86] Thus it was that Lloyd himself became a source for the late Victorian era, as shown most clearly in radio broadcasts during the Second World War in which he shared his reminiscences of his student years at Oxford, Tom Ellis and the early years of the university college at Bangor.[87] It was in his last years, too, that he assiduously researched his family history.[88] This may be seen as part of a broader concern – seen also in his diaries' noting of personal anniversaries – to seek coherence, and hence meaning, in his own life just as he sought to do on a much grander scale with respect to the life of his nation.[89] Although complemented by humility, generosity and what has aptly been described as 'a puckish sense of humour', such an attitude implies that Lloyd believed in his own worth and in the enduring value of his educational and scholarly achievements.[90] The 'lantern-bearer of the lost centuries' was acutely conscious that his work as a historian of Wales was inextricably bound to a life in Welsh history.[91]

1 Bryndifyr, Penygarnedd in August 2007.

2 Isis Society, Lincoln College, Oxford, 1884. Lloyd standing at back, second from left.

"Monsieur Hercules" - Dec. 20, 1888

3 J. E. Lloyd (third from left) acting in *Monsieur Hercules,*University
   College of Wales, 20 December 1888.

4 The Senate of the University College of North Wales, Bangor, 1 November 1923, on the occasion of opening the North Wales Heroes' Memorial and laying the foundation stone of the science buildings. Those present include (seated in front row, third from right going left) Professor Sir John Morris-Jones, Professor J. E. Lloyd, Sir Harry Reichel (principal), the prince of Wales (chancellor of the University of Wales), Lord Kenyon (president of the college); Professor Ifor Williams in second row behind the prince of Wales and Reichel, and next to Major W. P. Wheldon on the right, Lloyd's successor as registrar.

5 The Cambrian Archaeological Association, Riversdale, Ramsey, Isle of Man, 4 September 1929. Lloyd second from left in front row, with his wife Tina and daughter Eluned.

6 Portrait of J. E. Lloyd by Elliott & Fry, 14 October 1932. National Portrait Gallery, London.

PART TWO

THE MAKING OF A NATION

5

A Nation Revived: Lloyd and Modern Wales

On 27 February 1937 over two hundred guests at the St David's Day dinner of the Cardiff Cymmrodorion Society heard Lloyd deliver an address, in Welsh, which reveals much about his attitude towards Wales and its past. Looking back over the years since he had first addressed the society almost half a century earlier, what struck him most was the survival of the Welsh language, which, he declared, was essential to preserving the traditions and culture of Wales. However, in what was clearly a riposte to the nationalist ideas of Saunders Lewis (who had recently begun a prison sentence for his part in setting fire to the bombing school at Penyberth in the Llŷn peninsula), Lloyd went on to warn against those leaders who wished to take Wales back to an idealized Middle Ages, whose dark side of poverty and disease was conveniently overlooked. Such a scholarly construct was no substitute for a living tradition. In fact, Lloyd observed, the only elements of contemporary Welsh culture transmitted continuously from the medieval period were the Welsh language and its strict-metre poetry; the rest was essentially a creation of the religious revival of the eighteenth century.[1] The address thus highlights that Lloyd's understanding of Welsh history extended well beyond his particular field of expertise in the Middle Ages and, indeed, attached great significance to developments in the modern period. This prompts two sets of questions that will be addressed in the following

discussion. First, how far did Lloyd write about modern Welsh history and how did he interpret it? Secondly, given his belief that the Wales of his day was in many respects a recent creation, why did he devote the bulk of his scholarly energies to a study of the country's early and medieval past?

Modern Welsh history

Before examining Lloyd's approach to modern Wales it is important to stress that the period had figured only marginally in Welsh historical writing down to the end of the nineteenth century and, indeed, did not become securely established as a field of study until the second half of the twentieth.[2] This was partly a consequence of the widespread assumption among the new 'scientific', professional historians that emerged in nineteenth-century Europe that history should be concerned mainly with states and their politics. By that yardstick, Wales since the fall of Llywelyn ap Gruffudd in 1282 was plainly deficient, for, deprived of any semblance of independent statehood, it could boast neither the constitutional continuity of England nor the revolutionary ruptures of France and other continental countries, coupled in some cases, including the United States, with violent struggles for independence, that gave sustenance to the writing of a wide variety of modern history elsewhere.[3] Small wonder, then, that the Welsh proved reluctant to integrate the post-medieval centuries into narratives of national history, confining their treatment of the modern period largely to localities (including studies of industrial communities in south Wales), individuals (not least, preachers and other religious leaders) and other aspects of religion, notably accounts of Nonconformist denominations and chapels.[4]

However, the marginalization of the modern past in accounts of Welsh history was not simply a by-product of dominant historiographical approaches in the nineteenth century. It also had deep roots in the tradition of Welsh historical writing established in the Elizabethan period. As Humphrey Llwyd put it at the end of his *Cronica Walliae* (1559), after the late thirteenth century 'there was nothinge done in Wales worthy memory, but that is to bee redde in the Englishe Chronicle'.[5] In other words, Edward I's conquest meant that the political history of Wales was henceforth indistinguishable from that of England. True, David Powel, in his adaptation of Llwyd's work, briefly took the story on into his own time, and coverage was extended further forward by subsequent writers who adapted or were influenced by his *Historie of Cambria* (1584). Yet this later material was scanty and episodic, being no more than an appendix to the main account of the early and medieval past – a notion made explicit by the full title of the substantial Welsh-language history published by Thomas Price (Carnhuanawc) in 1842, which translates as 'A History of Wales, and the Nation of the Welsh, from the Early Ages to the Death of Llywelyn ap Gruffudd; together with Some Records Relevant to the Times Down from Then'.[6] Accordingly, only some sixty of Price's almost eight hundred pages were devoted to the centuries after 1282, and only twenty to the period commencing with Henry VII's accession in 1485.[7] Although the coverage of later events increased somewhat in the last two major histories of Wales published in the nineteenth century, they, too, remained firmly focused on the period down to the Edwardian conquest.[8]

The first coherent analyses of modern Welsh history appeared in two works published at the beginning of the twentieth century: John Rhys and David Brynmor-Jones's *The Welsh People* (1900) and O. M. Edwards's *Wales* (1901). Though not strictly a work of history, the former provided a thematic account of the Welsh, based partly on material drafted for the Report of the Royal Commission on Land in Wales and Monmouthshire (1896), that was largely historical in approach and covered eighteenth- and nineteenth-century developments in some detail.[9] For, although the authors were strongly influenced by traditional assumptions that in significant respects Welsh history had ended in 1282, the consequences they drew from this allowed for the continuation of that history, albeit in a circumscribed form, into the modern period. From Edward I's conquest

> the history of the Welsh in regard to wars, foreign policy, and general affairs becomes so merged into that of Great Britain that it is hardly susceptible of separate treatment in a continuous narrative form. They

have, however, a particular history as to many of the institutions, conditions, and activities, that create or maintain the life of a nation.[10]

Moreover, their interpretation of the making of the modern Welsh people resembled – and thus may well have influenced – that of Lloyd, notably in its emphasis on the transformative effect of the eighteenth-century Methodist movement, which was presented as much more than a religious revival: rather, it resulted above all in 'the new birth of a people', and 'profoundly changed and strengthened the mental and moral qualities of the Welsh-speaking people' – the linguistic qualification is significant – through preserving the Welsh language as well as stimulating literary activity and the demand for education.[11] The following statement would also have struck a chord with Lloyd: 'It is hardly too much to say that the chief event in the special history of Wales during the last fifty years has been the modern educational movement which has culminated in the system now existing . . .'[12]

O. M. Edwards's *Wales* offered a more coherent account of Welsh history than *The Welsh People*. Developing an interpretation of the past which the author had outlined in Welsh-language articles and books in the 1890s, it was the first book on Welsh history that devoted more space to the centuries after 1282 than to those before it.[13] However, despite its avowed aim of showing how the Welsh princes of the Middle Ages had been succeeded by a self-educated and self-governing peasantry in the modern era, the work remained predominantly medieval in focus, as 75 per cent of it deals with the period down to Henry VII's accession in 1485 and less than 4 per cent with the period 1730–1894 that witnessed the peasantry's ascendancy.[14] This latter period was examined in two chapters divided chronologically in 1832, the first of which presented the Methodist revival as a national awakening that affected education and literature as well as religion.[15] In its essentials, the sketch resembled the interpretation given in *The Welsh People*, but its emphasis differs as it lacks an explicit declaration that the revival had created a new Welsh people and ends by stressing the awakening's peasant character. The difference in emphasis is more marked still in Edwards's final chapter, 'The Industrial Revolution', which attributes a quickening of political thought in nineteenth-century Wales to economic forces: 'The cause of so great and so rapid a change is a very definite one. It is the rise of the great industries.'[16] Edwards develops the point by emphasizing that 'it was in the nineteenth century that agriculture became less important in Wales than the mining and manufacturing industries', and depicts the effects of the industrial revolution as both all-pervasive and progressive, observing, for example, that '[c]oal and steel and tinplate, of world-wide reputation, have given energy to the labour once bestowed indolently on peat and sheep and homespun'.[17] He concluded the chapter by highlighting developments in local government, facilitated in part by 'the new wealth' which gave the Welsh 'political independence', as well as the educational advances culminating in the establishment of the University of Wales.[18]

Lloyd's interpretation of modern Welsh history bears resemblances to the views expressed in both *The Welsh People* and *Wales*. This is hardly surprising, as he shared with those authors a general outlook on the past and future of Wales which was typical of Welsh intellectuals of a Liberal and patriotic persuasion. His writings on the subject were occasional and generally brief, lacking the coherence and depth of his 1911 *History*, and fall into two broad, though interrelated, categories. One consists of personal reminiscences. As R. T. Jenkins observed, Lloyd could have written an account of Welsh history from *c.*1870 onwards based primarily on his own recollections.[19] Although he never produced a coherent study of this kind, Lloyd was clearly conscious of his role in the national revival of the late nineteenth and early twentieth centuries and shared his memories of particular aspects, be they his student days in Aberystwyth and Oxford, the preaching of Gwilym Hiraethog, his early years at the university college in Bangor, his friendship with Tom Ellis or the history of the Welsh Language Society.[20] However, these autobiographically informed essays and addresses were only one element in a broader and much more substantial engagement with the history of Wales from the Tudors onwards.[21] In particular, he contributed over eighty articles to the *Dictionary of National Biography* on individuals from this period, including many from the nineteenth century.[22] True, in common with his other articles on aspects of post-medieval Wales, these contributions were short, and even his general *History of*

Wales (1930), though devoting its second half to the period from 1485 onwards (as had O. M. Edwards's *Wales*), offered no more than a sketch in thirty-nine small pages.[23] Nevertheless, these writings not only bear witness to the breadth of Lloyd's interests as a historian and his grasp of periods well beyond his specialist field but also, crucially, disclose some important assumptions about the course and significance of modern Welsh history and thus on how Lloyd saw the Wales of his own day.[24]

The mature reflection embodied in the 1930 *History of Wales* provides a convenient point of departure for analysing Lloyd's interpretation of modern Wales. Of course, in part its account was a product of its time and reflected both recent events – notably the Labour Party's electoral dominance of the south Wales coalfield – and recent scholarship: for instance, Lloyd acknowledged his great debt to R. T. Jenkins's volume on Welsh history in the eighteenth century.[25] Yet the work's overall approach finds echoes in Lloyd's earlier writings and, as he also acknowledged, although he had not undertaken detailed research on the modern period covered in the second half of the booklet, his task in that respect was eased by his contributions to the *Dictionary of National Biography*.[26] Likewise, an early article anticipated the identification of what Lloyd, like other Welsh historians of his age, considered to be the first major turning point in the making of modern Wales: the accession of Henry VII in 1485, with the consequent creation of closer relations with England, later formalized by the Acts of Union, which are presented as largely beneficial to the Welsh.[27] By contrast, the Reformation was carried out 'without any marked commotion or upheaval', while the seventeenth century is presented in a negative light in which Wales suffered from 'Stuart neglect' and then, under the Commonwealth, 'lost the virtual independence it had hitherto enjoyed and came directly under English rule'.[28] However, this sterile interlude was decisively ended by the most important turning point in modern Welsh history, namely the Methodist revival, which helped to create the unprecedented changes of the nineteenth century.

At the beginning of the eighteenth century the stage was set for the movement which beyond any other has made the Welsh people what it is to-day. In its ultimate effects, the Methodist revival was far more than a religious upheaval; through its agency the political and cultural life of Wales was raised to a new level – a new language and a new literature were evolved, new habits altered the routine of daily life, new organizations came into being, and a new social atmosphere was created.

The Wales of Victoria differed as widely from that of Queen Anne as did the latter from the Britain of Boudicca.[29]

It is a measure of the importance Lloyd attached to the nineteenth century, which he had long viewed as an era of major progress in Wales, that he divided his coverage of it into two chapters, which were followed by a chapter surveying developments in the early twentieth century; the treatment of the period from 1800 onwards thus accounted for 25 per cent of the whole work.[30]

The importance Lloyd attached to the Methodist revival echoed the emphasis of *The Welsh People* and, to a lesser extent, that of O. M. Edwards's *Wales*. Yet, if Lloyd was influenced by those works, this stemmed from a common outlook of long standing rather than slavish imitation. After all, there was nothing new in his positive assessment of the nineteenth century, which contained a strong element of celebrating the Nonconformist, Liberal Wales in whose values and aspirations he had been raised and with which he closely identified. As a young man Lloyd had depicted the nineteenth century not only as a golden age of Welsh literature, culminating in the poetry of Ceiriog (1832–87), but also as an era of progress that surpassed all that went before it.[31] Thus he contrasted the Wales of 1188 with that of 1886: 'The fertile fields, the fiery coal-mines and furnaces, the railways, the chapels, the miles of houses! As those who love our nation, we cannot be grateful enough for the alteration.'[32] As his rejection of calls to recreate a medieval, and thus by implication deindustrialized, Wales in his address to the Cardiff Cymmrodorion makes clear, he saw no reason to change this opinion fifty years later.[33]

However, it is not material progress that is emphasized most in his survey of 1930. One striking feature of that work is the priority given to religion, culture and education, though political developments affecting Wales's national status are a close runner-up; by contrast, while their importance is acknowledged, social and economic changes tend to be relegated to the background. In part, this was because Lloyd thought there had been little change until the nineteenth century; prior to that, Welsh economy and society were depicted as poor and overwhelmingly pastoral, and thus, it may have seemed, best passed over quickly.[34] Yet there was more to Lloyd's thematic emphases than that. Consider the last chapter of the work, covering 'modern developments'. This opens by singling out the foundation of the University of Wales as the most important new influence on twentieth-century Wales and arrives at political changes only via a survey of Welsh scholarship and literature, while industrial conflict, including the General Strike of 1926, goes unremarked.[35] The selection and order of topics no doubt reflected the personal perspective of an author who had played a significant part in the establishment of the university and the development of Welsh scholarship.[36] However, it also highlights a wider and more fundamental point, namely Lloyd's response to a challenge faced by all historians of stateless nations: should attention be focused on the nation's territory, or only on the ethnic group conceived to constitute the nation?[37] Lloyd clearly favoured the second of these options, and proceeded from the assumption that the history of Wales was synonymous with the history of the Welsh people, which possessed a distinctive national character.[38] Since, like the authors of *The Welsh People*, he believed that in the modern period Welsh nationality was expressed above all in the fields of religion, culture and education, it was these that principally engaged his attention – and had done so in various articles and essays since the late 1870s.[39]

This led to some tension in Lloyd's overall interpretation. On the one hand, as we have seen, the economic changes resulting from the industrial revolution were presented as beneficial modernization (in this, he was at one with O. M. Edwards); yet, on the other, they threatened the very culture and traditions that gave Wales claims to be a nation. Lloyd tried to resolve this tension in two ways. First, he emphasized the resilience of Welsh culture: just as this had weathered Edwardian conquest and Tudor union, so it had proved remarkably durable in the face of the anglicization resulting from industrialization.[40] Indeed, it had even benefited from that process to some extent. Thus, writing of the economic changes that swept across the south Wales coalfield in the nineteenth century, he commented:

In a large measure this signifies the submergence of all that was characteristically Welsh under a tide of foreign influence – the extension of England into what was once Wales. But hardly anywhere are the old landmarks entirely swept away, and in many regions it may with confidence be said that the Welsh tradition has survived the economic revolution. Such are the quarry districts of Caernarvonshire and Merionethshire, the Swansea Valley and the Carmarthenshire coal-field, the neighbourhood of Holywell and Mold. Interaction between these regions and the purely rural parts of Wales has enriched the life of the nation and infused new vigour into its politics, its literature, and its religion.[41]

Secondly, though, Lloyd acknowledged that culture alone could not ensure a future for Wales as a distinctive entity. Welsh unity could be preserved only through national institutions: hence the emphasis on the University of Wales, which, together with the Central Welsh Board (responsible for administering the new intermediate schools), National Library and National Museum, had been established precisely for this purpose.[42] Yet that was not enough. At the end of his survey Lloyd looked forward to a Wales that enjoyed a substantial measure of home rule. In words that almost certainly echo his own long-held convictions, he declared:

> For it is in the mind of many Welshmen that Wales cannot maintain its unity and distinctive characteristics without separate political, as well as educational and cultural institutions; their programme is home rule for Wales, with a local Parliament seated at Cardiff (or some other centre of the kind) and managing local, as distinct from imperial, affairs.[43]

If the prospects for the success of such a programme were far less promising than they had been during the high tide of the Cymru Fydd (Young Wales) movement some forty years previously, Lloyd does not seem to have been dismayed; in this and many other respects, the interpretation of Welsh history he published in 1930 restated views he had formed as a young man.[44]

Looking back to early and medieval Wales

The convictions that sustained his support for home rule also motivated Lloyd's decision to concentrate on early and medieval Welsh history. That decision cannot be explained simply by invoking the weight of tradition. It is of course true, as we have seen, that from the sixteenth century onwards writers on Welsh history had concentrated heavily on the period down to the Edwardian conquest, and thus Lloyd's 1911 *History* may be seen as essentially deploying the latest techniques and components to refit an existing model of the nation's past rather than designing a completely new one based on radically different assumptions. Yet this does not in itself explain why Lloyd believed that the existing model was still serviceable. One key premise, shared widely by Welsh intellectual patriots of the late nineteenth and early twentieth centuries (and having many European parallels), was that the Wales of their day was experiencing a revival, reawakening or rebirth, which in turn implied that the nation had come into existence at some previous point in the past.[45] In other words, the concept of national renewal begged the question of national origins and thus gave urgency to the study of the nation's history. Lloyd was explicit about this in some of his earliest writings. For example, he observed in 1882:

> I cannot but feel that, while the Welsh language is on the lips of over a million of this world's inhabitants, and scores of printing presses are sending into the world Welsh newspapers and periodicals, no Welshman has a right to consider the study of his national history and literature a barren and aimless pursuit.[46]

More specifically, a few years later he rejoiced in the renewal of national life in Wales and declared that this made it especially timely to look back at the origins of the nation: 'The nation is awakening, is casting away the shackles of sleep and apathy, is preparing itself for a new period of activity. No other moment, therefore, can be more timely for looking back at the nation's beginning . . .'[47] Likewise, advocates of such contemporary causes as home rule or land reform could find relevant example and inspiration in the medieval past.[48] In addition, Lloyd implied that investigating the early history of Wales was an imperative driven not merely by the particular circumstances of national revival but also by an innate quality of the Welsh, as he maintained, like Matthew Arnold, that one of their distinctive attributes was a keen sense of the past that differentiated them from the forward-looking Teutons or English.[49]

However, the fundamental reason for focusing on the Welsh past was that this gave legitimacy to claims that modern Wales was a nation reborn. Lloyd made this particularly explicit in an address given to the Liverpool Welsh National Society as the First World War drew to a close in November 1918. The presentation of the argument was coloured by current events, notably in its references to the inspiration Czech and Serbian nationalists drew from the past in their aspirations to self-government (in the latter case, through mourning the battle of Kosovo on 15 June 1389, which led to over four centuries of Turkish rule), but the convictions it expresses are entirely consistent with Lloyd's earlier views and surely help to explain why he wrote the *History* that had appeared almost eight years earlier. Declaring that 'Welsh literary and historical research' was 'a matter of lively interest for present day Welshmen and as worthy of a Welshman's consideration, yes, even of his enthusiasm, as politics or sport or business', Lloyd continued:

> The study of national history and of national literature is not a mere fad, the occupation of amiable people who have nothing more useful to do; it is essential to the growth of national self-respect and it has been one of the most powerful instruments in forming the national spirit of those new communities which are now claiming their independence.[50]

Nevertheless, as in most of his pronouncements on national history, Lloyd did not explicitly explain why the early and medieval past deserved particular attention as opposed to more recent periods. The nearest he came to providing such an explanation appeared ten years later, in an article challenging tendencies to concentrate mainly on the nineteenth century in the teaching of history in secondary schools. Here, Lloyd's message was unambiguous. He began with general principles, which he supported

by invoking the authority of the political theorist Ernest Barker
(1874–1960):

> The truth is that for the serious historian, who probes beneath the
> surface and seeks to discern the hidden springs of action, recent
> history deals only with superficial changes; for fundamentals, one
> must go back to much earlier times, to mediaeval, and even, it may
> be, to prehistoric days. For a full understanding of the history of
> modern Italy, it is not enough to study Cavour and Mazzini; Julius
> Caesar and Gregory I also belong to the picture. The civilization of
> the United States is rooted in that of English Puritanism; the key to
> the orientalism of Russia is to be found in the Tartar invasion. Many
> factors, as Professor Barker has recently shown, enter into the web
> of national character and some of them are of very great antiquity.[51]

Lloyd then turned specifically to Wales:

> In spite of the keen national consciousness of the Wales of to-day
> . . . there is a danger that Welsh history may disappear altogether
> from the Welsh secondary schools, and that Welsh boys and girls
> may grow up altogether ignorant of the forces which have gone to
> [*sic*] the moulding of the Welsh race. For with medieval history, the
> core of Welsh history must vanish also; no nation can less afford
> than ours to be explained in terms of the nineteenth century; we
> cannot sacrifice Arthur and St. David and the two Llywelyns and
> Owain Glyn Dwr to the Wales which was the product of the industrial
> revolution.[52]

These passages shed invaluable light on how Lloyd understood
his task as a historian. Of course, their rhetoric was aimed at a
specific target – the privileging of nineteenth-century history over
that of the Middle Ages – and the views expressed oversimplify
Lloyd's understanding of the relationship between modern Wales
and its early past as revealed by some of his other writings. Thus,
while acknowledging that the Wales of his own day was in many
respects a modern creation, he effectively played down its distinctively Welsh character by making its midwife the Industrial Revolution rather than, as elsewhere, the Methodist revival; significantly,

the model history syllabus he proposed placed the former under 'British' aspects of the period 1715–1914, whereas the 'Welsh' topics were entirely religious, educational and literary.[53] It is true, too, that Lloyd's case for the importance of medieval and earlier history relies on assertion rather than argument. We are not told *how* Mazzini's Italy was shaped by that of Julius Caesar, or *why* Arthur or Owain Glyndŵr were crucial to an understanding of 'the moulding of the Welsh race'. What we have, then, are assumptions: nineteenth-century evolutionary assumptions that the explanation of phenomena – be they nations, languages or biological species – lay in their origins and subsequent development over time, coupled with historicist notions, derived ultimately from Herder, that each nation possessed a unique individuality.[54] Lloyd's point seems to be that, although Wales had been transformed in the nineteenth century by the Industrial Revolution or the Methodist revival or by a combination of both, the Welsh were an ancient people whose distinctiveness had been forged by much earlier events. His task as a historian, therefore, was to confer legitimacy on the modern sense of Welsh nationality by demonstrating that it had deep foundations whose features could be established more authoritatively than ever before by using the most modern scholarly methods. Indeed, as we shall see in the next chapter, it was precisely through his adoption of those methods that Lloyd brought his own age to bear most directly on his country's early and medieval past.

6

Assumptions and Methods

Thirty years after the publication of the *History of Wales* in January 1911 Lloyd's daughter Eluned recorded her father's assessment of the work's significance:

Daddy Said,
    That the compliment on his History that pleased him most, he thought, was R. T. Jenkins saying that he 'created Welsh history'. This, he said, recognized the fact that he was the first to disentangle the mass of legend, records etc. . . . that he had really to pick out and decide who <u>were</u> the important people, what <u>were</u> the significant events. This had not been done before, and the foundation was really laid in the 3 little school history books published first. He said that when collecting material and compiling it, he made a point of not reading anything that had been written in the way of history by a modern writer. He drew it all from records, M.S. [*sic*] and other original sources. One job of [*sic*] tracking down legends and accretions to the sources, and debunking them.[1]

Though more succinct, the preface to his *History*, dated 1 November 1910, proclaims a similar purpose:

In this work it has been my endeavour to bring together and to weave into a continuous narrative what may be fairly regarded as the ascertained facts of the history of Wales up to the fall of Llywelyn ap Gruffydd in 1282. In a field where so much is matter of conjecture, it has not been possible altogether to avoid speculation and hypothesis, but I can honestly say that I have not written in support of any special theory or to urge any preconceived opinion upon the reader. My purpose has been to map out, in this difficult region of study, what is already known and established, and thus to define more clearly the limits of that 'terra incognita' which still awaits discovery.[2]

Likewise, Lloyd later acknowledged his debt to four scholars – John Rhys, Egerton Phillimore, Alfred N. Palmer and Hugh Williams – 'for the pioneer work which has so greatly facilitated the scientific study of Welsh history. I owe to them what cannot be expressed in the debit of citation and reference, namely, outlook and method and inspiration.'[3] Presumably this meant a commitment to thorough and critical analysis of a wide range of evidence.[4] In a perceptive review published just over a year later, T. F. Tout considered that the *History* had more than met its author's objectives, declaring that it 'well supplied' the 'ever-increasing need' for 'a sound and scientific textbook which would set forth fully, clearly, and impartially the facts generally accepted by scholars who have busied themselves with this subject'.[5] Indeed, Tout went further in emphasizing the magnitude of Lloyd's achievement in words that anticipated R. T. Jenkins's compliment: 'It is not enough to say that it will supersede all other books on the subject. A book on such lines, or of such a type, has never previously been written.'[6]

As Oxford-educated historians who had known each other since the late 1880s it is hardly surprising that Lloyd and Tout shared common assumptions about the writing of history: that it was a 'scientific' enterprise dedicated to establishing 'facts' about the past and ordering these in an 'impartial' narrative.[7] The following discussion will analyse those assumptions and explore how they shaped the *History*. Accordingly, whereas the previous chapter examined why the work privileged the early and medieval Welsh past, the emphasis here will shift to approaches and methods. What kind of book was Lloyd trying to write, and how did he go about his task? Although he never reflected at length on how history should be written, Lloyd furnishes sufficient evidence – in both general observations and the practice revealed by his *History* – to allow these questions to be addressed in the context of other works of his time.

'A sound and scientific textbook'

The nearest Lloyd came to explaining what he meant by 'scientific' history appears in an address given at the National Eisteddfod in Carmarthen in August 1911, some seven months after the publication of his magnum opus:

> the man who takes history seriously . . . starts with the assumption that there is a real past to investigate, and that it is of real importance to unlock its secret cabinets. He ranges himself by the side of the man of science, who knows that there are physical and chemical and biological laws to discover, of direct bearing upon daily life, and who does not suffer himself to be diverted by any subsidiary interest from the task of unravelling them. The serious historian thinks it important that historical truth, like scientific truth, should be established, and holds that, as in science, the facts which have the widest bearing and application have the first claim upon his attention.[8]

Lloyd went on to maintain that such a historian faced 'two opposing tendencies prevalent among those who are interested in his subject . . . the spirit of antiquarianism and the spirit of edification'.[9] Although the reference to 'laws' might seem to savour of Comtean positivism, Lloyd – in common with other advocates of 'scientific' history in Britain – was careful to avoid claiming that historians sought to discover 'laws' or that 'historical truth' was exactly comparable to 'scientific truth'; rather, the historian's task was analogous to that of scientists 'only in the sense that it involved the mastery of a definite objective and severe method and technique'. In other words, to characterize history as 'scientific' was to vindicate its authority as a serious enterprise, whose rigorous analysis of evidence enabled it to undertake 'a dispassionate and objective search for truth'.[10] While this search could include the presentation of hypotheses or the acceptance of tradition, the crucial thing was that it rested on a firm basis of evidence, which, if treated critically, alone could furnish 'facts' about the past.[11] Thus Lloyd justified some detailed criticisms he had offered in 1916 by stating:

> I daresay I am somewhat 'pernickety' in these matters, but in a subject like early Welsh history, in which the paucity of the material leaves so large a space for conjecture, it seems to me of cardinal importance that our conjectures – be they sound or unsound – should rest on an unassailable basis of fact.[12]

Moreover, Lloyd practised what he preached, carefully noting corrections he received to his *History* and revising later editions accordingly.[13]

This did not, of course, guarantee the work's impartiality: notwithstanding the denial of wishing 'to urge any preconceived opinion upon the reader', empirical rigour served to legitimize a 'whiggish' narrative of national origins informed by distinctly present-minded concerns about the identity and aspirations of the Welsh at the time Lloyd was writing.[14] It is also worth stressing that there were limits to his critical approach, which, in its determination to distil 'facts' from the written evidence, rarely went beyond questions of dating and provenance to engage closely with qualitative issues such as the genre, purpose and ideological perspective of individual texts. This is not to suggest that Lloyd was blind to such issues. However, he was reluctant to explore their full implications. His emphasis is, of course, comprehensible in terms of the scholarly context of the time and probably received added impetus from Lloyd's keen sense of the need to decontaminate Welsh history from later legendary interpretations: hence establishing the extent to which a source offered a contemporaneous witness to the events it recounted was particularly crucial. A good example of his priorities is provided by the following assessment of the Middle Welsh Life of Gruffudd ap Cynan (d.1137), king of Gwynedd, the only medieval Welsh ruler to be the subject of a medieval biography. This,

> though it is not the work of a contemporary, for it was composed during the reign of his son Owain, was written sufficiently near his time to be a valuable historical authority. Despite some inaccuracies

and the inevitable disposition to magnify the deeds of its hero, the *Ancient History of Gruffydd ap Cynan ap Iago* tells a story which is in general conformity with what is known of the history of the time, and in the following pages the evidence yielded by it is used without hesitation.[15]

By contrast, when discussing the division of Wales between the sons of Rhodri Mawr (d.878), Lloyd dismissed the late twelfth-century claim by Giraldus Cambrensis that Cadell ap Rhodri in the south outlived his brothers and secured the monarchy of all Wales for his descendants as being 'in flat opposition to the testimony of the chronicles and was no doubt concocted to support certain South Welsh claims'.[16] Lloyd subsequently upheld the veracity of the Welsh chronicles known generically as *Brut y Tywysogyon* ('The Chronicle of the Princes') by declaring that, unlike Geoffrey of Monmouth's *Historia Regum Britanniae* ('History of the Kings of Britain'), '"Brut y Tywysogion" owes nothing to flights of fancy; it is sober pedestrian chronicle, occasionally waxing eloquent, but as a rule content to record the simple facts'. He proceeded to analyse the relationship of the different versions of this chronicle both with each other and the Latin texts known as *Annales Cambriae* ('The Annals of Wales'), as well as to demolish the long-established attribution of the former to the twelfth-century author Caradog of Llancarfan.[17]

That Lloyd did not analyse sources in depth in the *History* also reflected practical constraints. In the preface he explained that he 'had originally intended to include a critical account' of the Welsh chronicles, 'but afterwards came to the conclusion that the task was too ambitious for the present occasion and must be separately undertaken'.[18] This brings us to the kind of work he was aiming to write. In describing the *History* as a 'textbook' and 'work of synthesis' Tout may seem to play down its achievement, given its wealth of references to primary sources and detailed additional notes on textual and other problems. However, the characterization appears in the context of warm praise for the book and was clearly not disparaging; rather, it points up an important aspect of Lloyd's aims, which were as much to do with providing a balanced synthesis as with demonstrating critical scholarship. While he was writing his magnum opus Lloyd gave a lecture which emphasized that a major obstacle to the teaching of Welsh history was that the subject had not been 'properly worked up' by scholars, in contrast to the history of England, for which the pioneering efforts of Clarendon, Hume and Sharon Turner had 'picked out salient points and provided a skeleton' that, despite subsequent changes, had not been 'substantially altered'.[19] Lloyd expanded on the point two years later, when he stated that the difficulty facing teachers of Welsh history was a 'want of books, not textbooks, but standard works', whereas for English history the 'labours of Hume, Lingard, Macaulay, Green, Stubbs, and Gardiner have provided [a] general outline in wh[ich the] story is told continuously with due regard to proportion – something for textbook makers to work upon'.[20] Tout offered telling corroboration of the latter part of this assessment when, also in 1905, he recommended Stubbs's *Constitutional History* and the work of Reinhold Pauli as the best modern 'general guides to the period' covered in his textbook on medieval English history.[21] Lloyd *was* the Stubbs or Pauli of Welsh history. In other words, his aim was to provide a 'standard work' that would establish a framework for his subject.

Lloyd evidently took it for granted that such a work should be written in English, and brought out by a major English publisher.[22] The most likely reason for this is that it would help to bestow on the history of Wales the dignity and prestige of a modern 'scientific' discipline and make it accessible to an international readership of scholars and students. Perhaps, above all, the use of English would bring that history to the attention of readers in England and thus help to enhance the status of Wales within Britain, a view already expressed by Thomas Stephens with respect to Welsh literature in the aftermath of the 'Treachery of the Blue Books' half a century previously.[23] It is true that Lloyd had been content to pave the way for his magnum opus by producing three bilingual textbooks for schools. However, since their bilingual format was designed to help Welsh-speaking children improve their grasp of English, the use of Welsh was essentially pragmatic, and did not reflect a belief that the native vernacular was the proper medium for writing the history of Wales. While praised for his commitment to the Welsh language, like many of his generation Lloyd seems to have assumed that, beyond the home, its use was appropriate only to particular spheres, especially religion and also aspects of children's education.[24] When it came to scholarship, though, English was the medium of choice, even for works on the Welsh language.[25] True, from the 1920s it became increasingly common for editions and studies of Welsh literature to be published in Welsh, a development later defended by Lloyd on the grounds that 'serious scholarship may very properly decline to cater for the requirements of the dilettante who wants to study an author whose work he cannot read in the original'. Welsh history, though, was 'on a different footing': here, 'the argument in favour of an English work is decisive'.[26] It is consistent with this view that, although the two most important new works of Welsh history in the nineteenth century, by Thomas Price and Gweirydd ap Rhys, were written in Welsh (indeed, Lloyd later declared the latter to have been 'the best book on the subject that had up to this date appeared'), he evidently did not regard them as models for the 'standard work' to which he aspired.[27] Rather, he drew comparisons with major works of English history, thereby implying that any worthwhile history of Wales had to measure up to the yardstick provided by these.

History and legend

The need to debunk legends and base history on soundly attested evidence was a central concern of Lloyd from his student days onwards.[28] However, while his determination to distinguish history from legend was genuine, his attitude to the latter was not entirely dismissive, being tempered by a readiness to accept traditions in some cases where contemporaneous evidence was lacking or inconclusive.[29] His approach is well illustrated by the introductions to his first two bilingual school textbooks, published in 1893 and 1896 respectively. The first announces an uncompromisingly revisionist objective:

> every effort has been made to ensure correctness in the facts. The true history of Wales has lain for so long under a heap of legends that some Welshmen may, perhaps, barely recognize their country in the pages that follow; but it was felt that a new beginning in

education in Wales asks for a change in this matter too, and that these history books should be truly historical, even at the expense of neglecting many entertaining and ancient traditions. It is true that the rising generation should be knowledgeable in the legends of the fathers, but they should not accept them instead of history.[30]

Lloyd returned to the difficulty of distinguishing history and legend in the introduction to the second volume, covering 400–1066. However, here he implied that legends merited careful consideration, for he added that the period was possibly the most difficult one for the Welsh historian, 'as there is so much truth in the legends, and no one, despite that, is able to say decisively how much'.[31]

As the weight of legendary interpretations lay particularly heavily on the early Welsh past, volume I of the *History* shows most clearly how Lloyd responded to the challenge these posed. In part, this was a matter of using recent discoveries in prehistoric archaeology to supersede mythical views: for example, in summarizing recent work on the Palaeolithic, Lloyd commented that, whereas the author of the Welsh Triads claimed that the first settlers of Britain found it full of bears, wolves, dragons and long-horned oxen, 'the truth revealed by science is a hundredfold stranger than his ingenuous fiction'.[32] He likewise gave short shrift to the notion that cromlechs were 'druidical altars'.[33] Indeed, following the lead of his Bangor colleague John Morris-Jones, Lloyd reserved his sharpest criticism for the grandiose edifice of druidism constructed by eighteenth- and early nineteenth-century writers such as Edward Davies: 'it will not do', he insisted,

> to assume, without trustworthy evidence and against historic prob-
> ability, that the Druids worshipped one God, that they sacrificed
> on cromlechs, that their lord was cast into the triadic form, and that
> it is represented in spirit and scope by the bards of Glamorgan in
> comparatively recent times.[34]

Likewise, Lloyd concluded, apropos of another devotee of druidism, William Owen Pughe: 'All ancient testimony is against him; Druidism, in short, represents, not the high water-mark of early British civilisation, but a survival from the less civilised past.'[35]

On the other hand, as the reference to 'historic probability' implies, a critical approach required discrimination: legends needed to be assessed carefully, with reference to a multiplicity of factors. As a young man, Lloyd had argued that tradition could reveal aspects of the past denied to those relying solely on 'the authoritative voice of History', and, though expressed less trenchantly, this view informed his *History* too.[36] Thus, in discussing the changing contours of the British Isles during prehistory, Lloyd thought it conceivable that science might in fact support legends of submerged kingdoms such as Cantref y Gwaelod, and wondered whether these were

> reminiscences handed down through many generations of the effects – at times, perhaps, startling – of this gradual subsidence attested by geology . . . it remains, however, for students of folk-lore to say whether this and kindred legends known to the Welsh people have any special features which show them to embody genuine traditional history, or whether they are merely specimens of a class of story known in all parts of the world.[37]

Moreover, he took pains to trace the evolution of the legend of Cantref y Gwaelod from a poem in the medieval Black Book of Carmarthen through sixteenth-century triads and early modern antiquaries to the nineteenth-century poetry of his childhood minister Gwilym Hiraethog.[38] Nor did the plausibility of legends depend only on the extent to which they might be correlated with sciences such as geology; it could be enough for traditional accounts to be internally consistent and compatible with other written evidence. Thus, after cautioning that the story of the Brythons' conquest of Gwynedd 'has not been recorded by any contemporary writer', and that its details were 'embedded in traditional narratives, of which the authority is not too high', Lloyd felt able to declare: 'Nevertheless, it does not seem impossible to construct with their aid a fairly consistent account of the Brythonic conquest.'[39] He then proceeded to relate the narrative of the expulsion of the Irish from Gwynedd by Cunedda and his sons given in the early ninth-century *Historia Brittonum* ('History of the Britons'), an event he placed *c*.400, four centuries before the composition of his source. It should be stressed that the account was far from uncritical: it scrupulously explained the date of the sources used, and drew the line at accepting some later developments of the legend; yet Lloyd expressed no fundamental reservation about relying on tradition as such.[40] He provided a fuller explanation of his reasons for accepting tradition with respect to the association of medieval Welsh law with Hywel Dda (Hywel the Good), king of most of Wales by his death in 950. After admitting that the earliest evidence for the attribution consisted of claims in manuscripts of Welsh law, none of which (so he held) was copied earlier than *c.*1200, Lloyd went on:

> But the unanimity with which they ascribe this great legal reform to the 'good' king, and the unchallenged assumption throughout Welsh literature that the work was his, without suggestion of a rival for the honour, constitute as strong a proof as tradition can supply; if Hywel was not the author of the code which bears his name, how came he to be singled out from among his fellows and invested by later generations of Welshmen with this unique distinction?[41]

Thus the argument relied on deductions from the available evidence, including the latest scholarship on the nature and date of the surviving legal texts, to whose manuscripts and editions Lloyd devoted a lengthy note reflecting his extensive knowledge of the field since the later 1880s.[42]

Sources

This note is but one illustration of a grasp of primary sources that was both precise and thorough.[43] Indeed, this is a key hallmark of the *History* that has given it enduring value. True, the work's exclusive reliance on printed materials has sometimes been seen as a limitation.[44] However, in assessing Lloyd's treatment of primary sources, it is important to take account of his synthesizing ambitions and to set his approach in the context of other comparable works. To judge by the *History*, what mattered above all was to attain a comprehensive mastery of printed materials (accorded the status of 'authorities').[45] To venture beyond these into unpublished manuscripts and archival records seems to have been considered neither practicable nor necessary. In part, this may be attributed to the relatively late development in Britain of the notion, first given systematic expression in Germany, whence it spread to France and other continental countries as well as the United States, that 'scientific' historians should go beyond printed materials and enter the archives.[46] However, there were two more specific, and mutually reinforcing, reasons for Lloyd's choice. First, the sources for the period down to 1282, though by no means insubstantial, were fewer than those for subsequent periods and, crucially, the bulk of them had been published by the time Lloyd embarked on his great work; by contrast, as he himself noted, any attempt to deal with the centuries from 1282 to 1603 would be largely dependent on the holdings of the Public Record Office.[47] Given the scope of the *History*, the challenge of getting a comprehensive grip – for the first time – on the wide and diverse range of published sources was daunting enough, without having to consult unpublished materials as well (and in any case his administrative duties as registrar would have made it difficult for Lloyd to undertake lengthy visits to archives and libraries outside Bangor).[48]

Secondly, the approach to sources was adapted to the nature of Lloyd's magnum opus. It was one thing to delve deeply in the archives for a monograph on a specific aspect of Welsh history, as both J. E. Morris and E. A. Lewis did in the early twentieth century; quite another for a 'standard work' designed to reconfigure the whole of the history of Wales from the Palaeolithic to the Edwardian conquest.[49] A possible implication of this contrast is that the former specialized studies were considered to be works of 'research', whereas the *History* was not.[50] Lewis's book on the boroughs of north Wales originated as a thesis submitted for a research degree in London and had been completed while a 'research fellow' of the University of Wales, while Morris declared that his account of Edward I's wars in Wales had involved 'close research'.[51] Lloyd, on the other hand, avoided this terminology in characterizing his *History*, preferring to describe it as an attempt to create 'a continuous narrative' of 'the ascertained facts' of the period covered, and 'to map out . . . what is already known and established'.[52] True, the lack of any explicit mention of 'research' in the work's preface is not itself conclusive. Lloyd does, after all, explain that his chapter on 'tribal divisions' depended mainly on his own studies, and there can be no doubt that, from a twenty-first-century perspective, the *History* as a whole embodies a vast amount of painstaking, detailed research by its author.[53] Nevertheless, there are further grounds for doubting whether Lloyd would have defined it primarily in such terms. As we have seen, Tout's praise of the *History* referred to it as a 'textbook' and 'work of synthesis'. In addition, it conforms only partly to Lloyd's own definition of 'original research' as given in an eisteddfod adjudication in 1918, namely

> the discovery of new facts previously unknown to the world of letters and the co-ordination of material, whether new or old, so as to lead to new views and conclusions. As a rule, such research will involve the use of material to be found only in manuscripts, or rare books, or printed papers not easily obtained: the arrangement of matter which can be obtained from the books on the shelves of an ordinary library, however carefully and competently done, unless there is re-interpretation and 'new light,' cannot be considered original research.[54]

The use of unpublished sources was highlighted as a prime virtue of the winning essay, on the Puritan movement in Wales, which had 'involved as thorough an examination of the printed and MS. evidence on this subject as any scholar could undertake'.[55] Of course, it needs to be borne in mind that these passages belong to the context of an eisteddfod competition rather than a discussion of academic writing, and are in any case somewhat ambivalent about the necessity of using unpublished sources. Yet their general thrust seems clear, and they merit careful consideration in assessing how Lloyd conceived of the *History*.

A reliance on printed sources was certainly not unusual in the Edwardian era. Like other historians of his day, Lloyd benefited from the increasing number of published sources available during the nineteenth and early twentieth century, whose appearance re-sulted from the desire of individual nation states to produce collect-ions of sources that served to define and legitimize their distinctive pasts and was reinforced by the emerging historical profession's emphasis on archival materials in particular.[56] From the 1920s Lloyd sought to extend this approach to Wales through helping to ensure that the Board of Celtic Studies published sources of Welsh interest in the Public Record Office.[57] These were intended to supplement the major British collections on which he had drawn extensively in the *History*: the Record Commission volumes of royal documents, the chronicles, letters and other sources edited in the Rolls Series and the calendars (summaries) of medieval documents issued by the Public Record Office. However, he also benefited from nineteenth- and early twentieth-century developments in Welsh and Celtic scholarship in his use of editions of Welsh literary and other texts, mainly the fruits of individual scholarly enterprise, sometimes appearing in the journals of antiquarian societies, though Gwenogvryn Evans's detailed descriptions of Welsh manuscripts were financed by the government's Historical Manuscripts Commission.[58] It should be stressed, too, that Lloyd was well aware that some editions were more reliable than others: for example, he contrasted the 'scrupulous care' shown by Phillimore in editing early Welsh Latin annals and genealogies with Ab Ithel's earlier and '[l]ess satisfactory' edition of the former.[59] Likewise, he maintained that the scholar could use Gwenogvryn Evans's facsimile editions of medieval texts 'with the same confidence as though he had the precious MSS. themselves in his hands'.[60] This critical discrimination was based in part on practical experience, for Lloyd did not shy away from consulting such materials himself on occasion, as shown, for example, by his edition of the portion of the *Annales Cambriae* covering the years 1035–93, by his detailed collation of Ab Ithel's edition of *Brut y Tywysogyon*, based primarily on the text in the Red Book of Hergest, with the version in Peniarth MS 20, and by his later work on Owain Glyndŵr.[61]

Lloyd's reliance on printed sources is paralleled in the work of some of his English contemporaries. Thus A. L. Smith opened his study of the thirteenth-century papacy by emphasizing the shift in the principal sources favoured for historical study from chronicles to documents, observing of the latter: 'Vast masses of these have been collected, critically sifted, and *calendared*.'[62] Furthermore, in noting that the opening of the papal archives by Pope Leo XIII (1878–1903) had hugely increased the amount of material available to scholars, Smith referred to published texts of the papal registers, and he relied exclusively on these in the rest of the work.[63] Tout also insisted on the superiority of records to chronicles and, indeed, believed that English historians should follow their continental counterparts and tackle archival materials at first hand.[64] Thus his 1906 lecture urging the creation of schools of history recommended that these should provide postgraduate training that included instruction in the technical skills needed to read manuscripts and documents, and he also undertook substantial archival research himself, most conspicuously in a massive study of royal administration that made extensive use of materials in the Public Record Office.[65] Yet the following passage, also from the 1906 lecture, suggests that the issue here was one of practical necessity rather than of any objection in principle to the use of published texts: 'Our national archives are being rapidly calendared and made accessible, and the cult of the record grows, since the labours of the last generation have made available for us competent and scholarly editions of most of our chronicles.'[66] Moreover, Tout was content to rely on printed editions and calendars in textbooks and interpretative essays.[67]

Constructing a coherent narrative

The critical use of evidence was not an end in itself, but rather an essential means to producing a coherent account of the past that would give shape and significance to Welsh history. Lloyd probably agreed with the ideal proclaimed in one of the works he was expected to read as an undergraduate at Oxford, namely Ranke's *History of England*:

> It is the ambition of all nations which enjoy a literary culture to possess a harmonious and vivid narrative of their own past history. And it is of inestimable value to any people to obtain such a narrative, which shall comprehend all epochs, be true to fact and, while resting on thorough research, yet be attractive to the reader; for only by this aid can the nation attain to a perfect self-consciousness, and feeling the pulsation of its life throughout the story, become fully acquainted with its own origin and growth and character.[68]

In other words, clarity and readability should not be sacrificed in the pursuit of methodological rigour.[69] Lloyd implied as much himself when he complained that Gweirydd ap Rhys's *Hanes y Brytaniaid a'r Cymry* ('The History of the Britons and Welsh', 1872–4), though 'very critical' and 'valuable as clearing the ground', was 'not constructive – no general idea given of course of W[elsh] hist[ory]'.[70] (Asser's *Life of King Alfred* is criticized in similar terms: 'the arrangement is confused and shows no unity of purpose'.[71]) As we have seen, Lloyd took particular pride in the assertion that he had 'created Welsh history' by identifying its important individuals and events, while the preface to the *History* declared that it sought 'to weave into a continuous narrative . . . the ascertained facts of the history of Wales up to . . . 1282'.[72] Particular aspects of that narrative are examined in the following three chapters; here attention will be focused on the *History*'s structure in general.

According to the recollections recorded by his daughter, Lloyd had laid the foundations for his magnum opus in the three bilingual textbooks for schools published between 1893 and 1900. These covered respectively prehistory to the end of the Roman occupation; 410–1066; and 1066–1282.[73] As the third volume was significantly longer than the first two, the chronological balance was broadly similar to that of the *History*, whose first volume took the narrative down to the early eleventh century, with the second, slightly longer volume continuing to 1282. More significantly, the *History*'s twenty chapters fall into three main groups that indicate a clear pattern of development: the formation of the Welsh people from the Neolithic onwards and its eventual restriction, by the mid-seventh century, to the territory of Wales (I–VI); the consolidation of early medieval Wales as a distinctive social and political entity (VII–X); and, occupying the whole of volume II and thus over half of the work, the response of this entity, under its native kings and princes, to the challenge posed by foreign conquest over the two centuries from the Normans to Edward I (XI–XX).[74] In short, volume I presents the foundations of medieval Wales, while volume II traces its subsequent fate, with a prime focus on the vicissitudes of the Welsh dynasties whose independence finally came to an end with the death of Llywelyn ap Gruffudd in 1282.[75] Moreover, an overarching theme running through the whole book is Welsh nationality and the impact on it of external conquerors: whereas from the prehistoric to post-Roman periods three successive racial groups, ultimately originating from the European continent, amalgamate to create the Welsh, thereafter the nationality of the latter is fixed, being consolidated rather than compromised by its contact with further invaders, especially the English.[76]

Of course, Lloyd's depiction of early Welsh history was richer and more complex than this summary may suggest. The coherence of the *History* lies not just in its overall architecture, but in the arrangement and design of its individual elements. For example, in contrast to Gweirydd ap Rhys's strict separation of political, social, literary and religious history, Lloyd sought to weave these different aspects into a single narrative.[77] This was achieved by adopting a mainly chronological approach, with chapters being devoted to successive periods defined by themes such as 'The age of the sea-rovers' or, especially in volume II, by individual Welsh rulers, although the two chapters on 'The tribal divisions of Wales' and 'Early Welsh institutions' in volume I were more synoptic. Each chapter was then subdivided into three or four sections. In some cases, this offered a means of imposing some order on the potentially bewildering kaleidoscope of events in a politically fragmented country by examining different regions or individuals separately: thus the two chapters on the Norman conquest that open volume II have sections on the Welsh rulers Gruffudd ap Llywelyn and Rhys ap Tewdwr as well as on 'The Normans in north Wales', 'The predominance of Powys' and 'South Wales under Henry I'.[78] This structure also meant that, though his sequence of chapters followed a chronology based largely on political developments, Lloyd was able to integrate other topics into his narrative – in particular, while chapter V, 'The age of the saints', is the only one bearing an explicitly religious title, Christianity and the church are the subject of eight sections in other chapters of the work.[79]

Lloyd also took great care in structuring each chapter section so that it formed a coherent entity in its own right, opening with a scene-setting paragraph before proceeding to provide detailed narrative to sustain his argument and often concluding, perhaps just in the final sentence, with a brief assessment of the topic's wider significance. The chapter on 'The national revival' provides a good example of his method.[80] Its first section opens dramatically by asserting the momentous consequences of a single event:

> The death of Henry I. on 1st December, 1135, brought about an immediate change in the position of affairs in Wales. Everywhere the foreign yoke was cast off, the power of the new settlers was dauntlessly challenged, and a new spirit of daring seemed to have seized the whole Welsh race.[81]

The subsequent account of events down to the burial in Bangor cathedral of Gruffudd ap Cynan of Gwynedd in 1137 ends with a brief epitaph: 'So rested at last a man whose life had been troubled and stormy in no common degree.'[82] Lloyd then moves on to the chapter's second section, 'The great revolt', whose opening sentences again leave the reader in no doubt of the subject's significance:

> The great revolution in Welsh affairs which now took place was long remembered by the foreign settlers as a turning-point in the history of their adopted country. The day of Henry's death was for them as fearful as was for another aristocracy in a later age the day of the capture of the Bastille.[83]

Likewise, the section ends by summarizing the long-term impact of Stephen's reign on Wales: 'While party spirit reigned through the length and breadth of England, the Welsh had nothing to fear, and they succeeded in winning during these years advantages which they did not again lose until the extinction of Welsh independence.'[84] The final section, 'The national awakening and the Church', follows in seamless succession, its first paragraph emphasizing that the Welsh revolt also had effects on the Church; true, 'the results achieved were not so striking as in the secular sphere, but the new spirit of independence nevertheless made itself felt'.[85] Having related the main developments in each Welsh diocese, Lloyd ends the section, and thus the chapter, with a conclusion that deftly sums up the revolt in general: 'It was an easier matter to shake off the yoke of the English crown than to escape from the control of the English primate, in this age when ecclesiastical power was at its height in England.'[86]

111

As these passages make clear, Lloyd took pains to delineate the broader significance of the events he related and to show how they fitted into his narrative as a whole. This perspective is also reflected in occasional references to taking 'a wide view of Welsh history' when considering particular problems or events, be it the extent to which the native tribes of Wales were Romanized or the consequences of the death of Rhys ap Tewdwr in 1093, and in comments on the importance of individual Welsh regions in the history of the nation as a whole.[87] In addition, the passages cited above illustrate how the narrative was given momentum by a stately yet incisive style. While it is doubtful that he would have gone so far as Ranke and maintained that '[t]he best-written histories will be accounted the best', Lloyd evidently believed that historical writing required literary skill.[88] As a perceptive obituarist observed, 'he was able to write – to write finely, sometimes colourfully, very often majestically', thanks to a late Victorian education that had steeped Lloyd in the Latin and Greek Classics as well as in historical works produced at a time when it was expected that history should be well written.[89] The style of the *History* is, indeed, essential to its author's ambition of creating a coherent synthesis. The results of critical analysis are expressed clearly and precisely in a story that skilfully blends both narrative and description, yet without getting bogged down in points of detail or dispute, which are swept into the numerous footnotes whose presence at the bottom of almost every page visibly underpins the work's claims to 'scientific' scholarship.[90] At the same time, though, the elevated tone – lightened by the occasional touch of typically dry humour – gives a dignity to the *History* commensurate with Lloyd's estimation of its significance.[91] The dignity is heightened at key moments by rhetorical flourishes, including a penchant for maritime and meteorological metaphors that reflects a romantic sensibility evident also in the work's lyrical descriptions of particular localities and its author's fondness for the poets Ceiriog and Islwyn.[92] Not for nothing was Lloyd described by one contemporary as the last example in Wales of the 'grand manner'.[93] Thus Owain Gwynedd (d.1170) is a 'trusty pilot' and Llywelyn the Great (d.1240) a 'dexterous steersman' in the face of political storms.[94] The pathos of Llywelyn ap Gruffudd's death in 1282 is dramatically conveyed by paraphrasing the lament of the poet Gruffudd ab yr Ynad Coch, 'who read the tragedy of the hour in the beating of the wind and of the rain, the sullen wash of the waves upon the grey beach, the roar of the wind-whipt oaks that miserable and more than wintry December'. However, Lloyd switches gear in the following – and final – sentence, concluding the work on an optimistic note that encapsulates his contemporary purpose: 'It was for a far distant generation to see that the last Prince had not lived in vain, but by his life-work had helped to build solidly the enduring fabric of Welsh nationality.'[95] Here, as elsewhere in the *History*, Lloyd's rhetoric is as revealing as his rigorous empiricism.

7

Origins: From Prehistoric to Post-Roman Wales

In December 1910, shortly before the publication of Lloyd's magnum opus, James Harvey Robinson, professor of history at Columbia University, New York, read a paper to the American Historical Association in which he urged the need for historians to take far more serious cognizance of the new human sciences of geology, anthropology and sociology that had emerged in the nineteenth century. In particular, he declared that the new insights into the age of the earth made it imperative to break down the barrier between prehistory and history and to adopt an interdisciplinary approach to human development as a continuum stretching back to the earliest times.[1] Despite the passion with which it was expounded, the prescription was not itself new, as it had already been advocated by some archaeologists and historians in Britain over the previous generation. Yet attempts to put it into practice by integrating recent discoveries in prehistory – itself a relatively new concept – into accounts of history had been few and limited in scope; indeed, Robinson himself had gone no further back than the fall of the Roman Empire in a textbook on the history of western Europe published in 1903.[2] One of the notable things about Lloyd's interpretation of Welsh history from the 1880s onwards was that it took the 'deep past' or 'deep history' seriously, and presented prehistory as a formative epoch in national development. In short, he assimilated intellectual currents to which he had been exposed in the late nineteenth and early twentieth centuries and deployed these to reconfigure previous interpretations of Welsh origins whose essentially legendary character had drained them of their legitimacy.

The following discussion will begin by summarizing those legendary interpretations together with criticisms of them down to the 1870s before moving on to consider new approaches to national origins in late nineteenth-century Britain and, in particular, Lloyd's adoption of these approaches in order to explain the making of the Welsh. The aim, therefore, is to shift the focus from Lloyd's critical treatment of earlier legendary accounts, examined in the previous chapter, towards the key features of the interpretation he offered in their place.

Earlier interpretations of Welsh origins

Until well into the Victorian period the predominant view of the origins of the Welsh was one elaborated in the Middle Ages, albeit expanded to embrace Celticist vistas from the early eighteenth century onwards. The creation of origin legends was widespread in medieval Europe, and these continued to have considerable purchase well into the early modern period, although from the sixteenth century some claims to a Trojan pedigree, deriving ultimately from classical sources, were rejected in favour of a scripturally based, and hence more authoritative, descent from Noah.[3] Wales was no exception. In the early ninth century the *Historia Brittonum* ('History of the Britons') included traditions connecting the Britons with a man called Brutus or Britto who gave his name to Britain. According to one tradition, Brutus was a descendant of Aeneas who had fled to Italy following the fall of Troy, while another claimed that he was a descendant of Japhet son of Noah and thereby of Adam, the first man.[4] But it was Geoffrey of Monmouth who was responsible for elaborating a full account of the alleged prehistory of the Britons, in his pseudo-historical epic, the *Historia Regum Britannie* ('History of the Kings of Britain'), completed *c*.1138 and translated into Welsh in the thirteenth century. According to Geoffrey, Brutus had occupied the island of Albion and renamed it Britain and his Trojan followers Britons; then, after

116

his death, the island was divided between his three sons – Locrinus, Albanactus and Camber – who gave their names to Loegria (England), Albania (Scotland) and Cambria (Wales).[5] Geoffrey's work offered a glorious picture of the Britons which was warmly welcomed by their Welsh descendants, both in the Middle Ages and, indeed, later.[6]

From *c.*1600 onwards Brutus and the Trojans faced new, though no less legendary, rivals as the founding fathers of the Britons and the Welsh. For example, several English writers claimed that the Welsh were descended from the Phoenicians, a belief still held in some quarters in the nineteenth century.[7] However, in Wales itself the most important development since the Middle Ages was the publication in 1716 of *Drych y Prif Oesoedd* ('A Mirror of the First Ages') by Theophilus Evans, a work that 'even by the twilight years of the Victorian age . . . was still far and away the most popular history book in Welsh'.[8] Admittedly this accepted the truth of Geoffrey's history. Yet Evans offered a new interpretation that tended to diminish the significance of that history, in that – following the derivation of the Celts argued by the Breton scholar, Abbé Paul-Yves Pezron – he traced the ultimate origins of the Welsh, not to Troy, but rather to the Tower of Babel and to Gomer, eldest son of Japhet, son of Noah.[9] According to the 'Mirror', it was only some centuries after the arrival of Gomer and his fellow speakers of Gomeraeg (Evans's fanciful derivation of *Cymraeg*, 'Welsh') that Brutus turned up and the island was named after him.[10] Other eighteenth- and nineteenth-century Welsh scholars – most notably Edward Williams or Iolo Morganwg (1747–1826) – added a further dose of Celticist legend through their emphasis on druidism and bardism, and these notions retained considerable purchase for many decades following Iolo's death in 1826, co-existing with the more critical perspectives of those who challenged them.[11] For example, in 1857 different components of this legendary past were presented in seamless succession by R. W. Morgan, whose *British Kymry, or Britons of Cambria*, opened with chapters entitled 'The Gomerian period', 'The Trojan period' and 'The Druidic religion of Britain'.[12]

As late as 1900, John Rhys and David Brynmor-Jones lamented that such origin legends still formed 'the view popularly taken of their own history by the Welsh'.[13] Admittedly they were by no means the first authors to adopt a critical stance. Geoffrey of Monmouth's account of early British history had, after all, been questioned by William of Newburgh at the end of the twelfth century and, more influentially, subjected to searching criticism by Polydore Vergil in the early Tudor period. However, such criticism was framed in essentially textual terms, as it was pointed out that authentic post-Roman sources offered scant corroboration of Geoffrey's colourful epic.[14] Similar criticism continued to be offered in the nineteenth century. One strand proceeded from the assumption – shared also, for example, by many historians of England – that the written sources of classical antiquity provided the earliest reliable evidence for the writing of history, which meant that the history of Britain began with Caesar's first invasion of the island in 55 BC.[15] Thus William Coxe, in the introduction to his *Historical Tour in Monmouthshire* in 1801, began with the Roman invasion of south-east Wales and declared that, 'To repeat the fabulous stories of Geoffrey of Monmouth would be to insult the reader's understanding.'[16] Over the following decades a similar critical approach appears, for example, in the works of ecclesiastical and literary history published respectively by Rice Rees and Thomas Stephens.[17] From 1852 it also became dominant in the Cambrian Archaeological Association, founded five years earlier, as supporters of the mythical interpretation of the Welsh past, associated most recently with Iolo Morganwg, lost ground to their opponents.[18] However, as the debates among the Cambrians made clear, there was no smooth or uniform transition from mythical to more critical understandings of the early Welsh past. The tensions at play here are captured in the Revd Thomas Price's *Hanes Cymru* ('History of Wales'), published in 1842. Rather than jettison mythical interpretations of the Welsh past entirely, Price redesignated them as 'imagination', which, he held, should be distinguished from 'historical authority'. Thus he felt able to repeat the tales of biblical and classical origins centred on Gomer and Brutus, while asserting his critical credentials by adding that there was no 'historical authority' that could show how and when the ancestors of the Welsh had, in fact, first arrived in Britain.[19]

Nor did all of Lloyd's nineteenth-century predecessors content themselves with criticizing the evidence of written sources, for some also drew on the new human sciences in constructing narratives that challenged mythical accounts of Welsh origins – an approach anticipated by the antiquary Edward Lhuyd (*c*.1660–1709), who had difficulty reconciling geological observations with biblically based understandings of the earth's antiquity and undertook pioneering research on the Welsh past focused on linguistic and archaeological evidence for the 'ancient Britains'.[20] Thus *The History of Wales* (1853) by Bernard Bolingbroke Woodward, while conventionally declaring adherence to '[t]he most ancient and authentic authorities which were accessible',[21] reveals an innovative openness to other disciplines in its first two chapters, which offer a survey of the physical geography of Wales, including an account of succeeding geological epochs presumably indebted to Charles Lyell's *Principles of Geology* (1830–3), before proceeding to consider 'what conclusions the newly created science of Ethnology has established about the origin of the Kymry'. Here Woodward explicitly acknowledges his debt to James Cowles Prichard (1786–1848), the leading British ethnologist of the first half of the nineteenth century, who held that the Celtic peoples, including the Welsh, were a branch of the Indo-European family of peoples, and thus 'the Kymry are one of the most ancient peoples of Europe'.[22] Moreover, while laying particular emphasis on linguistic evidence, Woodward also paid attention to archaeology, namely burial monuments and their associated artefacts, and implied that advances in civilization were linked to a sequence in materials used from stone to bronze, silver and gold and then to iron.[23] This categorization bears an intriguing resemblance to the Three Age System – referring to the stone, bronze and iron ages – developed in Denmark in the 1830s and 1840s as a means of distinguishing different periods of prehistory. However, the Three Age System met considerable resistance in England until the 1860s, and if Woodward had heard of it, his knowledge was evidently slight.[24] After all, he makes no explicit reference either to the Three Age System or to prehistory; indeed, he turned to the Old Testament for parallels to the cairns and cromlechs he described, and was content to observe that Britain had been 'peopled in very remote times'.[25] Moreover, for all his pioneering use of geology and ethnology, Woodward concluded that neither of these sciences could provide an accurate chronological account of the past: 'history alone can furnish this'.[26]

A similar privileging of written sources is even more apparent in the next two major books to be published on Welsh history, namely Jane Williams's *History of Wales* (1869) and Gweirydd ap Rhys's *Hanes y Brytaniaid a'r Cymry* ('The History of the Britons and the Welsh', 1872–4). Williams included a few brief references to archaeological sites in the first chapter of her *History*, but showed little grasp of the date or significance of the material evidence presented, assigning it vaguely to the period preceding Caesar's invasion of Britain.[27] The same is true of Gweirydd ap Rhys, although his use of archaeological evidence was more extensive, and included brief mentions of the 'Stone Period' and 'Bronze Period' which may indicate some familiarity with the Three Age System.[28] He also drew on studies of ethnology and comparative philology by Prichard, Friedrich Max Müller and Isaac Taylor, and celebrated the progress of the Britons from their 'pitiful, barbaric condition' 2,000 years previously to 'the civilized, honourable condition' they had attained in his day.[29] However, he had difficulty integrating the fruits of his reading in the human sciences into a coherent historical narrative and, like Woodward and Jane Williams before him, based his account principally on written sources.

New approaches: Teutons and Celts

Although varying in their precise details, the legendary interpretations that continued to resonate well into the nineteenth century were all predicated on a common key assumption: that the Welsh were a people descended from a single powerful race – be it Trojan or Celtic – which had lost its former glory after being restricted, following the Anglo-Saxon conquests, to the land of Wales. New interpretations of Welsh origins developed from the 1880s onwards, as exemplified by the work of Lloyd, assumed quite the opposite: namely, that the Welsh were derived from an amalgam of primitive, albeit increasingly civilized, races and had reached their full glory as a people only in the reign of Queen Victoria.

These new interpretations belonged to a wider re-evaluation of the origins of peoples in Britain in the later nineteenth century and may be compared in particular with challenges to the Teutonist theory of English origins that had become predominant by the 1840s and remained influential for the rest of the Victorian period.[30] In brief, the theory held that the English were essentially a Germanic or Teutonic race descended biologically from the Anglo-Saxon invaders of post-Roman Britain; moreover, according to the theory's most ardent devotees such as Thomas Carlyle and E. A. Freeman, this racial descent was the key to the greatness of the English and their superiority over other peoples, including Celts.[31] One objection to these views was that, through asserting that the Anglo-Saxons had exterminated or at least totally overcome the Britons, a crucial link was eliminated that could have ensured continuity between Roman Britain and modern England, and thus between Roman civilization – including Christianity – and the imperial Britain of the Victorian era. This prompted Henry Charles Coote to argue in 1864 that the English had direct Roman ancestry, an argument he developed further toward the end of the following decade, and by the 1880s the idea that Romano-Britons had survived the Anglo-Saxon conquests and contributed to the making of the English had gained significant ground among scholars of Roman Britain including the archaeologist Pitt Rivers.[32] (A more eccentric attempt to forge a link with classical antiquity was made by Luke Owen Pike, who flatly rejected the view of Teutonic origins by arguing that the English not only differed markedly from the Germans but rather, thanks to their predominantly Celtic ancestry, bore striking resemblances with the ancient Greeks.[33])

A further challenge to Teutonist views came from archaeologists and physical anthropologists. In the 1860s and 1870s the idea of prehistory, extending countless millennia beyond 4004 BC, the year in which Archbishop Ussher had placed the biblical story of creation, gained considerable ground in England, thanks especially to the publication of Charles Lyell's *The Geological Evidences of the Antiquity of Man* (1863), John Lubbock's *Pre-historic Times* (1865) and William Greenwell's *British Barrows* (1877), all of which adopted the Three Age System.[34] One consequence of this acceptance of human antiquity was that it allowed nineteenth-century populations to be seen as descendants of races that had lived in prehistoric Britain. Moreover, the analysis of skulls discovered in burial monuments and other prehistoric sites facilitated the identification of different races or peoples in prehistory, whose physical features could in turn be compared with those of modern individuals and thus cited as evidence of racial continuity.[35] This was closely linked to another important development from the 1860s onwards, namely the adoption by ethnologists and scholars in related fields of a more rigorous, biological definition of race as essentially a matter of physical characteristics which, therefore, in contrast to the thinking of James Cowles Prichard, needed to be uncoupled from language, the evidence of which had been a mainstay of earlier ethnology.[36] True, the links with the prehistoric past were complex, as it was argued that the original races of mankind had disappeared through a lengthy process of amalgamation: 'Modern races were mainly mongrels.' Hence the challenge facing anthropologists was to identify different 'racial types' in modern populations.[37] A further corollary was that it became less acceptable to equate race with nationality, though some were reluctant to abandon such a well-established elision.[38] In England the new, predominantly physiological thinking on race was vigorously upheld by T. H. Huxley, who consequently dismissed racial notions of Teutonism, maintaining in 1865 that '[a] vast amount of Kelticism, not found in our tongue, very probably exists in our pedigrees'.[39] The trend in favour of attributing mixed origins to the English gained such momentum over the next two decades that John Beddoe felt obliged to emphasize that a Teutonic element remained an important part of the mixture, declaring: 'It is not very long since educated opinion considered the English and Lowland Scots an almost purely Teutonic people. Now the current runs so much the other way that I have had to take up the attitude of an apologist for the "Saxon" view.'[40]

Lloyd was not the first in the 1880s to produce a new general account of a people's past in Britain based on a synthesis of recent linguistic, ethnological and archaeological work, for this had already been done with respect to early England by Grant Allen and Charles Elton. Allen drew on a wide array of historians, archaeologists and other scholars, including Huxley and William Boyd Dawkins, and sought to steer a middle course between the Teutonists and their critics by distinguishing biological ancestry from political and cultural characteristics: 'The facts seem to indicate that while the modern English nation is largely Welsh in blood, it is wholly Teutonic in form and language.'[41] Indeed, he went further and maintained that, partly thanks to '[a] return wave of Celts' since the Tudor period, the Teutonic character of the English had also been modified; in particular, when its unimaginative nature was 'counteracted by the Celtic wealth of fancy, the race has produced the great English literature'.[42] Here, Allen was evidently indebted to Matthew Arnold. Elton likewise turned to Arnold to argue for the enduring influence of the Celts on England, and stressed that, while its 'principal ancestors' were Teutonic, 'the English nation is compounded of the blood of many different races'.[43] Thus, like Dawkins and others, Elton connected the English (and other peoples of Britain) not just to the Celts but to the long-headed inhabitants of the Stone Age, declaring 'it extremely probable that some part of the Neolithic population has survived until the present time, with a constant improvement no doubt from its crossing and intermixture with the many other races who have successively passed into Britain'.[44] This view of the English as a hybrid race whose history originated long before the arrival of the Anglo-Saxons, in the depths of prehistory, gained further traction in the late nineteenth and early twentieth century.[45] Indeed, in his inaugural lecture as regius professor of modern history at Cambridge in 1902, J. B. Bury insisted that research on the Celtic peoples was urgently needed in order to understand the making of western Europe as a whole, for 'the Celtic world commands one of the chief portals of ingress into that mysterious prae-Aryan foreworld, from which it may well be that we modern Europeans have inherited far more than we dream'.[46]

Lloyd and the origins of the Welsh

In many respects the interpretation of Welsh origins that Lloyd developed from the 1880s onwards was simply a variation on other recent work in Britain that presented successively more advanced races amalgamating to form a particular nation; indeed, like the myth of Brutus and his sons, the interpretation implied – though the point is never explicitly stated – that the Welsh shared a common origin with the English, an implication that may have held some attraction for a patriot like Lloyd who sought to affirm the distinctiveness of the Welsh within a wider British and imperial orbit.[47] However, there was one crucial difference from the English examples considered so far. As we have seen, even advocates of a racially hybrid English people accepted its predominantly Teutonic character, especially with respect to language and institutions (neither of which necessarily depended on racial transmission). By contrast, the territory that became Wales had escaped Anglo-Saxon conquest, though admittedly this contributed indirectly to its definition as a nation; nevertheless, Teutonic or English influences only began to make a significant mark on the country's institutions after the Edwardian conquest or even the union with England under Henry VIII.[48] Consequently, circumstances were far more favourable for the early peoples of the prehistoric and Roman periods to make an enduring contribution to the creation of the Welsh than to that of the English or lowland Scots.

This certainly seems to have been Lloyd's view, which combined Dawkins's synthesis of prehistoric archaeology with the interpretation of Welsh origins advanced by John Rhys in his *Celtic Britain* of 1882 and subsequent writings.[49] Lloyd had come to know Rhys at Oxford and held him in high regard, adhering closely to his views until the early twentieth century.[50] The debt to Dawkins was more durable. Over half a century after the publication of *Early Man in Britain* Lloyd recalled the volume's seminal influence on his own thinking about Welsh history, noting that it was one of the first books to break down the barrier between written and archaeological evidence, between the arts and the sciences, and thus 'to show how prehistoric and historical studies were of necessity interdependent'. Lloyd continued that Dawkins 'was the first ... to clothe in literary form ... the idea that in geology, prehistoric archaeology and history we have successive records of one continuous process'. He added that this point of view had always appealed to him:

I know that every effort of mine to delineate the course of events which has created the Welsh people, from a very crude eisteddfod essay in 1884 down to the present day [i.e. 1932], has taken its exordium, not from the Druids or even the Phoenicians, but from palaeolithic man. In other words, what I first learnt from 'Early Man in Britain,' I have never forgotten.[51]

These were no empty words, for even a cursory perusal of Dawkins's book reveals how far Lloyd shared some of its basic assumptions. Apart from its insistence on the need to combine the fruits of archaeology, ethnology and history, the book's vision of human development emphasized the importance of the *longue durée* in its assertion 'that the continuity between the Neolithic age and the present day has been unbroken'.[52] Moreover, like the ethnologists, Dawkins regarded the succession of races that peopled the island as representing increasing levels of civilization – a progressionist viewpoint that also informed Lloyd's understanding of the past.[53]

Rhys also adopted an interdisciplinary approach, albeit one focused on philological, literary and ethnological sources, and argued that the Welsh derived from three principal races, each of which had arrived successively in Wales from continental Europe. The earliest of these was the pre-Celtic population of Britain, the 'aborigines' or 'Ivernians' which corresponded to the Iberians described by ethnologists, and which Rhys – the latest in a long tradition extending back to the Roman historian Tacitus' comments on the Silures of south-east Wales – believed to have originated in Spain. These were followed by two Celtic, and thus Aryan, peoples: the Goidels, then the Brythons. All three peoples had mixed with each other to create the Welsh.[54] Rhys elaborated this theory over the following two decades by suggesting, for example, that the Goidels had arrived by the fifth or sixth century BC, and most of the Brythons in the second century BC.[55] However, it was the pre-Celtic 'aborigines' that had made by far the most important contribution to the racial composition of the Welsh, as this people had lived in Britain for probably thousands of years before the arrival of the Goidels and had thus had a much greater opportunity to acclimatize themselves to the country.[56] Drawing on the distinction between language and race that had gained considerable ground by the time he was writing, Rhys famously declared: 'Skulls are harder than consonants, and races lurk when languages slink away. The lineal descendants of the neolithic aborigines are ever among us, possibly those of a still earlier race.'[57] Yet, just as opponents of racial Teutonism such as Charles Elton, while insisting that the English were racially mongrel, had nevertheless accepted that their identity as a people owed significantly more to the Anglo-Saxons than to any earlier people, so Rhys held that the last of the early invaders, namely the Brythons, had contributed most to creating the nationality of the Welsh, during the post-Roman period.[58]

Rhys was aware of recent work in archaeology, including the distinction between the Palaeolithic and Neolithic eras in the Stone Age, but made little use of it by comparison with ethnology and philology, fields with which he evidently felt much more comfortable.[59] In this he differed from Lloyd, who broke new ground in the writing of Welsh history by making much more systematic use of archaeology and assigning it far greater value as evidence than any of his predecessors.[60] Let us turn, then, and look more closely at Lloyd's depiction of the early Welsh past. Although the particulars of this depiction changed over the fifty-five years from the essay for the eisteddfod at Liverpool in 1884 to the third edition of his *History* in 1939, its main features remained essentially the same. Here attention will be focused on the detailed interpretation offered in the opening chapters of the first edition of the *History*, which were largely written in 1901–2, a decade before the work's publication in 1911.[61] These chapters are particularly significant, not only because they provide the fullest exposition of Lloyd's views on prehistoric and Roman Wales but because of their inclusion in a work intended to redefine Welsh history. Nevertheless, reference will also be made to both earlier and later writings by Lloyd where these help to illuminate his approach and method.

The *History* opens with a chapter entitled 'The prehistoric epochs' which draws heavily on archaeological and ethnological writing of the later nineteenth century, and invests it with considerable significance in the explanation of Welsh history as a whole. The first section summarizes the evidence for human settlement in Wales during the Palaeolithic (Old Stone Age), and begins: 'The region now known as Wales was inhabited by man in the earliest period during which science has clearly shown him to have dwelt in the British Isles.'[62] However, since this population was believed to have died out, leaving no posterity behind, the survey is only a prologue to the book's main concern: the making of the Welsh. 'Welshmen have inherited neolithic blood and the neolithic civilisation; in the palaeolithic man of Britain it is probable they have no part.'[63] The next section, entitled 'Neolithic Wales', reiterates the point: 'With the opening of the Neolithic or New Stone Age begins, so far as is now known, the continuous history of man in Wales.' This was followed in turn by the Bronze Age and 'by the Age of Iron, which may be regarded as lasting to our own day'.[64] Thus, Lloyd followed Dawkins in identifying racial invasions with the main divisions established for European prehistory, with the Neolithic Iberians being succeeded in the Bronze and Iron Ages respectively by two Celtic peoples, which Lloyd termed Goidels and Brythons following the classification proposed by Rhys.[65] The Brythons' arrival in Britain was tentatively placed in about the middle of the third century BC, although it would be a further two centuries or more before they reached what became Wales, being represented there at the time of the Roman conquest by the Ordovices of the north-east, and completing their conquest of the country only in the post-Roman period.[66] Lloyd later modified this account of racial invasions in the light of subsequent archaeological research, notably by describing the second wave of immigrants, in the Bronze Age, not as Goidels, but as 'Beaker Folk', a label first applied almost three decades earlier to the users of Early Bronze Age beaker pottery. However, he continued to insist on the formative contribution of these pre-historic peoples to the making of Wales.[67]

Lloyd also shared the widespread assumption that such early peoples remained visible in modern populations, for he had no doubts that the Welsh of his own day owed their physical appearance, and perhaps also aspects of their temperament and character, to the succession of three prehistoric peoples – representing ever-increasing levels of 'civilization' – from whom they were ultimately descended.[68] With respect to the earliest of these, the Neolithic, he asserted that 'it is to this people the ancestry of the modern Welshman must in a large measure be traced'.[69] Moreover, he accepted the views of Dawkins that this Neolithic population was small, dark and of Iberian origin, and he drew on Beddoe's *Races of Britain* to claim that their descendants were especially prevalent 'in the two old-world centres of Rhayader and Beddgelert'.[70] Nor did Lloyd adhere strictly to physiological concepts of race; like other contemporaneous writers on the subject, he assumed that, although language was independent of race, a people's temperament and character – including its religious inclinations – could be explained in terms of racial characteristics.[71] Thus he also declared of the 'Iberian race': 'Its features and build are represented in modern Britain by the short, dark Welshman of South Wales, possibly its very qualities of soul and mind in the typical collier and "eisteddfodwr," impulsive and wayward, but susceptible to the influences of music and religion.'[72] Nevertheless, while by no means the only instance of this kind in Lloyd's writing, such rhetorical adherence to commonplace ideas is not necessarily a reliable indication of the explanatory power with which they were endowed. True, the early medieval Welsh kindred is attributed with prehistoric origins, and the servile class of bondmen identified with the conquered Iberians.[73] In addition, Lloyd occasionally characterizes medieval Welsh princes with reference to the extent to which they possessed allegedly 'Celtic' characteristics, though this seems to owe more to Matthew Arnold than to Lloyd's own account of racial migrations and assimilation.[74] Otherwise, however, the concept of racial inheritance is largely absent from the account of medieval Wales that forms the bulk of the *History*.[75] This is consistent with Lloyd's overriding emphasis on the nation, in whose creation early races play an important contributory part but whose subsequent history develops a dynamic of its own, driven by a variety of factors of which racial inheritance was only one.

Lloyd summarized his views on the significance of the three prehistoric peoples he had identified by declaring that the arrival of the Brythons

> marks the appearance in the island of the third and last of the three considerable race elements which have gone to the making of the Welsh people. If it be contended that the first of these, the Neolithic, was the most important in respect of its contribution to the national physique and character, and that the second, the Goidelic, was the

source of the early political and social institutions of the Welsh, it cannot be denied that it is to the third we owe the Welsh language.[76]

One important reason why these early races were so fundamental to the making of the Welsh was that they were largely unaffected by the influence of Rome. This was the main conclusion of the third chapter of the *History*, written in the summer of 1902.[77] There, Lloyd provided a characteristically careful account of the Roman conquest of Britain, based on Tacitus together with the work of modern scholars such as Theodor Mommsen, before drawing on archaeological evidence as well as written sources to examine the chronology, scale and nature of the Roman occupation of Wales, a theme he developed further in a survey of 'the subject tribes' in the chapter's final section.[78] The section opened by posing a question 'which must be answered ere any wide view can be taken of the course of development of Welsh history', namely the relationship of 'the conquered Silures, Demetae, Ordovices and men of Gwynedd' to the 'Roman civilisation' imposed over much of the country. 'Were they Romanised as well as subdued . . . ? Or did they live in tribal isolation, retaining their Celtic speech and institutions and learning little from the soldiers who moved in and out among them?'[79]

Lloyd essentially favoured the latter scenario. True, the interpretation he offered was more nuanced than that of his previous writings on the subject. In part, this reflected his great debt to recent work by Francis Haverfield (1861–1919), 'the most eminent Roman archaeologist in Britain of the late nineteenth and early twentieth centuries'.[80] Haverfield challenged the prevailing view that the Roman occupation of Britain was essentially military in nature, making little impact on the culture of the indigenous people, and thus similar to British rule in India – a comparison also made by Lloyd in his school textbook of 1893.[81] Thus, while the eisteddfod essay presented the whole of Roman Britain as a militarized province, the *History* accepted Haverfield's distinction between a civil zone in the south-east and midland areas of Britain and a military zone to the north and west.[82] However, since Wales belonged to the latter, this merely served to reinforce Lloyd's previous arguments for minimal Roman influence on the tribes inhabiting that region: it would be rash, he argued, to presume that Wales followed the same pattern as south-eastern Britain.[83] On the other hand, thanks perhaps partly to the new thinking represented by Haverfield's emphasis on the Romano-Britons' assimilation of Roman civilization, but more evidently to a recent study of Latin loan-words in the Brittonic languages, Lloyd modified his view to argue that the Brythonic ancestors of the Welsh had been Romanized to a limited extent, namely with respect to aspects of warfare, literacy and material culture.[84]

Overall, though, Lloyd held that the linguistic evidence pointed in the other direction: the survival of the Welsh language indicated that 'the inhabitants of Wales were so far divorced from the main current of Roman life as to speak a separate language, which linked them with the customs and traditions of the past'.[85] In other words, there was a fundamental continuity between the Celtic population, itself infused with the blood of a Neolithic Iberian people, and the Britons of the post-Roman era who subsequently became the Welsh.

> Roman civilisation, then, while it imported many new influences into the old Celtic society, did not break up its essential structure or sever its connection with the past. It left Wales richer in many respects, its parting gift of a new religion . . . being the greatest of all it bestowed, but the land remained a home of primitive ways and ideas, the dwelling-place of a people who, taken as a whole, had scarcely attained the level of the Britons of the south-east at the time of the Roman conquest.[86]

The emphasis on 'primitive ways' is already found in the eisteddfod essay, which is more explicit than the *History* on the long-term significance of their survival – apparently adapting the 'germ theory' Lloyd would have encountered through his reading of Stubbs, who held that the medieval English polity had developed from purely Germanic 'common germs' – and also situates it in the specific economic and social context of pastoralism.

> We have now watched the growth of the complex mass which forms the foundation of the Welsh people up to the eve of the Roman

occupation. It has been necessary to describe the process in considerable detail, because it furnished the key to a great part of Welsh history. In what has been said of the early British tribes we may find the germs of nearly everything that marks mediaeval Wales: the Brythons and the Goidels bend their heads to the storm of Roman conquest and reappear with the fall of empire in all their old simplicity, leading a pastoral, tribal life for century after century under the shadow of the sternest, most rigid feudalism.[87]

The concept of pastoralism is a further key element in Lloyd's depiction of Welsh origins in the prehistoric and Roman periods. For racial amalgamation and survival were not simply a matter of transmitting physical and other characteristics to the Welsh people; they were inextricably linked to a form of social organization that facilitated political independence in the medieval centuries. The *History* contrasted the Brythonic 'agricultural people' of south-eastern Britain at the time of the Roman conquest with 'the wild pastoral tribes of the hills, half Goidelic and half Iberian', observing of the latter:

As in later ages, the fact that they had no stake in the soil, no rich crops to rot in the ground, no well-built houses and barns which an enemy might burn, gave them infinite mobility . . . Moreover, Rome could not tempt them; in the barbaric simplicity of their life their one fierce desire was for independence.[88]

While the contrast between lowland agriculture and upland pastoralism implies adaptation to different geographical conditions, and other statements present those conditions as having fundamentally determined the course of Welsh history, on the whole Lloyd eschewed any crude geographical determinism.[89]

This is particularly clear from a lecture, first delivered in 1909, which crystallizes views he had been developing since at least the 1890s.[90] The lecture opens by dismissing any simplistic belief that environment could explain everything: 'no student of history can rest content with this short cut to the philosophy of his subject; other factors than the environment have undoubtedly to be taken into account – the factor of race, the factor of religion, the factor of foreign influence'.[91] True, he maintained that, in Wales, 'it is possible to trace the closest connection between the facts of physical geography and the course of the national history'.[92] However, Lloyd was at pains to insist that this connection was complex: 'To say that Wales is a land of mountains is to render scant justice to the situation.'[93] This reads like a rebuke to O. M. Edwards, who famously opened his popular history of Wales in 1901 by declaring that 'Wales is a land of mountains. Its mountains explain its isolation and its love of independence; they explain its internal divisions; they have determined, throughout its history, what the direction and method of its progress were to be.'[94] Note the verbs here: 'explain', 'determined'. By contrast, Lloyd sought to show that the geographical environment of Wales had favoured the development of pastoralism. However, this was not simply a case of a predominantly upland landscape being suited to the rearing of livestock, but also had a cultural dimension that implied some measure of human agency; in other words, the emphasis lay, not on geography itself but, rather, on human adaptation to it. Put briefly, the mountains of Wales had provided a refuge for the most ancient races of Britain, of which the earliest, the Iberians, had apparently reached only the pastoral stage in social evolution; moreover, though they may originally have practised agriculture in lowland Britain, the Goidels probably ceased to do so after Brythonic conquests led to their being 'thrown back upon the great pasture lands of the North and West'.[95] Both early races had clung tenaciously to pastoralism during the Roman period, and Lloyd implies that the Brythons, too, notwithstanding their centuries-long tradition of agriculture, adopted a largely pastoral form of society when they settled in Wales, thereby inheriting the institutions and traditions associated with that earlier stage.[96]

> Nature has thus decreed that Wales, which is geologically the oldest part of Southern Britain, shall also be the stronghold and refuge of the ancient races of the island. Just as Cambrian and Silurian are terms expressive in geology of high antiquity in the matter of rock-formation, so Welshman must always mean one who inherits older traditions, has behind him a more venerable past than can be claimed by the prosperous tiller of the eastern plains.[97]

According to Lloyd, then, the origins of the Welsh lay deep in prehistory. However, they clearly emerged as a nation only in the post-Roman period. As we have seen, the Brythons constituted the final element that eventually overcame, and fused with, the earlier Iberian and Goidelic races to create the Welsh, bestowing on them a crucial badge of identity – the Welsh language. By the end of the Roman period they had become the dominant race in Wales, a position they consolidated in the early fifth century through the expulsion of the Irish from Gwynedd, undertaken by Cunedda from the northern Brythonic territory of Manaw Gododdin around Edinburgh, and other subsequent acts of conquest.[98] However, so Lloyd argued (following Rhys), it was conflict with the advancing Anglo-Saxons that led to the final act in the making of Wales, and in particular the Northumbrians' defeat of the Cymry – as the Brythons (or Britons) of Wales and Cumbria were now known – at the battle of the Winwaed in 655, for this separated the Welsh from their compatriots in northern Britain.

> Thus the year 655 forms an epoch of great importance in the history of the Welsh people; it closes the period of definition, during which they were gradually marked off from the other inhabitants of these islands and constituted a separate people; it brings upon the stage a nation, isolated and self-contained, dependent henceforth upon its own resources for its development.[99]

A full quarter way into the *History*, Wales and the Welsh had finally become one.

That Lloyd devoted so much space to tracing the formation of the Welsh from prehistory to the post-Roman period indicates the importance he attached to establishing their credentials as a historic nation. This emphasis on origins reflected assumptions which were widespread during his formative years in the late Victorian period, and the deployment of an interdisciplinary approach that drew on philology, anthropology and archaeology, together with the written sources that had been the mainstay of earlier accounts, likewise signalled an allegiance to modern scholarship as it had developed by the end of the nineteenth century. Indeed, although he was by no means unique in his day in integrating prehistory into an account of national history, Lloyd went further than many historians in drawing on the new human sciences in order to achieve this goal. His approach was, of course, driven by the powerful critical impulse that informed all his historical writing: Lloyd took delight in confounding earlier legendary interpretations and contrasting them with the even more astounding, but far more reliable, conclusions of modern science.[100] However, there was more to his approach than that. A different critical mind could have decided that, such were the uncertainties concerning the remote past, it was best to pass over it quickly. The decision to devote so much attention to the origins of the Welsh surely indicates that Lloyd proceeded from essentially the same premise as his myth-making predecessors: that key moments in the making of the Welsh people had occurred in distant, mostly pre-Roman, ages. Thus the continuity once claimed from Gomer, Brutus and Camber was now traced back to the much more soundly attested people of the Neolithic. Lloyd's commitment to 'deep history' belonged to a very specific context, as he drew on new ideas in order to reconfigure – rather than fundamentally subvert – his nation's past. In short, by combining close textual analysis with the human sciences of the late Victorian period Lloyd was able to reaffirm the antiquity of the Welsh, possibly in implicit contrast to Teutonist interpretations of English origins, while at the same time demonstrating a decisive break with myth-making.

8

Tribal Wales: Society and the Church

If Lloyd presented the making of the Welsh people as a dynamic process of racial migrations and integration beginning in prehistory, his account of how that people maintained its distinctive identity through the medieval centuries invoked two different, but complementary, themes. In part, as we shall see in the next chapter, Lloyd emphasized movement and change through focusing on the political ambitions of Welsh rulers and especially the extent to which they provided leadership for national aspirations. However, he seems to have thought that the survival of the Welsh as a people owed at least as much to social continuity as to political change (indeed, in his view, rulers' actions were themselves conditioned by social structures): namely, to the durability of a distinctive kind of society, whose main lineaments came into view in Caesar's description of the tribes of the interior of Britain and proved remarkably resilient for well over a millennium thereafter, despite Norman conquest and settlement and even the conquest of Wales by Edward I. This is not to say that Lloyd believed that the Middle Ages held the key to the making of modern Welsh society – which, as shown in chapter 5, he regarded as the product of changes beginning in the eighteenth century – nor that, in contrast to some late nineteenth-century scholars who wrote about Ireland and Scotland, he was strongly motivated by a desire to show the relevance of medieval forms of land tenure to debates about land reform in his own day.[1]

As with his account of Welsh origins, though, Lloyd benefited not only from studies concerned primarily with Wales but also from work that sought to illuminate developments in England, and combined these different strands of scholarship in order to help achieve his broader objective of demonstrating the deep historical foundations of Welsh nationality.

The present chapter aims, then, to analyse Lloyd's account of Welsh society as it had emerged by the early Middle Ages.[2] It will begin by summarizing some key aspects of that account before setting it in the context of the sources Lloyd used and assessing its significance. Finally, the discussion will consider how he treated the Church, an institution that claimed the allegiance of all sections of medieval Welsh society. However, whereas Lloyd attributed the main elements of secular society to the adaptation by successive early races to the environment of Wales, the Church was presented as resulting from the absorption of different kinds of external influences, from the original introduction of Christianity in the Roman period to the foundation of houses belonging to reformed religious orders in the twelfth and thirteenth centuries. The approach taken to the Church therefore merits attention, not only because of the institution's importance in medieval Wales, but also because it had the potential to complicate the emphasis on continuity that was fundamental to Lloyd's interpretation of medieval Welsh society.[3]

Society

Of the twenty chapters of the *History*, only one, entitled 'Early Welsh institutions', is devoted entirely to social organization, although the preceding topographical survey of Wales contains much relevant material, and Lloyd later returns to the topic in a short section on 'Welsh society in 1200'.[4] 'Early Welsh institutions' is divided into four sections, dealing respectively with the kindred or clan (*cenedl*), hamlet or township (*tref*), the cantref – literally, 'hundred townships', but a major territorial subdivision of the kingdom presented as synonymous with the 'tribe', and whose functions were later taken over by a further subdivision, the commote – and the chief or king (*brenin*). These different institutions were bound into a single socio-economic framework by pastoralism. Although Lloyd depicted a mixed agrarian economy that included cultivation of crops, the accent is firmly on the keeping of livestock: Welsh society was '[l]argely pastoral in its activities' and only 'to some extent agricultural'.[5] He gave lapidary expression to the wider political, social and cultural ramifications of this in one of the note-books he compiled in preparing the *History*:

> Wales unsuited for tillage – most profitable industry of early times: hence invaders always drive settlers (Iberians, Goidels, Britons) into this region & then leave them there undisturbed. Any inhabitants of Wales forced to turn to pastoral mode of life. Pastoral life nomadic – hence no permanent settlements: people move easily about, leaving nothing for an enemy to seize: have no stake in the country. Agri-cultural community at mercy of superior military force: pastoral not. Hence Welsh able to maintain independence. Same causes favoured tribal isolation: no opportunity for conquest which creates strong monarchy. Pastoral habits further make ties of association personal and not local – hence strength of family and clan feeling. Pastoral way of life means much leisure – hence cultivation of poetry, music, tale telling, and oratory.[6]

The last point is duly developed in the *History* itself, which gives particular attention to the Welsh poetry composed during the twelfth century as part of the 'national revival' led by the native princes, and concludes its section on Welsh society in 1200 by affirming that 'it was only as representing the survival of tribal custom and morality that Welsh life could be termed barbarous. In intellectual ability and mental culture the race stood high . . .'[7]

The reference to 'survival' implies both antiquity and resilience. Lloyd's emphasis on the antiquity of the institutions he describes gives further point to his insistence on tracing the origins of the Welsh back to the Neolithic. Indeed, he explicitly declared that the most ancient of these institutions, the kindred, linked 'the Welsh of the Middle Ages with their prehistoric ancestors'.[8] It contained

> the oldest elements in Welsh society, those which had resisted the influence of Roman law and government, of Christian ethical teaching,

and of royal authority as exercised by Welsh chiefs. It carries us back into the Celtic foreworld, and discloses a system not at all unlike, in spite of variations of detail, that which prevailed among the Irish.[9]

Likewise, Lloyd followed prevailing scholarly fashion in attributing the fundamental division of Welsh society between free and unfree to early racial migrations, as he identified the servile population with 'the remnant of the Iberian people, the oldest tillers of the soil in Wales, reduced to servitude by wave after wave of Celtic conquest, by the might of the ancestors of the free tribesmen'.[10] In addition, he suggested that the action for claiming ancestral land known as *dadannudd* (literally, 'uncovering (the hearth)') had originated in Aryan ancestor-worship.[11] By contrast, kingship in medieval Wales, while having ancient Celtic origins, was essentially a post-Roman creation: 'This much had been done for the Celts of Britain by the spectacle of the majesty of Roman justice; they never abandoned the conception of the magistrate as one who "beareth not the sword in vain".'[12]

Moreover, according to Lloyd, the key institutions of early medieval Wales were extremely durable, continuing largely unchanged until the Edwardian conquest and, indeed, beyond it. This is made clear in both the chapter on institutions and the later discussion of Welsh society in 1200, and highlights a key characteristic of Lloyd's interpretation of medieval Wales, namely the conservatism of an ancient kin-based, pastoral society. Referring specifically to kinship, he declared: 'It was the continuance of this system far on into the Middle Ages, when feudalism and canon law had elsewhere wrought such mighty changes, which gave Welsh life its piquant interest, its individual tone and colour.'[13] The point is elaborated with respect to the late twelfth century, when 'in essentials Wales still retained its ancient social structure, remaining a tribal and pastoral community in spite of the great wave of feudalism which beat upon its eastern flank and daily threatened to engulf the older social system'.[14] Although the *History* offers no comment on Welsh society after 1200, his later writings show that Lloyd believed that little changed during the thirteenth century.[15] Even the Edwardian conquest had only a limited impact to judge by his assessment of the mid-fourteenth century:

Despite the continual conflict of the last hundred years, the cease-less tide of English influence, the essential Wales remains very much the same. Political change only slightly affected the economic and the intellectual life of the country. Wales presents the spectacle of a land dotted over with centres of foreign activity . . . but it is still inhabited in the main by its ancient population, whose culture goes back to a distant past.[16]

Indeed, he suggested that only the industrialization of the nineteenth century marked a decisive rupture with an ancient pastoral way of life, still evoked 'with true poetic instinct' by the poets Hiraethog and Ceiriog.[17]

Another important thread running through the chapter on early institutions is the tension between tribal freedom and monarchical power. Lloyd is careful to distinguish the people or tribe from the smaller entity of the kindred. Although, as we shall see, the tribe comprised kindreds, and thus partook of their characteristics, it is defined primarily by its occupation of a particular territory, namely the cantref.

In point of fact, there is good evidence that the cantref is the histor-ical successor of the 'gwlad' or 'tud', i.e. country or tribe, the body of free tribesmen who, either as ancient settlers or as Brythonic im-migrants, held sway as an independent community within bounds which clearly marked them off from their neighbours.[18]

This territorial conceptualization of the tribe is also fundamental to the preceding chapter, entitled 'The tribal divisions of Wales', which is presented as both 'a general survey of the political con-ditions of Wales during the period 650 to 850' and 'a topographical account of the country', and proceeds from the premise that each district had its own tribal identity, reflected in an independence em-phasized in the observation, for example, that the men of Powys were 'lovers of tribal freedom'.[19] However, such freedom was a mixed blessing, in that it could obstruct the advance of royal authority which alone could facilitate greater national unity.[20] Thus Lloyd suggested that the greater independence of the leading free tribesmen of south Wales compared with those of the north was:

the chief explanation of the fact that the princes who worked most successfully for Welsh unity were in the main of northern origin. At the stage of political development which the Welsh people had now reached, aristocratic freedom meant tribal isolation and weakness, while royal power in capable hands made for national union and strength.[21]

The last sentence conveys the complexity of Lloyd's thinking particularly well, as political change is presented in terms of the interaction of broader social structures with individual rulers.

Although the point is not made explicitly, tribal freedom depended to a considerable extent on the fact that, while defined territorially, from a social perspective the tribe was an aggregation of kindreds.[22] Indeed, the kindred was 'the basis of society, for the Welsh were, and long continued to be, in that stage in which the tie of kinship is paramount, overshadowing all other relations'.[23] More specifically,

[i]t was the body of kinsmen descended from a common known ancestor who, recognising their relationship, acted in concert in all family matters, such as giving in marriage, acknowledging sons, and, above all, waging the family feuds and ending them by the payment and receipt of compensation.[24]

Its autonomy as a social group was underlined, moreover, by its possession of an elected head, the *pencenedl* (chief of kindred), and was mapped on to the land through the scattered homesteads of the 'free tribesmen', the heads of whose households probably formed the court of the cantref.[25] On the other hand, the power of free tribesmen was limited by two factors. First, they had only a life interest in the land, which was divisible at death among kinsmen; accordingly, a tribesman was prevented from passing his landed wealth intact to a single heir and thus from building up the power of his direct descendants.[26] Secondly, from at least the sixth century, free tribesmen – and also, of course, the unfree population – were subject to the authority of chiefs or kings. Although Lloyd does not explain in detail how royal dynasties emerged, he seems to suggest that they originated as the leaders of individual tribes, which agreed to subject themselves to a single authority as a means of achieving security. Thus 'the monarchical element' was:

a costly burden from the economic point of view, but able to offer in return, not only guarantees for the preservation of order within the state, but also – what was no less prized – satisfaction to the spirit of tribal pride and security from the inroads of detested rivals.[27]

The key unit for the exercise of royal power was the cantref, for, while originally synonymous with the tribe, its centre was the royal court, sustained by the food renders of the free tribesmen and the labour of the bondmen settled around it in a nucleated township.[28] In addition, for six weeks each year the king was entitled to supplement the forces of his war band by calling on both the free and bond population to join him in a military expedition.[29] Yet if the cantref was an essential building block of royal power, it also contained the potential for political collapse, as, on his death, the ruler's kingdom was divided among his sons, resulting in fragmentation into its constituent cantrefs – for 'what was customary was the succession of the eldest son to the principal part of the royal inheritance, with the assignment to younger sons of certain cantrefs of less importance'.[30]

Lloyd's delineation of medieval Welsh society combined approaches taken in previous histories of Wales with broader currents of later nineteenth-century thinking about social development, particularly as mediated through specialized studies focusing on Welsh evidence. For example, the account of Welsh society in 1200 bears some affinities with Thomas Price's admittedly much less critical section translating and paraphrasing sections of Giraldus Cambrensis's *Descriptio Kambriae* ('Description of Wales') (1194), a source used for similar purposes by later historians of Wales, including Gweirydd ap Rhys, whose magnum opus of 1872–4 also anticipated Lloyd in concluding from Giraldus's evidence that 'the familial and social customs of the Welsh' had been 'remarkably changeless over many long ages'.[31] This conclusion appeared, moreover, in one of the sections on society contained in each of the main chronological divisions of Gweirydd ap Rhys's work.[32] Although those sections were much thinner than those on political events or literature, they broke new ground in strengthening the claims of social history to be considered an essential part of the history of Wales and may have helped to encourage Lloyd to follow suit.

Nevertheless, the extent to which his depiction of Welsh society was influenced by this or other earlier histories of Wales is difficult to gauge. By contrast, his debt to later nineteenth-century studies of Welsh and Celtic society, including works by Seebohm and Vinogradoff, is explicitly acknowledged at the beginning of the chapter on early Welsh institutions, and again illustrates his identification with what he considered to be modern 'scientific' scholarship – in this case, as the emphasis on 'institutions' reveals, an interpretation of society framed by the categories of legal and constitutional history, still the dominant paradigm for reconstructing early societies in the late nineteenth and early twentieth centuries.[33]

One key feature common to the depictions of Welsh society both in previous histories of Wales and in more specialized studies was a heavy reliance on the evidence of medieval Welsh law. Not surprisingly, the same was true of Lloyd, who had acquired a close familiarity with the legal texts since the later 1880s, when he edited for publication a lengthy volume on the subject by the barrister Hubert Lewis (whose treatment he later dismissed as largely worthless, which may explain why, *c*.1898, he started to write a book of his own on the laws, though he seems to have got no further than the introduction and first chapter).[34] According to the prologues prefacing most of the compilations, the laws had been codified at the behest of Hywel Dda (Hywel the Good), a king who exercised authority over all Wales apart from the south-east by his death in 950.[35] However, the earliest surviving Welsh law books dated from the twelfth and thirteenth centuries. This raised an important question for those wishing to use the laws as historical evidence: how much of the extant legal material reflected the tenth-century law codified by Hywel, and how much consisted of later amendments and accretions? Lloyd's answer was clear, and had been so since his undergraduate days at Oxford. While acknowledging that, because of their late date, none of the surviving versions represented the law exactly as it had been in the tenth century, he nevertheless insisted – reflecting, perhaps, his belief in the conservatism of Welsh tradition and its consequent, albeit qualified, credibility – that much of their content in fact went back well beyond Hywel's reign, and thus referred to the earliest phases of medieval Welsh society.[36] The laws thus provided crucial justification for asserting the early origins of the principal institutions of medieval Wales.

However, confidence in the antiquity of the social institutions and practices revealed by these texts was far from universal. True, Gweirydd ap Rhys assumed that the law books represented the law under Hywel Dda and drew on them as his principal source for Welsh society in the pre-Norman period, and Hubert Lewis, in the volume Lloyd had edited, went further through discerning elements in the laws that pre-dated Hywel and occasionally even bore affinities with what was identified as ancient Aryan custom.[37] However, already in the early 1850s, B. B. Woodward had adopted a more nuanced approach which attempted to distinguish tenth-century features of the laws from later developments.[38] In a work which, together with that of Lewis, was cited at the beginning of Lloyd's chapter on early Welsh institutions, Frederic Seebohm was likewise cautious, leaving the complex textual questions posed by the legal compilations to Celtic scholars and warning against the danger of exaggerating the laws' antiquity. The radical implications of this point were seized upon by the legal historian F. W. Maitland, whose review of Seebohm's *The Tribal System in Wales* highlighted the difficulty of disentangling old and new elements in the law books: 'We seem almost entitled to say that it is improbable *a priori* that the Welsh Laws, even in their purest form, represent to us the life of the people as it was being lived, really and truly lived, at any one moment of time.'[39]

Seebohm's apparent indifference to the precise antiquity of the laws was closely connected to his aim in deploying their evidence. This differed significantly from that of Lloyd in that, rather than focusing on the historical development of a particular nation, Seebohm wrote as an economic historian who sought to demonstrate the broader comparative significance of the Welsh evidence for an understanding of what he, following H. S. Maine (1822–88), considered to be a widely attested stage in the development of human societies: the tribal system.[40] Thus he stressed 'the importance of a knowledge of the Tribal System, wherever found, as an almost universal factor in the early development of European society, and in the formation of mediaeval institutions'.[41] More specifically, Seebohm's *The Tribal System in Wales* developed a chapter in his earlier *English Village Communities*, a work which had argued that the persistence of tribal organization – and thus tribal freedom – in medieval Wales provided an instructive contrast with the manor of medieval England, whose origins he traced, contrary to Teutonist scholarly opinion that English villages derived from free Anglo-Saxon communities, to the villa of Roman Britain and its attendant serfdom.[42] Seebohm's objective also explains why he sought to compare the evidence of the laws with that of early Welsh charters and, above all, the extents or surveys made after the Edwardian conquest that estimated the potential revenue of lands in Wales.[43] This approach allowed him both to demonstrate the remarkable longevity of the 'tribal system' down to the late thirteenth century and to corroborate the reliability of the laws. As Seebohm put it: 'The facts of the surveys are sure. If the Codes contain a body of customary law which in natural course would produce the condition of things described by the surveys, their authenticity will be substantially confirmed.'[44] Yet, while the scale and systematic nature of Seebohm's combination of the laws with the post-conquest surveys were unprecedented, the approach itself was not new: the German legal historian Ferdinand Walter (1794–1879) had drawn on published surveys as well as the laws in 1859, as had Hubert Lewis more recently.[45] This makes it all the more striking that, despite listing books by Walter, Lewis and Seebohm among 'the chief modern works' on early Welsh society,[46] Lloyd restricted his use of surveys to identifying royal centres or the owners of particular lands in the course of his topographical tour of 'tribal divisions'.[47] By contrast, references to the surveys in his chapter on early Welsh institutions are conspicuous by their absence. In other words, Lloyd viewed these records through the spectacles of the historical geographer rather than those of the social and economic historian.[48]

As with his account of the origins of the Welsh, Lloyd benefited, then, from recent fashions in scholarship which gave the evidence from Wales a significance within broader contexts of social development. Although the *History* generally eschews specific comparisons with other societies, the works Lloyd drew upon helped to influence his general assumptions about conditions in Wales.[49] Of course, some assumptions were so commonplace in his day that it would be futile to try to trace their derivation from any particular source: the belief in progress from primitive to more advanced stages of society is an obvious case in point.[50] However, several aspects of Lloyd's interpretation seem to relate to specific debates. For instance, he declines to follow Seebohm – here strongly influenced by Maine – in asserting that the head of a kin exercised patriarchal power, akin to the *patria potestas* of Roman law, over his family and other dependents; instead, Lloyd maintains that there were few traces of this with respect either to adult men or married women in medieval Wales.[51] He also implicitly challenges Seebohm's contrast of a purely tribal Wales with an England organized in a network of village communities, subject to lords exercising manorial authority, by observing of the nucleated bond vills that 'the village community is to be found on Welsh soil, though only among the unfree cultivators'.[52] Moreover, despite this qualification, Lloyd arguably attributes some of the defining features of Maine's village community to free landholders as well. Thus he maintains that each 'community' – evidently refer-ring to the hamlet or township (*tref*) in general, not just to the bond vill – 'was to a very great extent self-supporting and eco-nomically complete', and that the free township was occupied by 'a group of private owners, each pursuing his own way and holding his land separately', which, according to Maine's schema, implied that they had already moved a fair way along the road travelled by 'the progressive societies . . . from status to contract', that is, from a society based on kinship to one based on individual rights.[53] However, these parallels should not be pressed too far. Read as a whole, Lloyd's account clearly emphasizes the centrality of kinship to Welsh society and, indeed, as we have seen, states unequivocally that free tribesmen possessed only a life interest in the land they held – a far cry from the individual ownership of land which, according to Maine and others, emerged in the feudal stage of society.[54] Indeed, feudalism is presented both as a later phenomenon than tribalism and as something entirely foreign to Wales, being introduced by the Norman and English conquerors.[55]

145

The Church

Although Lloyd devotes considerable attention to the Church in the *History*, he makes little attempt to integrate this with his analysis of Welsh society. Thus, while he takes care to identify the most important early churches in his survey of 'tribal divisions', he does not go further and consider how these churches related to the kindred and other secular institutions as Seebohm and other scholars had attempted to do.[56] In part, this may be because he found such attempts unconvincing.[57] However, the main reason was probably that Lloyd regarded the Church as part of the history of the Welsh people in general rather than as an aspect of their social history in particular. There were precedents for this, as the Church figured prominently in previous works of Welsh history. Unlike some of his predecessors, however, Lloyd treated religious matters without any overt engagement in contemporary controversies, which he clearly felt had no place in a work of 'scientific' scholarship.[58] Thus, while the attention he gave to the Church may well have owed something to his own strong Christian commitment in an age when religion was central to notions of Welsh nationality, especially for a Nonconformist strongly in favour of disestablishing the Anglican Church in Wales, the nearest Lloyd comes to denying that Church legitimacy as a Welsh institution is his firm declaration that 'the notion' that the Celtic Church 'was the home of a kind of primitive Protestantism, of apostolic purity and simplicity, is without any historical basis'.[59] However, as the idea is not attributed to any specific group, Lloyd does not take the opportunity to point out that it was an Anglican creation, originating at the reformation and still espoused by some Anglicans in the nineteenth century.[60] Likewise, he avoids the strident anti-Catholicism of several earlier writers (and from which he had not been immune in his youth, to judge by a stinging denunciation of the papacy in his first sermon in January 1879), and displays instead a liberal-minded empathy whose origins may be traced to his student days in Oxford, when he suggested that Welsh appreciation of the fine arts may have been hindered by anti-Catholic prejudice – an empathy consonant with a wider change in Welsh Nonconformist attitudes towards Roman Catholicism by the late Victorian period.[61]

One main theme in Lloyd's treatment of the Church is an emphasis on monasticism as the key to both piety and ecclesiastical organization in medieval Wales; another is the struggle for ecclesiastical independence from the English. Beginning with the first of these, the characterization of the early medieval Welsh Church as essentially monastic was a commonplace of late nineteenth- and early twentieth-century scholarship, which emphasized the centrality of monasteries to the development and organization of the churches in all the Celtic countries.[62] While acknowledging that Christianity had been first introduced to Wales by the Romans, Lloyd shared the opinion of those who argued that the longer-term influence of Romano-British Christianity was slight, and that the crucial development was the monastic movement, which, while imported from Gaul, gathered momentum only under native leaders, namely the 'saints' or monastic founders of the long sixth century. It was these – figures such as St David and St Illtud – who completed the evangelization of Wales.[63] Thus, while of foreign origin, Christianity soon became an integral part of Welsh society. However, Lloyd accepted that the heroic 'age of the saints' was followed, from about the end of the eighth century onwards, by a lengthy period of decline: although the old austerity continued to be practised by hermits in some places, the monasteries became more worldly as territorial endowments increased and celibacy was abandoned. Nevertheless, Lloyd stressed that the monasteries remained fundamental to the ecclesiastical organization of medieval Wales, thereby implying that the Church, too, possessed antiquity and continuity, albeit with a significant degree of change which is absent from his picture of the development of lay society. Thus he insisted on the early monastic origin of what he called the *clas*, thereby adapting a medieval Welsh term for major churches, witnessed in sources mainly from the twelfth century onwards, comprising a community of clergy or laymen under a man bearing the title of abbot, and often also referred to as mother-churches with authority over extensive areas.[64]

Although the reorganization of the Church that followed Norman conquests in Wales meant that the days of the *clas* were numbered, this did not signal the end of monasticism as a sustaining force of Welsh religion and identity. Quite the contrary: thanks initially to the foreign conquerors, '[t]he monastery was restored to its ancient place in Welsh religious life'.[65] This was not due to the foundation of priories belonging to the 'luxurious' and 'degenerate' Benedictines.[66] It was, rather, the result of the arrival in the twelfth century of the Cistercians or white monks, whose austere life 'made a strong appeal to men who had not forgotten the traditions of Celtic monasticism in the days of its primal earnestness and warmth. The Cistercian abbot was a St. David or a St. Teilo restored to life.'[67] In other words, a monastic order originating in Burgundy became the instrument of Welsh religious renewal, rapidly securing the support of the native princes and aligning itself with Welsh culture and aspirations.[68] It is striking that, while he notes the attraction of the remote sites chosen by the white monks, Lloyd does not explicitly attribute the order's success in Wales to the country's landscape and the associated pastoralism that is so central to his depiction of Welsh society, but emphasizes instead the monks' affinity with native traditions of piety – sustained by a memory of early monasticism, whose invocation was consistent with Lloyd's insistence on the Welsh people's keen sense of the past – and the leadership of the Welsh princes.[69]

The contrast between the Cistercians as friends of the Welsh and the Benedictines 'as auxiliaries of baronial power' draws on the second major theme in Lloyd's treatment of ecclesiastical matters, and one highlighted by previous writers, namely the struggle for the freedom of the Welsh Church.[70] This makes its first appearance in a chapter entitled 'The struggle of the Cymry and the English', which argues that the main reason why British clergy from Wales refused to cooperate with Augustine of Canterbury (d.604) in preaching to the pagan Anglo-Saxons was his assertion of Canterbury's primacy over the whole of Britain, thereby provoking 'indignation at the thought that the British Churches, the origin of which lay far back in a distant past, were to be disposed and ordered at the will of a mere missioner to the English'.[71] However, the 'subjugation' or 'subjection' of the Welsh Church – which Lloyd had no hesitation in designating 'a national church' despite the lack of a formal unifying structure – 'under the yoke of Canterbury' becomes a much more prominent theme in volume II, which presents it as an ecclesiastical current in the broader story of the

Welsh struggle for independence.[72] For example, 'the Welsh spirit of independence . . . found expression, as had often been the case before, in ecclesiastical affairs' when Giraldus Cambrensis attempted to free the Welsh dioceses from the authority of Canterbury by seeking papal recognition of St Davids as an archbishopric for Wales.[73] On the other hand, Lloyd pays little attention to the impact of ecclesiastical reorganization and reform in the twelfth and thirteenth centuries with respect, say, to the formation of parishes or the standards of the clergy.[74] Thus, while noting the reforming zeal of Giraldus Cambrensis, at the end of his short section on Welsh society in 1200 Lloyd is content to follow Giraldus in asserting that, despite their warlike nature, 'the Welsh were not inferior to any nation in Christendom' in their religious devotion, as was shown by the respect given to hermits and the peace of the Church.[75] He also appears to accept Giraldus's contention that there was a lack of good bishops.[76]

Two main points emerge, then, from Lloyd's treatment of the Church with respect to the making of the Welsh people. First, the Welsh had a venerable religious tradition of their own that went back to the age of the saints and indeed to Roman Britain – a tradition, moreover, of which they could be proud, without needing to pretend that the early Welsh church was effectively Protestant or to qualify their admiration with anachronistic complaints about papist superstition. True, this did not amount to a tale of unchanging continuity and durability comparable to that told of Welsh society. Nevertheless, the story of a golden age followed by decline and, ultimately, revival (thanks mainly to the Cistercians) was predicated on the survival of a distinctive religious sentiment across the medieval centuries; indeed, Lloyd implies elsewhere that it would eventually find expression in the Methodist revival of the eighteenth century.[77] Religion was thus an aspect of another intangible but tenacious reality – likewise inextricably linked to memory of the past – whose strength ebbed and flowed: Welsh nationality. Secondly, moreover, attempts to defend the Welsh Church from foreign domination contributed to a wider struggle for independence, led by the native princes, that was fundamental to forging a lasting sense of nationhood. The significance of that struggle is assessed in the next chapter.

9

Princely Wales:
Rulers as Nation Builders

A defining feature of the histories of Wales written from the sixteenth century onwards was their emphasis on the activities of
medieval Welsh kings and princes, whose reigns provided a
chronological framework for the events they related that clearly
distinguished them from crown-centred narratives of English
history.[1] This emphasis in turn reflected the dependence of these
works on the medieval Welsh chronicles, in which the native rulers
occupied centre stage. True, both the chronological and the
thematic scope of the earliest of these texts, namely Humphrey
Llwyd's *Cronica Walliae* (1559) and David Powel's *Historie of
Cambria* (1584), was expanded and modified by some of their
successors – most obviously by Gweirydd ap Rhys in his *Hanes y
Brytaniaid a'r Cymry* ('The History of the Britons and the Welsh',
1872–4), a work already familiar to Lloyd from his childhood days,
which not only extended the narrative to the age of Gladstone
but supplemented its political narrative by including sections on
social, religious and literary history. Lloyd's *History* differed from
these earlier works in two important respects. First, Lloyd constructed a political narrative of unprecedented accuracy and detail,
and, secondly, he sought – unlike Gweirydd ap Rhys – to integrate
that narrative with analysis of ecclesiastical, literary, social and
institutional topics in order to present a coherent account of the
formation of the Welsh people.

These two points highlight an important premise of the *History*'s treatment of Welsh rulers. Leaders mattered and could shape the course of events, but their policies and actions were in turn affected by a wider context, including both the inner dynamics of Welsh society, as shown in the previous chapter, and the aspirations of other political actors, notably the kings of England.[2] Medieval Welsh history could not be reduced simply to a tale of its kings and princes. Even so, Lloyd evidently believed that it was important to shine a spotlight on Welsh rulers and, crucially, to appraise their response as individuals to the challenges and opportunities they faced. The task of appraisal was predicated on a belief in 'the permanence of human nature . . . Men are swayed by the same motives, torn by the same passions, smitten with the same fears, the wide world over and in every age alike.'[3] Accordingly, where the evidence allowed him, Lloyd treated Welsh rulers as individuals whose characters could be discerned and weighed in the balance. Moreover, as others have noted, he viewed medieval Welsh kings and princes through the patriotic spectacles of his own age, and focused above all on the extent to which they had contributed to ensuring the survival of a distinctive Welsh nationality.[4] At the same time, though, his approach reflected wider intellectual trends. The writing of national history with a predominantly political emphasis in which leaders held centre stage was, after all, the height of historiographical orthodoxy during Lloyd's formative years in the later nineteenth century, and his depiction of medieval Welsh kings and princes needs to be viewed against this wider background as well as compared with other works specifically on the history of Wales.[5] In particular, as with other aspects of the *History*, it is important to assess how far Lloyd was influenced by the approaches to historical writing he had encountered at Oxford and may be seen as having adapted that English tradition within the context of Welsh history.

The following discussion, then, will explore three closely related questions. How important was a political narrative focused on Welsh rulers in structuring the *History*; why were those rulers considered significant; and how were they judged as individuals? After offering a general overview of these issues I shall move on to a case study that will bring them into sharper relief: Lloyd's treatment of Llywelyn the Great.

Even a cursory glance at the *History*'s chapter and section titles reveals that kings and princes are far more prominent in the second volume, which covers the period from Gruffudd ap Llywelyn in the mid-eleventh century to the death of Llywelyn ap Gruffudd in 1282, than they are in the first. None of the ten chapter titles in volume I includes the name of a Welsh king, and the same is true of all but three of the volume's thirty-five sections.[6] By contrast, the titles of five of the ten chapters in volume II name rulers (with Llywelyn the Great appearing in two), as do at least one of the section titles in a further three chapters.[7] This contrast may simply reflect the increase in the amount and detail of source material from the eleventh century onwards: early medieval Welsh kings remained obscure because so little evidence survived for them. However, since this had not prevented previous historians of Wales from labelling the early medieval centuries by the reigns of native rulers, the main motive for Lloyd's approach presumably lay elsewhere. In part, his refusal to characterize this period primarily as a succession of kings was of a piece with his determination to present a complex analysis that rejected any simplistic conception of early Welsh history as merely the struggles of leaders. In addition, though, the patchy nature of the evidence curtailed the potential for plausibly presenting kings as nation builders. Thus, while Lloyd charted the activities of numerous rulers in the course of constructing a political narrative, special significance was attached only to those who could be shown to have contributed to the development of Welsh nationality.

Such figures were few and far between in the early Middle Ages, which Lloyd presents mainly as a period that bore witness to the definition of Wales as a territorial entity with a distinctive ethnic and religious complexion. One underlying theme is the relationship of Wales to the rest of Britain, and especially to the Anglo-Saxon kingdoms; another is the attempt by some rulers to establish authority extending beyond their own individual kingdoms to encompass most of Wales. Thus Cadwallon ap Cadfan, king of Gwynedd, through his defeat of Edwin, king of Northumbria (633), 'holds a place in the forefront of those who have earned the grateful remembrance of the Welsh race by vigorous championship of the national cause', although the destructiveness of Cadwallon's

year-long rule in Northumbria subsequently demonstrated that
the Welsh 'did not possess the secret of rule'.[8] The first major con-
tributor to nation building appeared only two centuries later in
the person of Rhodri Mawr (Rhodri the Great), whose reign
(844–78) coincided with both Anglo-Saxon and Viking attacks:

> No one will contest the right of Rhodri to a title ['the Great'] which
> he earned, not only by strenuous and gallant resistance to the northern
> marauders, but even more by his success in uniting the greater part
> of Wales, so long divided into petty states, in a single realm. The
> kingdom he founded, though it did not retain its unity for any length
> of time, afforded future ages an instance of what could be achieved
> in this direction and set before ambitious princes a goal towards
> which their efforts might be directed.[9]

Here, rather than analysing Rhodri's achievements in the context
of the ninth century, Lloyd seeks to uphold the king's claims to
greatness by emphasizing the legacy of his unifying efforts for the
future. Nor was unity achieved only through military might. Hywel
Dda (Hywel the Good) (d.950) was praised for

> having done something for Welsh unity by his career of conquest,
> but far more by his work as a legislator. The realm he founded died
> with him, but the code he gave to Wales was the beginning of Welsh
> jurisprudence . . . the conception of one law, valid for the whole of
> Wales, took its rise from the measures of Hywel and was developed
> by the activity of the legal commentators – in this domain the Welsh
> people early arrived at national self-consciousness.[10]

The fostering of national consciousness or spirit becomes an increasingly prominent leitmotiv in assessments of later Welsh kings
and princes. Although Lloyd is neither entirely consistent nor clear
as to how this fostering was accomplished, he generally presents
the ruler as inspiring a sense of nationality which, nevertheless,
remains independent of him, as it belongs to the Welsh people as a
whole. For example, we read that, during the ninety years following the death of Hywel Dda, 'the man had not yet arisen who could
gather the whole nation around his banner and breathe life and

force into the national aspirations'.[11] A saviour then appeared in the person of Gruffudd ap Llywelyn (d.1063), who achieved a temporary personal unification of Wales and expanded its borders through attacks on England.

> He founded no dynasty, but he bequeathed to the Welsh people the priceless legacy of a revived national spirit; in his vigour and daring the nation felt its youth renewed and no longer harboured the hidden fear that it had grown old and effete among the peoples of the earth.[12]

Here, the ruler's military success provides a rejuvenating tonic to a people personified as an individual actor in its own right. Elsewhere, on the other hand, the emphasis is predominantly on the leadership of the ruler, with the people cast in an essentially passive role. This is particularly true of a passage highlighting the significance of Owain Gwynedd (reigned 1137–70):

> It was fortunate for the Welsh people that after the emancipation at the beginning of the reign of Stephen [1135–54] they did not find themselves leaderless, a flock without a shepherd, but that a prince arose who was able to give them wise and enlightened guidance and to teach them how to harvest the gains they had won. Owain Gwynedd was the first of a succession of such leaders; his work was carried on, almost without a break, by Rhys ap Gruffydd, Llywelyn ab Iorwerth, and Llywelyn ap Gruffydd, to the latest years of Welsh independence – it was, in fact, under him that the Welsh nation attained the full measure of national consciousness which enabled it for a century and a half successfully to resist absorption in the English realm.[13]

Admittedly, Lloyd says that the Welsh became fully aware of their nationality 'under' rather than 'through' Owain, but the causal connection is strongly implicit. Likewise, the key role of princes in inspiring nationality is underlined by the portrayal of the decade between the death of Dafydd ap Llywelyn (d.1246) and the rise of Llywelyn ap Gruffudd 'as a national leader' as one of 'depression and subjection . . . during which the sense of national solidarity was for the moment lost'.[14]

155

Above all, then, Welsh rulers made a vitally important contribution to nation building through providing inspirational example; political achievements mattered, not because they resulted in durable authority or institutions, but because they stimulated a national consciousness in the Middle Ages that was sufficiently resilient to be revived – under new leaders such as Gwilym Hiraethog and Tom Ellis – in Lloyd's day.[15] On the other hand, comments on their personal moral qualities were muted. This is striking in that moral judgement was a prominent feature of the nineteenth-century historiography in which Lloyd was brought up, and evidently influenced him, when, as a young lecturer at Aberystwyth, he followed Lord Acton in urging that such judgement was incumbent on the historian.[16] However, in his own historical writing Lloyd generally eschewed the simple dichotomies of good and evil favoured by some Victorian historians. Instead, perhaps because of his generally liberal-minded disposition, he was inclined to seek balance. Thus he has nothing comparable to Stubbs's condemnation of John as 'the worst . . . of our kings' or to Freeman's unabashed admiration of Alfred the Great as 'the most perfect character in history'.[17] Even Gildas's searing denunciation of the murderous sixth-century king, Maelgwn Gwynedd, evokes some sympathy.

> Yet, heavy as is the catalogue of misdeeds laid to his charge, he is not without a certain tincture of nobleness. He is a liberal giver, and no common tyrant would, in the heyday of his greatness, have laid aside his royal dignity and have withdrawn, as Maelgwn did, to the austere seclusion of a monastic cell. All Christians must, it is true, deplore his sad relapse into a life no less worldly and sin-ridden than before, but the very making of the experiment proves him a prince of no ordinary mould.[18]

If Lloyd exercised moral judgement, then, it was concerned less with personal failings than with qualities of rulership. In this he followed in the footsteps of other Welsh historians, both in the nineteenth century and earlier, who assessed medieval Welsh rulers principally with respect to their patriotism and associated martial and political qualities.[19] However, there were probably other influences at work here, too. Lloyd's assessments of Welsh rulers according to the extent to which they fostered Welsh nationality arguably bear affinities with T. H. Green's moral philosophy with its insistence on the need to work for the common good. After all, Lloyd seemed to equate that good with Welsh patriotism in a tribute to his friend and political idol Tom Ellis (who in turn had been influenced by Green's pupil Arnold Toynbee), maintaining that those who had worked with him 'in public movements for the good of Wales' felt they had lost 'the man of all others who . . . was fitted to be the leader and captain of Welsh patriots'.[20] Another, more direct, influence may have been the History School at Oxford, which encouraged the exercise of judgement on individual political leaders in terms of their contribution to national development.[21] For example, in a lecture in 1886 Charles W. Boase pronounced that James I was 'a man of no little ability in some respects, with learning enough for a school master, and theology enough for a bishop, but woefully deficient in kingcraft'.[22] Lloyd's assessment of Cadwgan ap Bleddyn, ruler of Powys (d.1111), is in much the same vein: 'His was a weak character, amiable, no doubt, but wanting in the sterner qualities which were demanded by the problems of statecraft in that turbulent age.'[23]

If a willingness to judge individual rulers sometimes led to criticism, it more often resulted in praise. Here, Lloyd was influenced by the nineteenth-century preoccupation with heroes.[24] As a student in Oxford he rejected Carlyle's dictum that famous people were the most important thing in history writing.[25] More significantly, the treatment of kings and princes in the *History* was more complex and nuanced than that of many of his predecessors as well as some of his contemporaries, most notably Owen Rhoscomyl in his *Flame-Bearers of Welsh History* (1905). Indeed, explicit descriptions of individual leaders as 'heroes' or 'heroic' are rare in the *History*, occurring unambiguously only with reference to Boudicca, the Lord Rhys and Llewelyn the Great.[26] Nor was heroism always a virtue. Lloyd commented on Owain ap Cadwgan's abduction of Nest in 1115 that, 'fascinating as is this story of passion and daring, which breathes the spirit of the early heroic age, and which Homer might well have told, its other aspect is not to be forgotten, as a reckless escapade'.[27] Indeed, through his behaviour, Owain ap Cadwgan exemplified what Lloyd considered to be shortcomings all too common in princely dynasties. The greatest Welsh princes, on the other hand, are held to have possessed exemplary virtues that stemmed in significant part from a willingness to temper innately Welsh or even 'Celtic' characteristics. This is especially evident in the praise lavished on Owain Gwynedd and the shortcomings attributed to his younger brother Cadwaladr:

> Welsh history can scarcely show a nobler or a better balanced character . . . An outstanding feature of his character was his wisdom and prudence; in him the native impetuosity and fire of the Celt were subjected to a perfect restraint . . . Cadwaladr was the ordinary, as Owain was the exceptional, Welsh prince. He was restless, impulsive, quick to suspect and hasty to strike.[28]

The contrast seems predicated on that drawn by Matthew Arnold between Celts and Saxons, and repudiates the racial stereotyping of the former only to the extent of claiming that Owain, apparently through sheer strength of character, managed to overcome the weaknesses inherited from his Celtic forefathers.[29] It may even be that, for Lloyd, the greatest Welsh rulers were those who managed to behave most like the English – an attitude consistent with the insistence of T. C. Edwards and like-minded compatriots that modern Welsh culture needed to assimilate English elements.[30] This is particularly clear in the attribution of Hywel Dda's success to his alleged admiration of King Alfred and 'English civilisation', while 'the keen insight into affairs' of the Lord Rhys was demonstrated by his decision, after his rapprochement with King Henry II in 1171–2, 'to be recognised not only as a great Welsh chieftain but also as a great baron of the realm [of England]'.[31]

More generally, Lloyd depicted those he considered to be the greatest Welsh rulers as possessing virtues – wisdom, prudence, statesmanship, enlightened religious patronage and, above all, a dedication to national unity – that were likely to appeal to patriotic intellectuals and leaders in his own day. Nevertheless, Lloyd's account also reveals a tension, or perhaps it would be truer to say an interplay, between this emphasis on exemplary character and a Carlylean concept of the 'great man' remembered for his achievements, especially inspirational leadership which strengthened the

Welsh people's sense of nationhood.[32] For one of Lloyd's purposes was to show, through a critical analysis of the available evidence, that individuals traditionally deemed to be heroes of Welsh history – principally on account of their deeds rather than their character – deserved their high reputation. The aim is announced unequivocally in the preface to his volume on Owain Glyndŵr: 'I offer my readers, therefore, not a new Glyn Dŵr, but fair warrant for regarding him as the national hero we have always in Wales understood him to be.'[33] Indeed, Lloyd may be seen as placing a scholarly imprimatur on the popular image of Glyndŵr that had evolved by the early twentieth century.[34] Moreover, by stressing that particular rulers were worthy of grateful remembrance by the Welsh on account of their contribution to the national cause, the *History* implied that figures such as Rhodri Mawr or Llywelyn ap Gruffudd had good claims to be considered national heroes.[35]

The national spirit or consciousness evoked by the rulers is never defined precisely, but seems to have been perceived as a continuous, if at times dormant, sentiment inherent in the people which was essentially the same in Lloyd's day as it was in the Middle Ages. In this respect, Lloyd reflected common assumptions in the late nineteenth century, ultimately deriving from the thinking of Fichte, who insisted (albeit specifically of the Germans) on the continued development of an 'original' national character.[36] The closest parallel to the judgement on Llywelyn ap Gruffudd's legacy occurs in the work of Gweirydd ap Rhys, which declared, with respect to the final conquest of Wales (placed here in the time of Owain Glyndŵr or Henry VIII), that Wales 'has kept alive its national spirit, which centuries of foreign rule have failed to extinguish or weaken'.[37] Moreoever, the survival of that spirit was attributed to the poets and traditions which had preserved a memory of medieval Wales.[38] Although he never develops the point, Lloyd, too, seems to have regarded memory as essential to ensuring the longevity of Welsh nationality, notably in his occasional references to the Welsh people's strong sense of the past and the inspirational legacy of certain great rulers.[39] Indeed, his *History* may itself be seen as an attempt to renew that memory by delineating its features with unprecedented clarity and authority.

Stubbs also placed great emphasis on national 'character', 'consciousness' and 'spirit', declaring at the beginning of his *Constitutional History* that 'the national character has been formed by the course of the national history quite as certainly as the national history has been developed by the working of the national character'.[40] Likewise, Stubbs's pupil Tout had no difficulty in writing of 'Welsh national spirit', at least with respect to the period from the sixteenth century onwards; by contrast, he held that in the thirteenth century 'Welsh sentiment was clannish and local rather than national' and that, in the *History*, Lloyd may have been 'a little over-eager to accentuate the existence of Welsh national feeling'.[41] Yet, while Lloyd similarly conceived of the nation as a conscious body with its own character and spirit, his conception lacks the complexity and sophistication of Stubbs's analysis. This is largely because Lloyd was not writing a constitutional history; he saw the Welsh nation essentially as an ethnic entity that had been revived in the cultural, educational and political movements of his own day, not as a formative element in constitutional development. Moreover, although Stubbs recognized the nation as being distinct from rulers, his understanding of the relationship between the two differed from that of Lloyd, who presented princes as providing inspirational leadership that gave life to the Welsh people's sense of its nationality. By contrast, Stubbs attributed the emergence of English national consciousness in significant measure to conflict between the people and the Angevin kings, above all King John (1199–1216), who was compelled to issue Magna Carta (1215): 'The Great Charter is the first great public act of the nation, after it has realised its own identity.'[42]

Llywelyn the Great

One of the beneficiaries of Magna Carta was Llywelyn ap Iorwerth or Llywelyn the Great (d.1240), prince of Gwynedd. He plays a starring role in the *History*, where he is cast as the greatest native ruler of medieval Wales, and its account of him thus throws particularly revealing light on Lloyd's treatment of Welsh kings and princes. As we have seen, Llywelyn is unique in giving his name to the titles of two chapters, occupying between them some eighty pages, and the prince's rise is also the subject of a short section in the chapter that precedes these.[43] This emphasis on Llywelyn reflected a well-established perception of the prince's importance, a perception that Lloyd himself had shared and, indeed, helped to promote since his undergraduate days. Although its coverage was brief, the eisteddfod essay painted the prince in glowing colours, asserting that the military successes of 1214–16 were nothing less than 'the work of a master-mind – a military and administrative genius'. Above all, his ability was demonstrated by 'the marvellous celerity with which he accomplished a task that had hitherto defied the best efforts of the Welsh politicians – the union of the principalities of Wales into a single state'. Given these successes, it is hardly surprising that the young Lloyd had no hesitation in concluding his account of Llywelyn by declaring that he had 'justly earned the title of Great which was bestowed upon him by the enthusiasm of his contemporaries – certainly the greatest Welshman who ever wielded princely authority'.[44] He repeated this judgement in public lectures on Llywelyn while a lecturer at Aberystwyth.[45] A report of one of these, given at Bangor in December 1887, shows that Lloyd emphasized the prince's single-minded pursuit of political unity through the application of 'the feudal idea' to his relations with the other Welsh rulers, and its conclusion strikingly anticipates the final sentence on the prince's grandson Llywelyn ap Gruffudd in the *History* over twenty years later.[46]

> His dream of a United Wales for a brief space made a reality, vanishing again after his death into the region of phantoms and chimeras, and they could not think that he lived in vain. His labours bore fruit, if not in any visible organisation, at least in a more fervent spirit of unity; they helped to make Welshmen feel more keenly than ever their relationship to each other, and they in this age, when that sense of kinship was keener and livelier perhaps than at any former period of their history must gratefully recognise the services rendered to their race by the mightiest of Welsh princes.[47]

Lloyd's early assessments of Llywelyn followed a long tradition among historians of Wales of emphasizing successful resistance to the English, territorial expansion and the creation of political unity through asserting an overlordship that required the other Welsh rulers to hold their lands from the prince. Yet the insistence that Llywelyn was not merely 'The Great' but the greatest of the medieval Welsh princes was a new development of the late nineteenth century. This assessment depended in turn on elevating him above his famous grandson, Llywelyn ap Gruffudd or Llywelyn the Last, whose death in 1282 effectively marked the end of Welsh independence and who continued to be considered an outstanding hero of Welsh history.[48] More precisely, whereas earlier historians of Wales had tended to cast Llywelyn the Great in the role of a brave warrior upholding Welsh unity and independence, this script was now revised in order to present the prince as above all a skilled diplomat and prudent statesman, and thus to endow him with qualities deemed to be lacking in the more martial and less politic Llywelyn ap Gruffudd – qualities well attuned to the aspirations of Welsh Liberals committed to pursuing their patriotic aspirations through constitutional means, without undermining Wales's loyalty to the British Empire.[49] The novelty of favouring Llywelyn the Great at the expense of his grandson was acknowledged by Lloyd in his 1887 lecture, which began by explaining that, while less famous than his grandson, 'Llewelyn ap Iorwerth was probably a much abler man'.[50] Six years later Tout offered a highly positive account of Llywelyn in the *Dictionary of National Biography*, which declared that '[h]e was certainly the greatest of the native rulers of Wales'.[51] By contrast, Tout's article on Llywelyn ap Gruffudd for the *DNB*, though sympathetic, was far less laudatory, and his criticisms of the last Llywelyn became more pronounced in subsequent works – for example, in the period following the treaty of Montgomery in 1267, 'Llywelyn himself was the chief obstacle to peace. The brilliant success of his arms and diplomacy seems somewhat to have turned his brain.'[52] A. G. Little came to a similar conclusion:

> Llywelyn the Great refused to dispute the suzerainty of England. This may appear pusillanimous to the enthusiastic patriot, but subsequent events proved the old statesman's wisdom and clearsightedness [*sic*]. His successors were less cautious, were carried away by the patriotism round them and the syren [*sic*] voices of the bards.[53]

Soon after those lectures were delivered O. M. Edwards published his influential popular history, *Wales*, which both developed recent reassessments of Llywelyn the Great and echoed his deployment in political rhetoric. Its chapter on the prince opened by announcing its author's adherence to the new orthodoxy: 'Llywelyn the Great is the most important figure in mediaeval Welsh history.'[54] In support of this view the discussion deftly weaves together several strands in the estimation of Llywelyn that had developed by the end of the nineteenth century to create a portrait that was very much Edwards's own. In part, it reiterates the familiar theme of the prince's success in resisting the English and, above all, in establishing Welsh unity; in addition, though, the account emphasizes the prince's diplomatic skill and political insight, not least his far-sighted recognition of the constraints imposed by the unchanging geographical conditions Edwards had emphasized at the beginning of his book.[55]

> Llywelyn had discovered what the natural boundaries of Wales were . . . he had given up the Celtic luxury of scheming against the inevitable. He had seen that mountain and plain remained, while race and language changed. The new unity was not a racial one, neither was it based on common language: it was simply territorial.[56]

Thus the prince is praised as a role model with a clear political message for the present day:

> The policy of Llywelyn is more modern than that of any native prince of Wales. He foresaw the eventual political fate of the country he had consolidated . . . He saw that unity was impossible as long as any chief could appeal to a hostile king of England, and that the independence of Wales must be its independence as a part of a more extensive kingdom. The experience of his long reign, so full in its intensity and variety, had enabled him to see very far into the future . . . He had seen that the independence which is natural to Wales, and the unity which is natural to the islands of Britain, are not inconsistent.[57]

In other words, Llywelyn was the first exponent of home rule. Lloyd George had said as much a few years earlier, as he argued for the necessity of organizational unity among Welsh Liberals in pursuit of the nationalist goals of the Cymru Fydd movement, being applauded when he told a public meeting in Pontlottyn, Glamorgan that

> Llewelyn the Great fought for exactly the same object as they were fighting for now. He fought for the freedom of the land, and he fought for something in the nature of Home Rule for Wales – the right of the people to govern themselves in accordance with their own needs.[58]

However, according to Edwards, it would take over another two centuries before 'the ideas of Llywelyn were finally realised by a statesman who may be regarded as one of his descendants', namely King Henry VII (1485–1509).[59]

However, Edwards did not follow Thomas Price (Carnhuanawc), who, sixty years earlier, had claimed for Llywelyn a crucial role in securing Magna Carta, a point which had, moreover, recently received qualified scholarly sustenance from Tout as well as the exuberant advocacy of Lloyd George.[60] This interpretation of the prince's alliance with the barons who compelled King John to issue Magna Carta served to give the lie to the notion that the Welsh had contributed nothing to the constitutional development of the British state, and thus to the liberties they had enjoyed since the union with England under Henry VIII.[61] As Owen Rhoscomyl put it with characteristic extravagance in 1905:

> If ever you read a *full and true* history of England, you will see there how great a part Llywelyn played in the history of England as well as of Cymru. And when you come to read further still, you will see how principal a part he took in a yet greater history, the history of human freedom. For without him the barons could never have forced King John to sign the Great Charter (Magna Charta), which is the first step in the personal freedom of the British people of to-day.[62]

How, then, did Lloyd portray Llywelyn the Great when he came to write his fullest and most considered account of the prince for the *History*?[63] Not surprisingly, the main features of the portrait were recognizable from the historian's earlier accounts of the prince; the main difference was that it had become much fuller and more detailed. More particularly, Lloyd provided a political narrative that was unprecedented in its empirical depth, being based on a thorough and critical assessment of a wide range of printed primary sources. This in itself was a major achievement. For one thing, it brought new evidence to bear on the prince's reign. Moreover, in so doing it set Llywelyn firmly in the context of his own time and, by implication at least, served to dampen some of the wilder claims that had been made about his significance: for example, the treatment of Magna Carta in relation to Wales threw fresh light on its contemporaneous significance but avoided citing it as evidence for a vital Welsh contribution to British constitutional liberties.[64] Above all, though, the new narrative served to substantiate Llywelyn's claims to be considered the outstanding medieval Welsh leader, for it allowed the prince to be seen more clearly than before as an individual character who contended with a complex and changing set of circumstances whose chronology could be established with considerable precision. Thus, while Lloyd offered general assessments of the prince's achievements, the historical narrative went well beyond a biographical account and attempted to explain political developments in Wales by presenting the prince's actions as part of a broader story of relations between the English crown, Marcher lords and other Welsh rulers. The narrative introduces the reader to a variety of actors across the length and breadth of Wales, yet is never merely descriptive, as events are analysed in terms of competing political interests and the characters of the leaders who pursued them. In addition, as in his 1900 textbook, Lloyd argued that Llywelyn's political achievements had beneficial consequences for the Welsh as a whole: 'under the powerful protection of the lord of Gwynedd, Welsh society followed the lines of its natural development, and Welsh literature, law and religion quietly prospered'.[65] Not only did he, like the Lord Rhys before him, bestow 'enlightened' patronage on reformed religious houses, but his age was one of 'brilliant literary achievement'.[66]

However, it was Llywelyn's character as a successful and inspiring national leader that Lloyd emphasized above all. The prince is shown to have had clear goals as well as the energy and steadfastness to see them through successfully.[67] These personal qualities were apparent from an early age, as he defeated his kinsmen in order to secure mastery of Gwynedd: 'the young Llywelyn owed the lofty position which he attained to no other cause than his own fortitude and courage, which made light of difficulties that might have been for ever the prison of a less heroic soul'.[68] Yet this was only the beginning. Using a maritime metaphor similar to one already applied to Owain Gwynedd, Lloyd stressed that the prince was tested even more severely by King John's onslaught on Gwynedd in 1211: 'The dexterous steersman was to appear in a new light and to prove his fortitude by weathering the blackest and most desperate of hurricanes.'[69] And even after achieving de facto supremacy over native Wales in 1218, the prince 'had still before him many years of strenuous and successful work, of assured supremacy, of good fortune which scarcely knew a rebuff'.[70] While the last point might seem to detract from the prince's personal achievement, the subsequent discussion highlights the judicious exploitation of the opportunities created by political division in England that helped to make Llywelyn 'the strongest ruler Wales had known since the Norman Conquest'.[71]

Lloyd's final verdict on Llywelyn was informed by his larger aim of charting the development of Welsh nationality, perhaps with an allusion – though no more – to the goal of Welsh home rule in the vague reference to using 'the native force of the Welsh people for adequate national ends'. The phrase underlines the point made elsewhere in the *History* that, while Welsh nationhood realized its full potential under exceptional leaders like Llywelyn, its foundations were resolutely popular.

> Among the chieftains who battled against the Anglo-Norman power his place will always be high, if not indeed the highest of all, for no man ever made better or more judicious use of the native force of the Welsh people for adequate national ends; his patriotic statesmanship will always entitle him to wear the proud style of Llywelyn the Great.[72]

Moreover, in contrast to his eisteddfod essay over twenty years earlier, neither this judgement nor Lloyd's account as a whole characterizes Llywelyn's rule in terms of state-building.[73] Although attention is given to the political ties that enabled the prince to exercise supremacy over other Welsh rulers and thus foster greater unity, the term 'state' is conspicuous by its absence from the discussion, and the prince's administrative arrangements occupy fewer than two pages.[74] The emphasis in the 1887 lecture on applying 'feudal' ideas is also absent, perhaps because elsewhere in the *History* Lloyd had presented feudalism as alien to the Welsh, though his earlier thinking is detectable in the description of the princes of north Wales as Llywelyn's 'vassals'.[75] The reader's attention is held, rather, by his qualities as a national leader who achieved 'the unquestioned primacy of his race' through military victories and who demonstrated the foresight and prudence praised by O. M. Edwards.[76]

Likewise, it is these qualities that, in Lloyd's view, continue to make the prince superior to his grandson, Llywelyn ap Gruffudd.[77] True, the *History* designates the thirteenth century as 'the age of the two Llywelyns', and the second of these princes is accorded respect and significance.[78] However, his treatment of the last Llywelyn is briefer, less analytical and more critical than that of Llywelyn the Great.[79] Indeed, there is a tension in the account that may indicate that Lloyd had some difficulty in reconciling trad-itional perceptions of Llywelyn ap Gruffudd as a heroic warrior fighting for Welsh independence with more recent estimations of the prince's shortcomings by comparison with his grandfather: if the last Llywelyn's eventual failure could hardly be portrayed as heroic as it stemmed from his own personal failings, nevertheless, it was ultimately due to cosmic forces beyond his control.[80]

> The ruinous end of his career may justly qualify one's admiration and suggest that he had not, with all his merits, the statesmanlike insight and prudence of the elder Llywelyn, but it invests the whole with the light of romance, touches it with a most poignant pathos, and closes the narrative in a vein of dignified tragedy, as who should tell the vain struggle of weak human will against the resistless forces of Nature.[81]

Whereas the implicit contrast with Llywelyn the Great's success in weathering the 'hurricane' unleashed by King John in 1211 accurately captures the fact that the last Llywelyn faced a far more powerful foe in Edward I, Lloyd's romanticized conclusion – like his readiness elsewhere to ascribe the prince's fall to fate – serves to divert attention from the specific causes of Llywelyn ap Gruffudd's defeat, thereby endowing it with an inevitability that renders it acceptable.[82] This is of a piece with the *History*'s famous conclusion, whose upbeat (and long-held) assessment in turn encapsulates the long-term significance Lloyd attached to medieval Welsh rulers: 'It was for a far distant generation to see that the last Prince had not lived in vain, but by his life-work had helped to build solidly the enduring fabric of Welsh nationality.'[83]

Conclusion:
Creating Welsh History?

The day after his death *The Times* proclaimed Lloyd's lasting significance: 'His work in the field of Welsh history is the foundation on which all Welsh historians who come after him must build; to vary a famous saying, whatever else is read, Lloyd must be read.'[1] This view was shared by other commentators both during and after his lifetime, and is of a piece with the compliment which pleased Lloyd so much – that he had 'created Welsh history'.[2] The present book has been written on the assumption that Lloyd was, indeed, a pivotal figure in the historiography of Wales and has sought to set his work in the contexts of his life and his intellectual environment. What general conclusions may be drawn, then, about his achievement? In particular, why did Lloyd write the kind of history he did and how influential was he?

Lloyd had decided to dedicate himself to the history of Wales by the mid-1880s, and his approach was shaped by three principal factors. To begin with, as a schoolboy in Liverpool he had read earlier accounts of Welsh history, notably the recently completed work of Gweirydd ap Rhys, as part of a wider engagement with Welsh – and especially Welsh-language – culture, an engagement encouraged by his parents, particularly his mother. Secondly, this in turn laid the foundations for a strong commitment to what he and other contemporaries termed a Welsh 'national awakening' that was nurtured by friendship with like-minded students at Aberystwyth and then Oxford, aspirations Lloyd sought to realize not only in his work as a historian but also through his university teaching and administration in Wales, above all at Bangor. Thirdly, however, integral to these patriotic impulses was a commitment to modern forms and standards of scholarship. In part, this was a matter of building on the critical approach towards texts taken by some nineteenth-century Welsh scholars, particularly Thomas Stephens and Gweirydd ap Rhys, an approach to which Lloyd was further exposed through his study of Classics and history at Oxford.[3] In addition, Lloyd was influenced by developments in other disciplines – archaeology, ethnology, philology and also economic and social history focusing on law and institutions – which, unlike the standard works of English history by Stubbs, Freeman and Green, took a serious and largely sympathetic interest in Celtic societies, including Wales, as part of wider comparative investigations into the origins, character and social organization of different peoples.[4]

To pause at the second of these factors, it is clear, as previous writers have recognized, that Lloyd's *History* formed part of a larger movement of national renewal in Wales, especially in the field of education, a movement that had reached a critical stage when Lloyd was a young man in the 1880s and 1890s. This helps to explain not only the nature of his historical writing but also why his energies were exerted in other directions as well. Unlike historians in England, Scotland, Ireland and much of the European continent, including Henri Pirenne's Belgium, Lloyd did not have the benefit in Wales of an established university with a tradition of teaching history; accordingly, in common with patriots in some other countries – including Serbia, Croatia, Bulgaria and Slovakia – where nationalist movements were comparatively late in securing the establishment of universities, one of his chief priorities was to help remedy this deficiency through a commitment to the newly established university colleges of the late nineteenth century and the legitimizing framework of the federal University of Wales founded in 1893.[5] True, in many respects his commitment was matched by that of scholars at the new universities established in late nineteenth- and early twentieth-century England: his friend T. F. Tout at Manchester is an obvious example. However, there was also a crucial difference, as the University of Wales was the principality's first university and was designed specifically as a national – rather than regional or civic – institution.[6] Moreover, the Welsh university was intended as both the coping stone and beneficiary of a national system of elementary and secondary education, whose development Lloyd also supported, not least by producing three bilingual school textbooks in the decade before he began writing his *History* in January 1901. And, with the reorganization of the University of Wales following the recommendations of the Haldane Commission, Lloyd played a central role in creating and sustaining an institutional framework designed specifically to advance Welsh scholarship, including Welsh history, through his chairmanship of the Board of Celtic Studies (1919–40), thereby putting into practice ideas he had developed since the late nineteenth century. At the same time, as registrar (1892–1920) and professor of history (1899–1930), he played a key role in placing the recently founded university college at Bangor on a secure footing.

However, if Lloyd's *History* was begotten in the heat of national awakening, its character bore the imprint both of its historiographical ancestors and of the scholarly and intellectual environment in which its author was raised. Lloyd did not come to Welsh history from scratch: like most other historians, his approach was influenced by what had come before. This has usually been seen, following Lloyd himself, as an essentially reactive process by which a new kind of 'scientific' historian applied a critical solvent to the legends encrusting the history of Wales and forged a new synthesis that was impartial as well as coherent. There can be no doubt that Lloyd broke new ground in the painstakingly careful and detailed analysis of sources that underpins the *History*, together with his other scholarly work, as his numerous footnotes – and notebooks – demonstrate. Indeed, the 'very independent mind . . . always anxious to work things out for himself' noticed by his history tutor at Oxford is a fundamental feature of Lloyd's work: the quest for accuracy created a momentum of its own over and above that generated by patriotic inspiration.[7] Yet the contrast between his work and that of earlier historians of Wales was less stark than Lloyd implied. If his methods were new, they shone light on a terrain whose contours had already been mapped in significant measure by his predecessors. The emphasis on the period down to the Edwardian conquest was long established;

so too was the central role ascribed to Welsh kings and princes. Some found Lloyd's demolition of long-cherished notions disconcerting.[8] However, the resulting historical landscape still looked familiar, as, even after rigorous scientific refurbishment, its principal landmarks remained intact and, indeed, stood out more clearly than before.

As already mentioned, in liberating the Welsh past from the realm of legend and subjecting it to the brave new world of 'scientific' scholarship Lloyd was influenced by academic fashion and intellectual trends in late Victorian and Edwardian Britain. His readiness to adopt what today would be termed an interdisciplinary approach, exemplified by the deployment of prehistoric archaeology, ethnology and philology to trace the origins of the Welsh, is a good case in point. His openness to different fields of inquiry and readiness to make connections between them are important characteristics of his work and underline that Lloyd, in common with others of his generation in Britain, was largely self-trained as a historian. Although the two years he had spent reading history at Oxford doubtless provided a grounding in British and European history and also helped to instil important assumptions about how history should be written and taught, not least the value of critical and coherent synthesis, it did not offer training in historical research. Lloyd's first major venture into such research, the essay on Welsh history for the eisteddfod, was undertaken on his own initiative and written away from Oxford during a term at home in Liverpool. Nor did Lloyd proceed to postgraduate study. Viewed from a continental European perspective, his higher education illustrates the continuing resistance of late nineteenth-century Oxford to the German model of the research university, including Ranke's emphasis on training in the use of original documents.[9] After graduating in 1885 Lloyd honed his skills as a historian of Wales partly through consolidating his mastery of the crucial ancillary fields of Welsh language, literature and law, but also through his contributions to the *Dictionary of National Biography*, an enterprise that provided an apprenticeship for 'a formidable generation' of historians including Tout (1855–1929), Charles Firth (1857–1936) and Albert Pollard (1869–1948).[10] Moreover, just as these scholars sought to promote more formalized provision for historical training and research, so too did Lloyd – at least, up to a point.

Thus he voiced support for Tout's call to establish continental-style schools of history and established a dedicated history research room in the new college buildings at Bangor opened in 1911, while from the 1920s onwards he helped to ensure that original sources became more widely accessible by encouraging the Board of Celtic Studies to publish editions and calendars of archival materials relating to Wales held in the Public Record Office. On the other hand, Lloyd's teaching and supervision seem to have concentrated on the analysis of published sources, thereby following the example of his own work, and in general he was less ready than some of his contemporaries to turn his back on the world of late Victorian historical scholarship and embrace the astringent methods of 'modernist' English academic historians united in their assumption that facts about the past could be recovered by rigorous analysis of 'the evidence'.[11]

It is also worth pausing to consider how Lloyd's work related to other kinds of Welsh historical writing during his lifetime. One important reason why Lloyd remains such a prominent figure in Welsh historiography is that subsequent generations of historians – the present writer included – have seen themselves as his successors, be it in his medieval field of expertise in particular or more generally as practitioners of modes of enquiry into the Welsh past that may be labelled, and thus legitimized, as academic. However, as elsewhere, academic history was (and is) only one means of apprehending and presenting the past. In the efforts to disseminate knowledge of Welsh history in the late nineteenth and early twentieth centuries Lloyd's meticulous revisionist synthesis comes after monographs based on archival research at the self-consciously academic end of a spectrum that extends via the prolific popularization of O. M. Edwards to Owen Rhoscomyl's colourful evocations of heroes in both print and pageant. The comparison with Edwards is particularly revealing in that it points up how friends of a broadly similar educational background, sharing a common commitment to national revival anchored in the deep waters of a distinctive Welsh past, made different choices when it came to promoting an understanding of that past – choices that involved both gain and loss.[12] For Edwards, a university historian for almost two decades, the priority was to popularize Welsh history as an integral element of Welsh culture, whereas Lloyd, by seeking to establish Welsh history as an academic discipline endowed with 'scientific' credentials acceptable to a wider world of scholarship, effectively distanced it from that culture. Small wonder, then, that the terms in which he praised Edwards's book *Wales* – 'charmingly written' and '[a]n admirable general sketch' – implied that it was a far cry from the kind of historical work to which he himself aspired, or that Lloyd regarded Edwards above all as a talented literary artist who had opened a new chapter in Welsh prose writing.[13]

Lloyd's decision to deploy 'scientific' scholarship in the task of renewing a lengthy, and traditionally seminal, period of his nation's past was informed, of course, not only by the emphasis but also by the quality of previous Welsh historical writing, none of which, in his view, matched the pioneering work of historians of England from the seventeenth century onwards. This attitude in turn implies that, as for many Welsh patriots of his generation, he was motivated by a desire to prove that Wales could match the progress of its English neighbour, which simultaneously constituted the 'other' against which Welsh nationality was defined and the source of authoritative norms which helped to legitimate it. Thus Lloyd seized an opportunity bequeathed by his predecessors. That he was able to seize it so effectively reflects his ability, not only to combine close analysis of particulars with a clearly structured, cogent narrative, embellished at key moments by dramatic flourishes, that sustains an overarching vision of the whole, but also, crucially, to take advantage of scholarly developments by the beginning of the twentieth century, notably the availability in print of most of the relevant written sources and the approaches offered by the human sciences. In other words, the *History* drew upon several prevailing strands in the study of early societies, especially in Britain. Yet, if its origins lay in a dynamic engagement with recent trends in scholarship, once completed the work assumed an almost canonical status for Lloyd, who, while he went on for the rest of his life to revise points of detail and add new material to the notebooks used in composing it, saw no reason to move beyond its parameters and explore fresh approaches to the period he had covered so exhaustively in his forties. Nor did Lloyd look beyond his native country in his historical writing – unlike, say, Pirenne, with his pan-European range or, closer to home, J. Goronwy Edwards (1891–1976), who not only worked on Welsh history but published extensively on medieval England.[14] In these as in other respects, Lloyd remained true to the views and attitudes he had formed as a young man in the late Victorian and Edwardian eras. This is not to suggest that he was content to rest on his laurels. After finishing the *History* in 1910, Lloyd published many scholarly articles on aspects of both the centuries it covered and later periods of Welsh history, wrote an important volume on Owain Glyndŵr and contributed to major collaborative works, the Carmarthenshire county history and the dictionary of Welsh biography. However, he clearly believed that the *History* remained his greatest and most significant achievement: it was for this, after all, that he was praised as the creator of Welsh history.

Lloyd also contributed to the historiography of Wales in a broader sense. Few today might wish to go as far as asserting that the *History* 'has given new dignity to the Welsh nation the world over and for all time'.[15] However, the critical acclaim Lloyd received for his magnum opus almost certainly rubbed off on Welsh history in general, and helped to raise both its profile and its academic credentials. At the very least the reception of the *History* cemented Lloyd's position as the most distinguished Welsh historian of his day, and his reputation gave him authority to shape the development of the subject through leading, and lending prestige to, collaborative initiatives as chairman of the Board of Celtic Studies and also as an editor.[16] Moreover, thanks to his longevity, he remained a commanding presence in Welsh scholarship for over three more decades after his *History* first appeared in 1911. This dominance clearly allowed Lloyd to achieve a great deal. How far it inhibited developments that failed to attract his interest or sympathy is, on the other hand, hard to tell. While an attempt to persuade him to allow a goalkeeper and a boxer to join the hallowed ranks of saints, princes and literary figures who largely peopled the projected dictionary of Welsh biography was greeted with hearty but dismissive laughter, Lloyd could not impose his influence on all aspects of Welsh historical writing; nor is it likely that he wished to do so.[17] After all, among the numerous scholars to whom he gave help and encouragement were a fair number with different interests and approaches from his own. Several of these – including E. A. Lewis, William Rees, Thomas Richards, Caroline Skeel and David Williams – contributed to two significant, and partly interrelated, developments during his day which stand in contrast to his own priorities: the production of monographs based on extensive archival research, and the study of post-conquest Wales.[18] Lloyd did not create modern Welsh academic historiography single handedly. Nevertheless, his role in its creation was both singular and substantial, for he brought steadfast dedication, breadth of vision and meticulous verification of detail to a clearly conceived task: the renewal of a nation's past.

Notes

Introduction

1.   Robert Richards to Lloyd, 7 May 1940, LP 318, no. 221. Richards wrote a social and economic history of medieval Wales, *Cymru'r Oesau Canol* (Wrexham, 1933), with mention of Pirenne at p. 212.
2.   Key assessments include Jenkins, 'Lloyd'; Edwards, 'Lloyd'; Davies, 'Lloyd'; Evans, 'Men and mountains', 228–37. Lloyd George himself declared that Lloyd had made 'a contribution to [the] History of Wales which will be . . . an inspiration to those who look forward to build on the past a future which will place Wales forever in the foremost ranks of great little nations of the world', *North Wales Chronicle*, 14 March 1941, 5.
3.   Cf. Michael Bentley, *Modernizing England's Past: English Historiography in the Age of Modernism 1870–1970* (Cambridge, 2005), p. 12.
4.   See below, p. 95.
5.   See Bryce Lyon, *Henri Pirenne: A Biographical and Intellectual Study* (Ghent, 1974), with a list of publications at pp. 461–2; see below, p. 72.
6.   Lyon, *Henri Pirenne*, pp. 34–65.
7.   Ibid., pp. 127–36; Christian Koninckx, 'Historiography and nationalism in Belgium', in Erik Lönnroth, Karl Molin and Ragnar Björk (eds), *Conceptions of National History: Proceedings of Nobel Symposium 78* (Berlin/ New York, 1994), pp. 34–48; Gita Deneckere and Thomas Welskopp, 'The "nation" and "class": European national master narratives and their social "other"', in Stefan Berger and Chris Lorenz (eds), *The Contested Nation: Ethnicity, Class, Religion and Gender in National Histories* (Houndmills, 2008), pp. 144–5. On the nation-state and Lamprecht, see also Robert Harrison, Aled Jones and Peter Lambert, 'The primacy of

political history', in Peter Lambert and Phillipp Schofield (eds), *Making History: An Introduction to the History and Practices of a Discipline* (London/New York, 2004), pp. 38–42.

8   Marnix Beyen and Benoît Majerus, 'Weak and strong nations in the Low Countries: national historiography and its "others" in Belgium, Luxembourg and the Netherlands in the nineteenth and twentieth centuries', in Berger and Lorenz (eds), *Contested Nation*, pp. 297–303.

9   Huw Pryce, 'The Normans in Welsh history', in C. P. Lewis (ed.), *Anglo-Norman Studies XXX* (Woodbridge, 2008), pp. 2–3, 17; Max Engman, 'National conceptions of history in Finland', in Lönnroth et al. (eds), *Conceptions of National History*, pp. 49–63; Derek Fewster, *Visions of Past Glory: Nationalism and the Construction of Early Finnish History* (Studia Fennica Historica, 11; Helsinki, 2006), pp. 16–17, 116–42 *et passim*.

10   For recent wide-ranging discussions, see Stefan Berger, Mark Donovan and Kevin Passmore (eds), *Writing National Histories: Western Europe since 1800* (London/New York, 1999); Stefan Berger (ed.), *Writing the Nation: A Global Perspective* (Houndmills, 2007); idem and Lorenz (eds), *Contested Nation*; Daniel Woolf, 'Of nations, nationalism, and national identity', in Q. Edward Wang and Franz L. Fillafer (eds), *The Many Faces of Clio: Cross-cultural Approaches to Historiography, Essays in Honor of Georg G. Iggers* (New York/Oxford, 2007), pp. 71–103.

11   For instance, *Guardian*, 30 September 1911; *Times Literary Supplement*, 20 April 1911, 158; Ernest Rhys, *Manchester Guardian* (Welsh edition), 4 March 1911; R. Thurneysen, *Historische Zeitschrift*, 110 (1913), 405–6; reviews cited in Neil Evans, 'Finding a new story: the search for a usable past in Wales, 1869–1930', *THSC*, new ser., 10 (2004), 156–9.

12   *Western Mail*, 4 February 1911, cited in Evans, 'Finding a new story', 159. Lloyd's work is also linked to the wider promotion of a national revival in Edwards, 'Lloyd', 320–1; Kenneth O. Morgan, *Rebirth of a Nation: Wales 1880–1980* (Oxford/Cardiff, 1981), pp. 102, 108.

13   Thurneysen, review, 406.

14   John Williams, *Digest of Welsh Historical Statistics*, vol. 1 ([Cardiff] 1985), p. 7.

15   Prys Morgan (ed.), *Brad y Llyfrau Gleision: Ysgrifau ar Hanes Cymru* (Llandysul, 1991); Ieuan Gwynedd Jones, '1848 and 1868: "Brad y Llyfrau Gleision" and Welsh politics', in idem, *Mid-Victorian Wales: The Observers and the Observed* (Cardiff, 1992), pp. 103–65, 186–98; Gwyneth Tyson Roberts, *The Language of the Blue Books: The Perfect Instrument of Empire* (Cardiff, 1998).

16   Kenneth O. Morgan, 'Welsh nationalism: the historical background', *Journal of Contemporary History*, 6, 1 (1971), 153–72, quotation at 165. See also idem, *Wales in British Politics, 1868–1922* (paperback edn, Cardiff, 1991), chapters I–IV; Emyr W. Williams, 'Liberalism in Wales and the politics of Welsh home rule 1886–1910', *Bulletin of the Board of Celtic Studies*, 37 (1990), 191–207; Paul O'Leary, 'Accommodation and

resistance: a comparison of cultural identities in Ireland and Wales, *c*.1880–1914', in S. J. Connolly (ed.), *Kingdoms United? Great Britain and Ireland since 1500* (Dublin, 1999), pp. 123–34; Wil Griffith, 'Devolutionist tendencies in Wales, 1885–1914', in Duncan Tanner et al. (eds), *Debating Nationhood and Governance in Britain, 1885–1945: Perspectives from the 'Four Nations'* (Manchester/New York, 2006), pp. 89–117; John S. Ellis, *Investiture: Royal Ceremony and National Identity in Wales, 1911–1969* (Cardiff, 2008), chapter 1.

[17] *HW*, I, p. 275. Lloyd believed that the Welsh should fill posts in the empire: J. Gwynn Williams, *The University College of North Wales: Foundations 1884–1927* (Cardiff, 1985), p. 258. See also Aled Gruffydd Jones and Bill Jones, 'The Welsh world and the British empire, *c*.1850–1939: an exploration', *Journal of Imperial and Commonwealth History*, 31 (2003), 57–81; idem, 'Empire and the Welsh press', in Simon J. Potter (ed.), *Newspapers and Empire: Ireland and Britain, c.1857–1921* (Dublin, 2004), pp. 75–91.

[18] Morgan, *WBP*, pp. 98–102, 129–33, 218, 274, 286–91.

[19] Cf. D. Brynmor Jones, 'Introduction', in J. Hugh Edwards, *The Life of David Lloyd George, with a Short History of the Welsh People*, vol. I (London [1913]), pp. xxv–xxxii.

[20] Jones, '1848 and 1868', pp. 137–41; Roberts, *Language of the Blue Books*, chapter 15; Paul O'Leary, 'The languages of patriotism in Wales 1840–1880', in Geraint H. Jenkins (ed.), *The Welsh Language and its Social Domains 1801–1911* (Cardiff, 2000), pp. 533–60; Prys Morgan, 'Lingen, Arnold a Palgrave: tri Sais a'u hagweddau at Gymru', in Tegwyn Jones and Huw Walters (eds), *Cawr i'w Genedl: Cyfrol i Gyfarch yr Athro Hywel Teifi Edwards* (Llandysul, 2008), pp. 89–93.

[21] Matthew Arnold, 'On the study of Celtic literature', in *The Complete Prose Works of Matthew Arnold*, vol. III, *Lectures and Essays in Criticism*, ed. R. H. Super (Ann Arbor, MI, 1962), pp. 291–395. See also Rachel Bromwich, *Matthew Arnold and Celtic Literature: A Retrospect 1865–1965* (Oxford, 1965); Patrick Sims-Williams, 'The visionary Celt: the construction of an ethnic preconception', *Cambridge Medieval Celtic Studies*, 11 (summer 1986), 71–96; Joep Leerssen, 'Englishness, ethnicity and Matthew Arnold', *European Journal of English Studies*, 10, 1 (2006), 63–79; Daniel G. Williams, *Ethnicity and Cultural Authority: From Arnold to Du Bois* (Edinburgh, 2006), pp. 33–52; Robert J. C. Young, *The Idea of English Ethnicity* (Malden, MA, 2008), chapter 5.

[22] Arnold, 'On the study', pp. 296–7.

[23] Cf. R. T. Jenkins, 'The development of nationalism in Wales', *Sociological Review*, 27 (1935), 177: 'There are but two main ingredients in modern Welsh mental life – what is native, and what is English or has been mediated through England; and the proportion between them would in fact be difficult to assess.' See also Morgan, 'Welsh nationalism', 164–5; E. G. Millward, *Yr Arwrgerdd Gymraeg: Ei Thwf a'i Thranc* (Cardiff,

1998), pp. 289–90; Lowri Angharad Hughes, 'O. M. Edwards: ei waith a'i weledigaeth', in Gerwyn Wiliams (ed.), *Ysgrifau Beirniadol XXIX* (Denbigh, 2010), pp. 65–8; see below, p. 29; and, for 'national thought', Joep Leerssen, *National Thought in Europe: A Cultural History* (Amsterdam, 2006), esp. pp. 13–20.

24 Arnold, 'On the study', p. 291.
25 Morgan, 'Lingen', p. 101, n. 51; see below, pp. 33, 90–1.
26 Paul Readman, 'The place of the past in English culture, *c.* 1890–1914', *Past & Present*, 186 (2005), 147–99; Peter Fritzsche, *Stranded in the Present: Modern Time and the Melancholy of History* (Cambridge, MA/ London, 2004).
27 Gwyn Griffiths, *Land of My Fathers: Evan, James, Their Lives and Times* (Llanrwst, 2006), pp. [5–6], 10, 43–7.
28 E. G. Millward, '"Cenedl o bobl ddewrion": y rhamant hanesyddol yn Oes Victoria', in idem, *Cenedl o Bobl Ddewrion: Agweddau ar Lenyddiaeth Oes Victoria* (Llandysul, 1991), pp. 104–19; idem, *Yr Arwrgerdd Gymraeg*, chapter 10; Dot Jones, *Statistical Evidence relating to the Welsh Language 1801–1911 / Tystiolaeth Ystadegol yn ymwneud â'r Iaith Gymraeg 1801– 1911* (Cardiff, 1998), p. 498; Matthew Cragoe, 'Welsh electioneering and the purpose of parliament: "From radicalism to nationalism" reconsidered', *Parliamentary History*, 17 (1998), 118–19; Geraint H. Jenkins, 'Clio and Wales: Welsh remembrancers and historical writing, 1751– 2001', *THSC*, new ser., 8 (2002), 121–2.
29 Hazel Davies, *O. M. Edwards* (Cardiff, 1988), pp. 38–58, 75–9.
30 For the *cofiant* (memoir), see Llion Pryderi Roberts, '"Y mae efe, wedi marw, yn llefaru eto": mawl a moes yng nghofiannau'r pregethwyr', *Y Traethodydd*, 161 (2006), 78–97.
31 David Powel, *The Historie of Cambria, Now Called Wales* (London, 1584); R. T. Jenkins, 'William Wynne and the *History of Wales*', *Bulletin of the Board of Celtic Studies*, 6 (1931–3), 157–9; see below, pp. 82–3.
32 Jenkins, 'Clio and Wales', 123; Marion Löffler, *The Literary and Historical Legacy of Iolo Morganwg, 1826–1926* (Cardiff, 2007); see below, pp. 117–18.
33 Edwards, *Wales*; see below, pp. 83–5.
34 Edwards, 'Lloyd', 321–2; Huw Pryce, 'Modern nationality and the medieval past: the Wales of John Edward Lloyd', in R. R. Davies and Geraint H. Jenkins (eds), *From Medieval to Modern Wales: Historical Essays in Honour of Kenneth O. Morgan and Ralph A. Griffiths* (Cardiff, 2004), p. 19.

1 Welsh Liverpool, 1861–1877

1 LP 336: 1 January 1876.

2   LP 73, 336: 4 May 1876.
3   LP 2, 17. Margaret Lloyd's year of birth calculated by combining the age of thirty-six in the census taken on 2 April 1871 (RG10/3784, fol. 118, p. 2) and her birthday of 19 April in LP 2, although the latter gives the year as 1832.
4   Liverpool was given city status in 1880. For population numbers, see Colin G. Pooley, 'The residential segregation of migrant communities in mid-Victorian Liverpool', *Transactions of the Institute of British Geographers*, new ser., 2 (1977), 365, 366; P. J. Waller, *Democracy and Sectarianism: A Political and Social History of Liverpool 1868–1939* (Liverpool, 1981), p. 9; R. Merfyn Jones, 'The Liverpool Welsh', in idem and D. Ben Rees, *The Liverpool Welsh and their Religion* (Liverpool, 1984), pp. 21–2, 34; John Belchem and Donald M. MacRaild, 'Cosmopolitan Liverpool', in John Belchem (ed.), *Liverpool 800: Culture, Character and History* (Liverpool, 2006), p. 344.
5   Jones, 'Liverpool Welsh', pp. 23, 26–7. For the Liverpool Welsh in the later nineteenth and early twentieth centuries, see also Jen Llywelyn, '"The sun in splendour": George M. Ll. Davies (1880–1949), pacifist, conscientious objector and peace-maker, and the creation of a Nonconformist saint' (unpublished Ph.D. thesis, Aberystwyth University, 2010), 20–43.
6   Cf. Colin G. Pooley and John C. Doherty, 'The longitudinal study of migration: Welsh migration to English towns in the nineteenth century', in Colin G. Pooley and Ian D. Whyte (eds), *Migrants, Emigrants and Immigrants: A Social History of Migration* (London/New York, 1991), pp. 143–73, esp. pp. 163, 169–70.
7   Leonore Davidoff and Catherine Hall, *Family Fortunes* (revd edn, London/New York, 2002), pp. 219–21.
8   Biographical details largely based on LP 2, 17, supplemented by TNA, HO107/2499, fol. 703, p. 1 (1851 census); RG10/3784, fol. 118, p. 1 (1871 census), and David Adams, 'Edward Lloyd, Y.H., Lerpwl', *Y Dysgedydd*, 96 (1917), 217. That the business was located in the family home is indicated by its address in Richard Brooks to J. E. Lloyd, 31 December 1935, LP 317, no. 16, i.e. 200 and 202, Falkner Street; Lloyd recorded that he was born in 184, 'today 200', Falkner Street: LP 17. The business at 200 and 202 Falkner Street was closed and the premises put up for sale in August 1939: LP 25.
9   For the economic context, see Graeme J. Milne, *Trade and Traders in Mid-Victorian Liverpool: Mercantile Business and the Making of a World Port* (Liverpool, 2000), p. 9; Roderick Floud, 'Britain, 1860–1914: a survey', in idem and Donald McCloskey (eds), *The Economic History of Britain since 1700*, vol. 2, *1860–1939* (2nd edn, Cambridge, 1994), pp. 1–28, esp. pp. 2–3, 16–19; and, for the sharp commercial downturn in Liverpool in 1878, W. Nicholson, 'Anerchiad', *Adroddiad Eglwys Gynulleidfaol Grove Street, Liverpool, am 1878* (n.p., n.d.), p. [2].

[10] TNA, RG10/3784, fol. 118, pp. 1–2 (1871 census); cf. John Felix, 'Y wraig rinweddol', *Yr Eurgrawn Wesleyaidd*, 114 (1922), 57, for the affection Margaret Lloyd's maids showed her. Neither this nor the Falkner Street house survives. Edward and Margaret Lloyd later moved to 31 Falkner Square. On the middle-class home and its separation from work, see Davidoff and Hall, *Family Fortunes*, chapter 8.

[11] LP 336: 2, 5 February, 22, 28 April, 5, 15 May 1876.

[12] LP 336: 10, 16 June, 4 August 1876; 337: 30 March, 2 April 1877.

[13] LP 337: 10 March 1877.

[14] Cf. J. Glyn Davies, *Nationalism as a Social Phenomenon* (Liverpool, 1965), p. 27; Jones, 'Liverpool Welsh', p. 25.

[15] LP 336: 14 February, 19 September 1876; cf. 10 February 1876.

[16] LP 336: 24 March, 8, 26 April, 28 September, 10, 13, 16, 24 October, 6, 7 November, 25 December 1876; 337: 10, 31 January, 10 February, 10 March, 2 April 1877.

[17] LP 336: 6 January, 26 April, 5, 21 June, 20 December, 1876; 337: 25 January 1877.

[18] LP 336: 4 February, 8 July, 31 August, 6 October 1876; 337: 19 March 1877. Cf. Richard Shannon, *Gladstone and the Bulgarian Agitation 1876* (London, 1963), esp. pp. 36–81.

[19] LP 18. For Veitch, see TNA, RG10/3873, fol. 103, p. 27 (1871 census); RG11/3623, fol. 94, p. 28 (1881 census).

[20] LP 18 (results in 1875 and 1877); 336: 30 August 1876.

[21] LP 336: 23, 26 May, 5 September 1876.

[22] Ibid., 10 February, 30 March, 8 April, 28 May, 21 September 1876; LP 337: 24 February 1877.

[23] LP 336: 9 February 1876.

[24] David Adams, 'Yn llefaru eto: marwolaeth a chladdedigaeth y diweddar Thomas Arthur Lloyd', *Y Dysgedydd*, 96 (1917), 83.

[25] Evan Lewis, Congregational minister, to Edward Lloyd, 12 September 1872, LP 204; Glanystwyth, 'Mrs. Lloyd, Falkner Square, Liverpool', *Y Gymraes*, 3 (1899), 146; Felix, 'Y wraig rinweddol', 56.

[26] Lloyd certainly thought that his upbringing made him appreciate that no denomination had a monopoly of virtue: LP 224, pp. 3–4. One contemporary reportedly declared that Edward Lloyd was the 'broadest in his sympathies' among the men in the chapel: Owen Evans to Edward Lloyd, 28 July 1875, LP 204.

[27] For Grove Street chapel, see T. Rees and J. Thomas, *Hanes Eglwysi Annibynol Cymru*, vol. IV (Liverpool, 1875), pp. 419–21; John Thomas, *Hanes Eglwysi Annibynol Cymru*, vol. V (Dolgellau [1891]), pp. 406–13, 527; T. Eli Evans, *Hanes Cymanfaoedd Annibynwyr Lerpwl* (Liverpool, 1902), pp. 12–13 and photograph facing p. 58. Cf. R. A. Johnson, revised M. A. Williams, 'Rees, William [*pseud.* Gwilym Hiraethog] (1802–1833)', *ODNB*.

28 Cf. Jones, 'Liverpool Welsh', p. 26.

29 Rees and Thomas, *Hanes Eglwysi Annibynol Cymru*, p. 421; *Adroddiad Eglwys Gynulleidfaol Grove Street, Liverpool. 1876.* ([Liverpool, 1877]), pp. 1, 5; *Adroddiad Eglwys Gynulleidfaol Grove Street, Liverpool. 1877.* ([Liverpool, 1878]), pp. 3, 7; Adams, 'Edward Lloyd', 218.

30 LP 202; 203; 336: 2–3, 8, 30–1 January, 2–6, 9–10 March, 10, 18, 26 October, 5–6, 9, 20, 22 November, 19, 21, 31 December 1876; Thomas, *Hanes Eglwysi Annibynol Cymru*, p. 412; *DWB*, pp. 141, 685–6.

31 *Adroddiad 1877*, p. 11. Cf. Adams, 'Edward Lloyd', 217. Lloyd's paternal grandfather had been the first to break the family's allegiance to Wesleyan Methodism and become a Congregationalist: LP 17.

32 *TLWNS*, 1 (1885–6), xii, xviii; Adams, 'Edward Lloyd', 217–18. Cf. Davies, *Nationalism*, pp. 27–8, 30–2, 45.

33 LP 18, 221, p. 1.

34 Cf. Davies, *Nationalism*, pp. 26, 28. Lloyd provides revealing recollections of his Nonconformist upbringing in Liverpool in LP 221 (1932).

35 LP 336: notes on sermons at back.

36 LP 336: 23 July ('Mr J. Evans, Llangynog, preached indifferently on Heaven. He committed some magnificent geographical errors à la Bardd.'), 27 August 1876.

37 J. E. Lloyd, 'Hiraethog a'i gyfnod', *Adroddiad Cyfarfodydd yr Undeb*, new ser. 10, 4 (Undeb yr Annibynwyr Cymraeg; Swansea, 1932), p. 21; Jenkins, 'Lloyd', 87.

38 LP 337: 1 January 1877.

39 LP 221, p. 8. Cf. below, p. 49.

40 LP 74 ('Cytundeb Daeareg ac Ysgrythyr'); 221, pp. 6–7. Cf. M. A. Taylor, 'Miller, Hugh (1802–1856)', *ODNB* (quotation); Ioan Williams, 'Gwilym Hiraethog (William Rees, 1802–83)', in Hywel Teifi Edwards (ed.), *A Guide to Welsh Literature c.1800–1900* (Cardiff, 2000), p. 57; Peter J. Bowler, *The Invention of Progress: The Victorians and the Past* (Oxford, 1989), pp. 175–8.

41 LP 74 ('Yr Awyrgylch'); 337: 6 April 1877; [J. E. Lloyd], 'Yr awyrgylch', *Y Beirniad*, 19 (1877), 61–7.

42 LP 337: 5 January 1877.

43 LP 336: 14 October, 9, 27 December 1876. Cf. ibid.: 21, 22 August, 9 October 1876; LP 337: 29, 30 January 1877. The first English translation of the novel was published in 1876.

44 Cf. R. Tudur Jones, *Congregationalism in Wales*, ed. Robert Pope (Cardiff, 2004), pp. 172–5, 188–9.

45 The International Order of Good Templars, 'a pseudo-Masonic organization of extreme temperance zealots', was founded in the United States and reached Wales in 1871, shortly after its arrival in England: W. R. Lambert, *Drink and Sobriety in Victorian Wales c.1820–c.1895* (Cardiff, 1983), pp. 89 (quotation), 102–4.

46   LP 337: 14 February 1877. The addition of 'all' to the quotation from Ecclesiastes 9:10 perhaps indicates that the verse was quoted from memory.

47   Davies, *Nationalism*, p. 27.

48   *Adroddiad Eglwys Gynulleidfaol Grove Street, Liverpool. 1877*, p. 11; LP 336: 3 January, 2, 3, 17 March 1876.

49   Topics discussed: LP 336: 21 April, 7, 28 October, 2 December 1876; 337: 24 March 1877.

50   LP 336: 11 February, 3 April, 12 December 1876; 337: 21–2 February 1877. Cf. Jones, 'Liverpool Welsh', p. 27.

51   LP 337: 9 March 1877.

52   Cf. John Tosh, *A Man's Place: Masculinity and the Middle-Class Home in Victorian England* (New Haven, CT/London, 1999), pp. 113–14; Felix, 'Y wraig rinweddol', 55–7.

53   Ibid., 57; Glanystwyth, 'Mrs. Lloyd', 147; David Adams, 'Y ddiweddar Mrs. Edward Lloyd, Falkner Square, Liverpool', *Y Dysgedydd*, 101 (1922), 65; Robert Hughes to Lloyd, 3 November 1928, LP 316 no. 172.

54   After his father had promised to join the recently established Good Templar lodge at Grove Street, Lloyd commented that '[i]t will be a great thing to us to have somebody of position in the church to strengthen us and keep up the name of the "Cyfrinfa"'. LP 337: 30 January 1877.

55   LP 336: 16 September, 13, 27 October, 16 November 1876; 337: 10 January, 6, 8 March 1877.

56   Davidoff and Hall, *Family Fortunes*, pp. 215–22.

57   LP 337: 12, 13, 20 January, 31 March, 5 April 1877 (quotation).

58   Jenkins, 'Lloyd', 77.

59   Useful background on the Tanat valley, including Pen-y-bont-fawr, is provided by Clwyd-Powys Archaeological Trust, 'Historic landscape characterisation: the Tanat Valley': *http://www.cpat.org.uk/projects/longer/histland/tanat/tanat.htm* (last accessed 28 May 2010). Population: Pooley, 'Residential segregation', 365; *Census of England and Wales, 1871. (33 & 34 Vict. c. 107.) Population Tables. Area, Houses, and Inhabitants*, vol. I, *Counties* (London, 1872), C. 676, p. 544; Melvin Humphreys et al., *Llanfyllin: Portrait of an Age* (Llanfyllin, 2002), pp. 121–2. In the Llanfyllin census registration district, over 70 per cent of the population spoke Welsh in 1891, over half of whom were monoglot: Dot Jones, *Statistical Evidence relating to the Welsh Language 1801–1911 / Tystiolaeth Ystadegol yn Ymwneud â'r Iaith Gymraeg 1801–1911* (Cardiff, 1998), p. 226.

60   Richard Kretchmer, *Llanfyllin: Ei Hanes trwy Luniau* (Welshpool/Llanfyllin, 1992), p. 170; LP 336: 19 June 1876.

61   LP 337: 10, 11 January, 8 March 1877; cf. 336: 4 January 1876. Lizzie and Maggie were daughters respectively of Margaret Lloyd's sisters Eliza and Mary Ann.

62   In 1886 the lease of Bryndifyr was transferred from Eliza Williams (who had held it since 1881) to her brother-in-law Edward Lloyd, who bought

the house for £300 in 1901 (having already bought the adjacent property of Bronynant in 1897, which had been leased to Thomas Ridge since 1885): 'Family notes', back of LP 303 (1936 diary).

63 Davies, *Nationalism*, pp. 48–50, 63, 67–9.

64 LP 17: 'Eu gwir gartref, gwlad a anwylir gennyf hyd y dydd hwn, ar gyfrif cyfathrach agos a'i [*sic*] phobl a llu o adgofion bore oes, oedd Dyffryn Tanat, lle mae Sir Drefaldwyn yn ymylu ar Sir Ddinbych. Ni bu adeg yn fy mywyd pryd nad oeddwn yn gartrefol iawn ym Mhenygarnedd a Phenybont Fawr, ac yn Llanfyllin, eu tref farchnad.' Later visits to Penygarnedd: e.g., Lloyd to Edward Owen, 16, 24 August, 1 September 1910, NLW MS 18099C; LP 283: 29 July 1916.

65 LP 17.

66 LP 336: 19 June–3 August 1876.

67 Thomas Ridge was married to Margaret Lloyd's sister, Mary Ann.

68 LP 336: 4 July 1876. His description of Pennant Melangell written three decades later clearly drew on personal familiarity with the site: *HW*, I, p. 247; cf. below, chapter 8, n. 4.

69 LP 336: 25 October 1876.

70 LP 336: 21 March 1876. Cf. Hywel Teifi Edwards, *Coffáu Llywelyn 1856– 1956* (Llandysul, 1983), pp. 9–11; Llinos Beverley Smith, 'Llywelyn ap Gruffudd and the Welsh historical consciousness', *WHR*, 12 (1984–5), 25–7.

71 J. E. Lloyd, 'The teaching of history', *UCW Mag.*, 10 (1887–8), 101; LP 336: 11 February 1876.

72 *Cynghanedd*: LP 336: 29 August, 7 November, 30 December 1876.

73 For example, Lloyd held that the one redeeming feature of Radnorshire was that its people 'all speak English', and commented, apropos of the National Eisteddfod, that 'The "Saeson" [English] are just opening their eyes to the importance of our festival!': LP 336: 23 August 1876; 337: 5 March 1877. See also ibid.: 10 February 1877; Lewis Morris, 'The principle of national development in relation to Wales', *TLWNS*, 1 (1885–6), 1–15; Jones, 'Liverpool Welsh', pp. 29–35.

74 Also mentioned are *Y Dysgedydd* ('The Instructor'), *The Liverpool Critic* and *Y Tyst Cymreig* ('The Welsh Witness'): LP 336: 25 January, 26 March, 30 April, 25 August, 9 September, 21–2 October, 6, 24–5, 30 November, 5, 30 December 1876; 337: 27 January, 3, 10 February, 6 March 1877. For the Welsh titles, see Aled Gruffydd Jones, *Press, Politics and Society: A History of Journalism in Wales* (Cardiff, 1993), pp. 120–1, 133–4; Huw Walters, 'The periodical press to 1914', in Philip Henry Jones and Eiluned Rees (eds), *A Nation and its Books: A History of the Book in Wales* (Aberystwyth, 1998), pp. 199, 204–5. Lloyd saw a prospectus for *Y Genedl Gymreig* on 3 January 1877 in the shop of Isaac Foulkes (1836–1904), the prominent Liverpool-Welsh publisher. Cf. J. E. Lloyd, revised R. Rhys, 'Foulkes, Isaac [*pseud.* Llyfrbryf] (1836– 1904)', *ODNB*.

75   Lloyd commented on his purchase of the score of Handel's *Messiah*: 'It is wonderful how cheaply the modern press turns out well-known and generally sought works.' LP 337: 16 January 1877.

76   LP 336: 19 February, 18 March, 4 April 1876; 337: 6, 21 March 1877. Grant: newspaper obituary preserved in BU, Bangor MS 13843; LP 18, letter, 9 September 1942, informing Lloyd that the *Liverpool Mercury*, 29 May 1877, had an announcement that 'on that day General Grant would be entertained to luncheon at the Town Hall and would be shown various objects of interest in the City, including St. George's Hall'.

2 Expanding Horizons: Aberystwyth and Oxford, 1877–1885

1   Cf. Peter Lambert, 'The professionalization and institutionalization of history', in Stefan Berger, Heiko Feldner and Kevin Passmore (eds), *Writing History: Theory and Practice* (London, 2003), pp. 42–51.

2   Aberystwyth's population in 1871 and 1881 was about 7,000: John Williams, *Digest of Welsh Historical Statistics*, vol. 1 ([Cardiff] 1985), p. 62.

3   For the foundation and early years of the college, see Ellis, *UCW*, chapters 1–2.

4   *UCW Cal. 1878–9*, p. 21; Ellis, *UCW*, p. 48.

5   *UCW Cal. 1879–80*, p. 19; J. E. Lloyd, 'A retrospect, 1877–1881', in Iwan Morgan (ed.), *The College by the Sea* (Aberystwyth, 1928), pp. 70–1.

6   J. Gwynn Williams, *The University Movement in Wales* (Cardiff, 1993), p. 61.

7   Edward Lloyd to J. E. Lloyd, 24 January 1878, LP 19. For Edwards, see *DWB*, pp. 197–8.

8   Cf. Ellis, *UCW*, p. 57. Later Lloyd clearly saw the founding of the college as a turning point in Welsh education: J. E. Lloyd, 'Addysg uwchraddol yng Nghymru', *Y Traethodydd*, 55 (1900), 69–70.

9   Ellis, *UCW*, pp. 10–19, 43–4, 61; Gwyn A. Williams, 'Ambiguous hero: Hugh Owen and Liberal Wales', in idem, *The Welsh in their History* (London, 1982), pp. 151–70; J. Gwynn Williams, 'Owen, Sir Hugh (1804–1881)', *ODNB*. Members of the council are identified in the list of the college's court of governors in *UCW Cal. 1877–8*, pp. 17–18.

10   *DWB*, pp. 197–8; D. Densil Morgan, *Lewis Edwards* (Cardiff, 2009), pp. 177–87, 221. Cf. H. S. Jones, 'Pattison, Mark (1813–1884)', *ODNB*; idem, *Intellect and Character in Victorian England: Mark Pattison and the Invention of the Don* (Cambridge, 2007); Peter Hinchcliff and John Prest, 'Jowett, Benjamin (1817–1893)', *ODNB*.

11   T. C. E[dwards], 'Introductory', *UCW Mag.*, 1 (1878–9), 4.

12   Mark Pattison, 'An address to the students', *UCW Cal. 1877–8*, pp. 23–31 (quotation at p. 27).

13 Ibid., p. [2]; Matthew Arnold, *Schools and Universities on the Continent* (1868), in *The Complete Prose Works of Matthew Arnold*, vol. IV, ed. R. H. Super (Ann Arbor, MI, 1960–77), p. 332.

14 *UCW Cal. 1877–8*, pp. 39, 41–4.

15 Ellis, *UCW*, pp. 50–1. See also Thomas Parry, 'Daniel Silvan Evans, 1818–1903', *THSC*, 1981, 109–25.

16 *UCW Cal. 1877–8*, pp. 5–16; *DWB*, p. 295. The inclusion only of Welsh-men is praised in T. E. E[llis], 'The college calendar', *UCW Mag.*, 1 (1878–9), 171. By contrast, the newspaper published in Aberystwyth was more cosmopolitan in the people and events it commemorated: *The Cambrian News Almanack for the Year 1878*.

17 H. N. Grimley, 'How to spend the vacation', *UCW Mag.*, 1 (1878–9), 184–9.

18 Ellis, *UCW*, pp. 38–40.

19 T. C. E[dwards], 'A nation's wish', *UCW Mag.*, 3 (1880–1), 107.

20 *UCW Cal. 1877–8*, p. 83; *UCW Cal. 1878–9*, pp. 71, 75; *UCW Cal. 1879–80*, p. 80; LP 25. For the matriculation examination, see John Roach, *Public Examinations in England 1850–1900* (Cambridge, 1971), p. 261.

21 Edward Lloyd to J. E. Lloyd, 24 January 1878, LP 19.

22 His diary shows that Lloyd did not return to the college after Easter 1881: LP 248. Compare how Tom Ellis, after passing the London matriculation, prepared for Oxford by focusing primarily on the classical languages and English literature: T. F. Roberts, 'Gyrfa athrofaol y diweddar Mr. Thomas Ellis', *Y Traethodydd*, 54 (1899), 269–70.

23 Jenkins, 'Lloyd', 81; LP 23; 248: 1, 5 December 1881; *The Examination Statutes . . . Revised to the End of Trinity Term, 1882* (Oxford, 1882), pp. 16–17.

24 *UCW Cal. 1877–8*, pp. 42–3; *UCW Cal. 1878–9*, pp. xxiii–xlvii. Some of the pages on the 'Cymdeithas Lenyddol Gymreig' in LP 19 (discussed below, p. 33) contain, on the back, notes on Goethe's verse drama *Iphigenie auf Tauris*, one of the set texts for the German paper in 1878.

25 Aberystwyth University, UW A/D/M6/14; Ellis, *UCW*, p. 171.

26 Lloyd, 'Yr iaith Gymraeg', *Y Dysgedydd*, 59 (1880), 116. Lloyd was among the six or so who attended these lectures, and was subsequently deemed sufficiently expert to take over the Welsh teaching after Evans's resignation: *Thomas Charles Edwards Letters*, ed. T. I. Ellis (Aberystwyth, 1952–3), p. 241 (no. 418); see below, pp. 45, 50.

27 LP 19–20, 25.

28 J. E. L[loyd], 'The rise of periodical literature in Wales', *UCW Mag.*, 1 (1878–9), 32–7; idem, 'Two Welsh prose authors of the XVIIIth century', ibid., 246–52.

29 Lloyd, 'Rise of periodical literature', 33. He largely endorsed this view ten years later in idem, 'Some characteristics of modern Welsh poetry', *UCW Mag.*, 11 (1888–9), 242.

30 J. E. L[loyd], 'The Welsh romance', *UCW Mag.*, 3 (1880–1), 66–70.
31 J. E. Lloyd, 'Athrylith y Celt', *Cenad Hedd*, 1 (1881), 179–81, 335–9; idem, 'Yr iaith Gymraeg', 114–17. Cf. above, p. 7.
32 Roberts, 'Gyrfa athrofaol', 273.
33 Ibid.; Edward Anwyl, review of *HW*, *Y Brython*, 13 April 1911; J. Hugh Edwards, *The Life of David Lloyd George, with a Short History of the Welsh People*, vol. I (London [1913]), p. 243.
34 LP 19; Lloyd, 'Retrospect', p. 71, n. *.
35 [W. Nicholson] to Lloyd, 4 October 1877, LP 19; notes in Welsh of sermons at Aberystwyth, 9 January 1879–7 March 1880, LP 337. Miles (1841–1914) was minister of Baker Street chapel 1873–1907: R. Tudur Jones, *Yr Undeb: Hanes Undeb yr Annibynwyr Cymraeg, 1872–1972* (Swansea, 1975), p. 152, n. 5.
36 Edward Lloyd to J. E. Lloyd, 24 January 1878, LP 19.
37 Lloyd recorded that his first sermon, on Matt. 13:58, was given at Grove Street, 5 January 1879: LP 25, 337.
38 Lloyd, 'Retrospect', pp. 71–2. Residence: *UCW Cal. 1880–1*, p. 23; R. W. Genese, 'When the college was residential', in Morgan (ed.), *College by the Sea*, pp. 73–6. For the latter episode, see *Cambrian News*, 20 June 1879; Ellis, *UCW*, pp. 58–60.
39 *UCW Mag.*, 1 (1878–9), 95; 2 (1879–80), 37–8, 136–7, 183–4, 223–31 (esp. 230–1); 3 (1880–1), 146–7, 196–7.
40 Ibid., 1 (1878–9), 51; 2 (1879–80), 281–3; 3 (1880–1), 98–101. In March 1881 he supported another motion in favour of the continuation of the Welsh language at the debating society of the English Congregational chapel in Portland Street: LP 248: 17 March 1881; text of speech in LP 77.
41 *UCW Mag.*, 3 (1880–1), 104; LP 19; 248: 8 March 1881; Lloyd, 'Retrospect', p. 72. For the controversy surrounding Parry, see also Ellis, *UCW*, pp. 55–6.
42 Lawrence Stone, 'The size and composition of the Oxford student body 1580–1909', in idem (ed.), *The University in Society*, vol. I (Princeton, NJ, 1974), pp. 65–9. Ibid., pp. 91, 95 (tables 1, 4), show that the number of annual matriculants in the decade 1880–9 averaged at 766, of which 592 (77 per cent) obtained BAs four years later.
43 Fees at Aberystwyth were £10, and the charge for boarding in college £35 (plus fuel), per session: *UCW Cal. 1877–8*, p. 33; *UCW Cal. 1880–1*, p. 25; Genese, 'When the college was residential', p. 74. By contrast, a surviving battels bill from March 1883 shows that Lloyd paid Lincoln College £29 9s. 9d for ten weeks of tuition and residence (including fuel and the services of a laundress, but not meals) in the first quarter of 1883, and apparently £27 19s. 3d for the previous quarter, suggesting a total for three terms of about £85: LP 23. Allowing for a modest increase in costs, this tallies quite closely with the charges of £90–£100 at Lincoln

by the 1890s: Vivian Green, *The Commonwealth of Lincoln College, 1427–1977* (Oxford, 1979), pp. 588–9.

44 Green, *Commonwealth of Lincoln College*, pp. 480, 492–3; M. C. Curthoys, 'The colleges in the new era', in M. G. Brock and M. C. Curthoys (eds), *The History of the University of Oxford. Volume VII: Nineteenth-Century Oxford, Part 2* (Oxford, 2000), p. 123; J. R. de S. Honey and M. C. Curthoys, 'Oxford and schooling', in ibid., pp. 551–2.

45 Green, *Commonwealth of Lincoln College*, pp. 480, 649; M. C. Curthoys and Janet Howarth, 'Origins and destinations: the social mobility of Oxford men and women', in Brock and Curthoys (eds), *The History of the University of Oxford*, pp. 578–80.

46 J. E. Lloyd, 'Cymry yn Rhydychen – atgofion o'r blynyddoedd 1881–1885', *Yr Eurgrawn*, 135 (1943), 17; LP 249: 16 February, 15–17 June 1882; 251: 20 May 1884. See J. E. L[loyd], 'Oxford letter', *UCW Mag.*, 6 (1883–4), 271–2; see above, p. 16.

47 LP 248: 23 October, 7, 9, 12 November 1881; 249: 15 February, 14 March, 1 May 1882.

48 R. H. D[avies], 'Yr Athro J. E. Lloyd, M.A., D.Litt., Bangor', *Y Dysgedydd*, 113 (1933), 164–5 ('y mae ei leferydd a'i feddyliau yn ei gyhuddo o fod wedi ei fwydo yn ei [sc. Oxford] hawyrgylch'). See also de S. Honey and Curthoys, 'Oxford and schooling', pp. 548–9; Edwards, *Life of David Lloyd George*, p. 248.

49 W. Silvanus Jones, 'Our Oxford letter', *UCW Mag.*, 5 (1882–3), 153–4; Curthoys, 'Colleges in the new era', pp. 139–41.

50 LP 251: January–April 1884. For example, in January Lloyd attended meetings in support of the college at Aberystwyth and Welsh disestablishment: Lloyd to T. E. Ellis, 8 February 1884, NLW, T. E. Ellis Papers 1431. The college still expected Lloyd to pay room rent while non-resident as he had given short notice of his absence: W. Warde Fowler to Lloyd, 19 January 1884, LP 22. See also W. S. Jones to Lloyd, 13 March 1884, ibid. Eisteddfod: 'Official list of subjects, second issue' (Liverpool, 1884), LP 23; Lloyd, 'History of Wales'.

51 J. E. L[loyd], '"The Blind Harper," by Ceiriog, in English verse', *UCW Mag.*, 4 (1881–2), 122–4; idem, 'A word about prose-writing', ibid., 265–8; idem, 'Welsh words for three of Schubert's songs', ibid., 5 (1882–3), 66–8; idem, 'Oxford letter', 269–72.

52 LP 25; 249: 1 June 1882 ('Began "History of Welsh Literature"'). As Lloyd noted (LP 25), the prize was won by Gweirydd ap Rhys. The last of four notebooks in Welsh used in compiling material for the essay (LP 26–9) ends with incomplete drafts of a discussion of 'Y Traddodiadau Cymreig a Thaliesin', which bear resemblances to John Edward Lloyd, 'Taliesin Ben Beirdd', *Y Geninen*, 2 (1884), 145–8; 3 (1885), 65–9.

53 Lloyd, 'Cymry yn Rhydychen', 13–18. For the end of the ACC, see also W. S. Jones, 'Our Oxford letter', *UCW Mag.*, 6 (1883–4), 80

(12 December 1883); LP 24 ('ACC formed May 1881 (18 members) collapsed – end of 1883?').

54 E. Morgan Humphreys, *Gwŷr Enwog Gynt: Argraffiadau ac Atgofion Personol* (n.p., 1950), p. 78.

55 NLW MS 877 C (minutes of the ACC); LP 80.

56 Ellis 'showed a sound judgment and an appreciation of the purpose of an Oxford education': Lloyd to W. J. Gruffydd, 21 July 1942, NLW, W. J. Gruffydd Papers, 542. See also Lloyd, 'Cymry yn Rhydychen', 16.

57 L[loyd], 'Oxford letter', 271. See also LP 248: 23 October 1881.

58 Peter Hinchcliff, 'Religious issues, 1870–1914', in Brock and Curthoys (eds), *The History of the University of Oxford*, p. 103 and n. 30.

59 Lloyd, 'Cymry yn Rhydychen', 15; LP 248: 16 October 1881; 249: 6 June 1882; 250: 4 February 1883; 251: 11 May 1884; 337 (notes of sermons). Lloyd also attended meetings of the Wesley Guild, a literary society which Hughes founded: LP 251: 7 June, 15 November, 4 December. 1884. See, further, Christopher Oldstone-Moore, *Hugh Price Hughes: Founder of a New Methodism, Conscience of a New Nonconformity* (Cardiff, 1999), esp. pp. 90–106. Lloyd also heard the Americans Dwight Moody and Ira Sankey during their revivalist mission to Oxford: LP 249: 16, 19 November 1882; cf. Curthoys, 'Colleges in the new era', p. 139.

60 LP 248: 22 November 1881; 249: 27 January, 25 March, 21 April, 6 June, 20 October, 5 November 1882. Oxford, Mansfield College Library Archives, minute book of Oxford University Nonconformists' Union, 1–5, 8, 10, 12, 19–20. Quotation: Jones, 'Our Oxford letter', 82. See also T. I. Ellis, 'Rhydychen yn yr wythdegau', *Y Llenor*, 21 (1942), 28, 30; Hinchcliff, 'Religious issues', p. 103; Elaine Kay, 'Horton, Robert Forman (1855–1934)', *ODNB*.

61 LP 78 (16 May 1882), 82 (11 November 1883).

62 LP 249: 5, 8 December 1882. Cf. W. H. Walsh, 'The zenith of Greats', in Brock and Curthoys (eds), *The History of the University of Oxford*, pp. 318–23; Morgan, *WBP*, p. 70; Alon Kadish, 'Toynbee, Arnold (1852–1883)', *ODNB*.

63 T. Hughes to Lloyd, 25 March 1883, LP 23; ibid. 251: 18 October 1884. Cf. Jones, 'Our Oxford letter' (1882–3), 154–5; Tim Hilton, *John Ruskin: The Later Years* (New Haven, CT/London, 2000), pp. 456–60, 492–7.

64 LP 251: 9 May, 11 November 1884. By March 1885 this seems to have been renamed, or replaced by, the Pattison Society: LP 252: 28 January, 14 March 1885.

65 LP 249: 27 April, 19 October, 30 November 1882; 251: 12 June 1884. For opposition to vivisection, see e.g. 'Vivisection in Oxford. Convocation of the University, 2 p.m., Tuesday, Feb. 5, 1884', Bodleian Library, G. A. Oxon. b. 140 (4).

66 LP 251: 8 May 1884; Lloyd, 'Oxford letter', 270. For the statute passed in Convocation on 29 April 1884, see Bodleian Library, G. A. Oxon.

b. 140 (4), and discussion in Janet Howarth, "'In Oxford but . . . not of Oxford": the women's colleges', in Brock and Curthoys (eds), *The History of the University of Oxford*, pp. 256–7.

67 LP 23; *OU Cal. 1883*, p. 134; *OU Cal. 1884*, p. 143 and n. 2.

68 Jenkins, 'Lloyd', 81.

69 Percy M. Wallace to Lloyd, 8 July 1883, LP 21.

70 *The Examination Statutes . . . Revised to June 30, 1881* (Oxford, 1881), pp. 20–1, 30–3; W. S. Jones to Lloyd, n.d., LP 21; W. Warde Fowler to Lloyd, 17 July 1883, ibid. See also Richard Jenkyns, 'Classical studies, 1872–1914', in Brock and Curthoys (eds), *The History of the University of Oxford*, p. 327.

71 Warde Fowler to Lloyd, 17 July 1883, LP 21. Cf. Green, *Commonwealth of Lincoln College*, pp. 518–22.

72 For the Oxford history school at this period, see Peter R. H. Slee, *Learning and a Liberal Education: The Study of Modern History in the Universities of Oxford, Cambridge and Manchester, 1800–1914* (Manchester, 1986), chapter 6; Reba N. Soffer, 'Nation, duty, character and confidence: history at Oxford, 1850–1914', *Historical Journal*, 30 (1987), 77–104; eadem, *Discipline and Power: The University, History, and the Making of an English Elite, 1870–1930* (Stanford, CA, 1994); eadem, 'Modern history', in Brock and Curthoys (eds), *The History of the University of Oxford*, pp. 361–84. Figures for finalists: *OU Cal. 1883*, p. 75 (98), *OU Cal. 1884*, p. 78 (74), *OU Cal. 1885*, p. 81 (68), *OU Cal. 1886*, p. 247 (96), *OU Cal. 1887*, p. 250 (98), *OU Cal. 1888*, p. 254 (108).

73 *The Examination Statutes . . . Revised to the End of Trinity Term, 1883* (Oxford, 1883), pp. 84–9; *Oxford University Examination Papers. Second Public Examination. Honour School of Modern History. Trinity Term, 1885* (Oxford, 1885). Lloyd's choice of special subject may be inferred from the close correspondence with the honours course on 'The Age of the Renaissance' (1453–1527) he later taught at Bangor, whose set texts, like those of the Oxford course, included works by Commynes, Villeneuve and Machiavelli: ibid., p. 87; see below, p. 56.

74 Although new regulations had come into force after Lloyd completed the course in 1885, its content remained essentially the same: *The Examination Statutes . . . Revised to the End of Trinity Term, 1884* (Oxford, 1884), pp. 95–101.

75 C. R. L. F[letcher], 'Honour school of modern history', Bodleian Library, G. A. Oxon b. 140 (4), discussed in Slee, *Learning and a Liberal Education*, pp. 102–5 (where the document is mistakenly attributed to Charles Firth). Cf. C. H. K. Marten, revised Richard Symons, 'Fletcher, Charles Robert Leslie (1857–1934)', *ODNB*.

76 Slee, *Learning and a Liberal Education*, pp. 88–9, 95–101; Soffer, 'Modern history', pp. 372–4.

77 Charles Oman, *Memories of Victorian Oxford and of Some Early Years* (London, 1941), p. 105; Slee, *Learning and a Liberal Education*, p. 109.

78 In contrast to Tom Ellis, who appears with Stubbs in a photograph of the Modern History Society in the winter of 1882–3: Oman, *Memories*, facing p. 106. Lloyd, 'Oxford letter', 270–1, reported Stubbs's last lecture on 8 May 1884, but at second hand.

79 Lloyd to O. M. Edwards, 16 February [?1889], NLW, Sir O. M. Edwards Papers, AG/4/16.

80 Jones to Lloyd, 25 January 1888, LP 314, no. 246. Jones obtained a third in modern history: *OU Cal. 1890*, p. 258.

81 LP 232 (testimonial of Richard Lodge, 28 June 1891).

82 See esp. below, pp. 108, 157.

83 Soffer, 'Nation', 80–1, 84–6; eadem, 'Modern history', p. 373.

84 Slee, *Learning and a Liberal Education*, pp. 90–1, 109 (quotation at p. 90); Soffer, *Discipline and Power*, pp. 140–2.

85 Soffer, 'Modern history', pp. 380–1.

86 LP 252: 2, 31 March 1885; Lloyd, 'History of Wales'.

87 Owen M. Edwards, 'An Oxford letter', *UCW Mag.*, 7 (1884–5), 269–70. For Freeman's fierce criticism of J. A. Froude (1818–94), see Rosemary Jann, *The Art and Science of Victorian History* (Columbus, OH, 1985), pp. 135–6.

88 Edwards, 'Oxford letter', 269.

89 Paul Frédéricq, *The Study of History in England and Scotland*, trans. Henrietta Leonard, Johns Hopkins Studies in Historical and Political Science, 5th ser., 10 (Baltimore, MD, 1887), pp. 32–48, 50–4; quotation at p. 51.

90 LP 232 (testimonial of Richard Lodge, 28 June 1891).

91 Idris Foster, 'Sir John Rhŷs', in D. Ellis Evans, John G. Griffith and E. M. Jope (eds), *Proceedings of the Seventh International Congress of Celtic Studies, Oxford, 1983* (Oxford, 1986), pp. 10–14.

92 LP 249 (1882 diary); Lloyd, 'History of Wales', pp. 354, 359; 'Adjudication of Professor John Rhys, M.A.', ibid., p. 339.

93 LP 251: 23, 30 November 1884.

94 David N. Klausner, 'Evans, John Gwenogvryn (1852–1930)', *ODNB*.

95 Ellis, *UCW*, p. 84. Cf. *Thomas Charles Edwards Letters*, ed. Ellis, p. 233, no. 403 (Lloyd to Edwards, 26 December 1884).

96 *UCW Cal. 1885–6*, p. 29; testimonial of Richard Lodge, 28 June 1891, LP 232: 'I think I am justified in saying that he was quite the best man of his year.'

97 I. Edwards J[ones?] to Lloyd, 7 July 1885, LP 22. By contrast, W. Warde Fowler's congratulations praised the example set for other Lincoln men in history: Fowler to Lloyd, 10 July 1885, ibid.

98 Hazel Davies, *O. M. Edwards* (Cardiff, 1988), pp. 19–20, 23, 38. See also J. E. Caerwyn Williams, 'Cenedlaetholdeb haneswyr Cymru gynnar

Rhydychen', in Geraint H. Jenkins (ed.), *Cof Cenedl XIII: Ysgrifau ar Hanes Cymru* (Llandysul, 1998), pp. 1–32.

3 *Towards* A History of Wales, *1885–1911*

1. LP 252: 24–30 October 1885; 253: 26–30 October, 3 November 1886; O. M. Edwards to Lloyd, n.d. [1885 or 1886], LP 314, no. 90; Richard Lodge to Lloyd, 10 October 1886, ibid., no. 284.
2. Lloyd's salary at Aberystwyth was initially £45 a term: Aberystwyth University Archives, Council Minutes, C/MN/2.
3. Ellis, *UCW*, pp. 66–70, 71–2, 74–84; J. Gwynn Williams, *The University Movement in Wales* (Cardiff, 1993), chapter IV, esp. pp. 65–70, 78, 81–3.
4. Thomas Jones, 'College memories: Aberystwyth in the nineties', in idem, *Leeks and Daffodils* (Newtown, 1942), p. 6; Ellis, *UCW*, pp. 88–9; Williams, *University Movement*, pp. 99–101; LP 234.
5. *UCW Cal. 1885–6*, p. 32.
6. Ibid., pp. 25–6, 29. In 1889 the grant was made permanent, and the college received its charter: Ellis, *UCW*, p. 94.
7. The number rose to 177 in 1888: *UCW Cal. 1889–90*, p. 26.
8. C. H. Herford, 'Impressions of Aberystwyth, 1887–1901', in Iwan Morgan (ed.), *The College by the Sea* (Aberystwyth, 1928), p. 96.
9. LP 207; 254: 15 April 1887; 255: 4–6 January 1888; 256: 14 June, 28 August 1889; Morgan, *WBP*, pp. 98–104; J. R. Webster, 'The Welsh Intermediate Education Act of 1889', in Owen E. Jones (ed.), *The Welsh Intermediate Education Act of 1889: A Centenary Appraisal* ([Cardiff] 1989), pp. 11–26.
10. D. Isaac Davies to Lloyd, 2 April 1887, LP 314 no. 50; LP 256: 11, 24, 31 May 1889; J. E. Lloyd, 'Cymdeithas yr Iaith Gymraeg: trem ar hanes y mudiad', *Y Llenor*, 10 (1931), 207–14; J. Elwyn Hughes, *Arloeswr Dwyieithedd: Dan Isaac Davies 1839–1887* (Cardiff, 1984).
11. *UCW Cal. 1885–6*, p. 63; LP 232 (ninety extension lectures to groups across west and mid Wales by the summer of 1891). His diaries show that Lloyd preached most weeks while at Aberystwyth, including twenty-five new sermons: LP 325 nos 12–20; 326 nos 5–20.
12. LP 325 no. 11 (1885); 326 no. 5 (1886); 221, pp. 12–14 (1932); Jenkins, 'Lloyd', 84.
13. *UCW Cal. 1885–6*, pp. 41–6; *UCW Mag.* 8, 1 (November 1885), 37.
14. *UCW Cal. 1886–7*, p. 55; *UCW Cal. 1887–8*, p. 56. For example, at the end of Michaelmas term 1888, the elementary paper for the junior class extended from the Anglo-Saxons to Oliver Cromwell and also included questions on place-names and geography, while the four advanced papers for the intermediate and senior classes were divided chronologically in to periods that between them covered 1558–1740: *UCW Cal. 1889–90*, pp. 59, xiii–xvii, lxxviii–lxxix.

15   T. R. Dawes, 'Aberystwyth in '85 – or life in the Queen's Hotel '85', in
     Morgan (ed.), *College by the Sea*, p. 83.
16   *UCW Cal. 1885–6*, pp. 25–6, 29.
17   Lloyd to T. C. Edwards, 27 April 1885, in T. I. Ellis (ed.), *Thomas Charles
     Edwards Letters* (Aberystwyth, 1952–3), p. 241 (no. 418); *UCW Cal.
     1885–6*, pp. 50–1; *UCW Cal. 1886–7*, pp. 52–3, xcvi–xcvii, clvi.
18   *UCW Cal. 1887–8*, pp. 57, xli–xlii, xcix–c, cxli–cii; *UCW Cal. 1888–9*,
     pp. 50, cxi–cxii; *UCW Cal. 1889–90*, pp. 60, xcv, clxviii–clxix, ccviii.
19   Teaching hours: *UCW Cal. 1885–6*, pp. 50–2; *UCW Cal. 1886–7*,
     pp. 54–5, 68; *UCW Cal. 1888–9*, pp. 49–50, 63–4; *UCW Cal. 1889–90*,
     pp. 59–60.
20   J. E. Lloyd, 'Ffurfiad y genedl Gymreig. (Cyfres o ddarlithiau ar hanes
     y Cymry, o'r bummed hyd y ddeuddegfed ganrif.)', *Y Geninen*, 4 (1886),
     264–70; idem, 'How England and Wales became united', *TLWNS*, 1886–
     7, 83–99.
21   'List', 97; *UCW Mag.*, 12 (1889–90), 26; 14 (1891–2), 201.
22   J. E. Lloyd, 'The personal name-system in Old Welsh', *Y Cymmrodor*, 9
     (1888), 39–55; idem, 'Welsh place-names: a study of some common name-
     elements (with notes by the editor [Egerton Phillimore])', ibid., 11 (1892),
     15–60; Hubert Lewis, *The Ancient Laws of Wales*, ed. J. E. Lloyd (London,
     1889). See also J. E. Lloyd, 'Law and lawyers among the ancient Welsh',
     TLWNS, 1890–1, 96–113; idem, *Early Welsh Agriculture* (Bangor, 1894).
23   Lloyd to Thomas Richards, 8 September 1903, BU, Bangor MS 16717.
     Lloyd also corresponded with J. Gwenogvryn Evans concerning manu-
     scripts of the laws: Evans to Lloyd, 25 July 1889, 31 July 1899, LP 314,
     no. 155; NLW, T. I. Ellis Papers F29.
24   See below, pp. 142–3.
25   J. E. Lloyd, 'Some characteristics of modern Welsh poetry', *UCW Mag.*,
     11 (1888–9), 241–9; cf. ibid., 263, 309–10.
26   LP 256: 13 December 1889; *UCW Cal. 1885–6*, pp. 82–3; *UCW Cal.
     1886–7*, pp. 96–7; *UCW Cal. 1887–8*, p. 100; *UCW Cal. 1888–9*, p. 94.
27   LP 253: 15 December 1886; BU, Bangor MSS 21062–4; *UCW Cal. 1886–
     7*, p. 95; *UCW Cal. 1885–6*, p. 98; *UCW Cal. 1888–9*, p. 92; *UCW Cal.
     1892–3*, p. 168.
28   *UCW Mag.*, 14 (1891–2), 253–4; J. E. Lloyd, 'Mendelssohn's "St. Paul."',
     ibid., 219.
29   LP 252: 19 November 1885; 253: 13 February 1886; 258: 24 November
     1891. Tennis: LP 253: 8 May 1886; 254: 10, 25 May 1887; 255: 31 May,
     7 June 1888.
30   *UCW Cal. 1892–3*, pp. 187–9; LP 339 (class book 1887–8, 1888–9). Perhaps
     this relationship explains Lloyd's decision to spend a holiday in Scotland
     in August 1890 (though this does not seem to have taken him to Aber-
     deen): LP 257: 11–26 August 1890. Tina first appears in Lloyd's diaries
     when she visited him late in 1891, and he noted her birthday the following
     year: ibid. 258: 19 December 1891; 259: 17 February 1892.

31   Ellis, *UCW*, pp. 99–100; LP 232.

32   LP 233, esp. Lloyd's letters to his brother-in-law W. R. Owen; 259: 3 March, 20 April 1892; *UCNW Mag.*, 1, 4 (June 1892), 4, 37. Cf. *UCW Mag.*, 14 (1891–2), 201, 260; Williams, *UCNW*, p. 104.

33   J. E. Lloyd, 'Sir Harry Reichel 1856–1931', in idem (ed.), *Sir Harry Reichel 1856–1931: A Memorial Volume* (Cardiff, 1934), pp. 1–28, esp. p. 10.

34   John Williams, *Digest of Welsh Historical Statistics*, vol. 1 ([Cardiff] 1985), pp. 62–3; above, p. 14. (In 1891 the population of Aberystwyth was 6,725, that of Bangor 9,892.)

35   *UCNW Mag.*, 2, 1 (December 1892), 3; Williams, *UCNW*, p. 119.

36   Williams, *Univ. Wales*, pp. 9–12. However, preparation for London continued at Bangor until the end of the 1897–8 session: Lloyd, 'Sir Harry Reichel', p. 17.

37   Aberystwyth University Archives, Council Minutes, C/MN/2, show that by the time he left Aberystwyth Lloyd's salary was £66 13s. 4d per term, with additional payments of £1 1s. for each extension lecture; Williams, *UCNW*, p. 60, n. 134; LP 341 (1894–7 accounts).

38   LP 260: 14 February–2 March 1893.

39   *UCNW Mag.*, 2, 1 (December 1892), 3: 'ar neges bwysig dros ben'.

40   NLW MS 8843E, no. 7; LP 341; LP 264: 25 November 1897.

41   LP 271: 14 January (move), 24 September (birth) 1904; Bangor MS 20176 (family Bible).

42   'Family notes', back of LP 303 (1936 diary). Electric light was installed in 1921.

43   LP 341 (1894–5). The piano cost £40, and the servant's wages were raised from £14 to £15 per annum in September 1894. While only four account books survive (ibid. 341–4), covering 1894–7, 1910–14, 1917–21, 1945–7, presumably Lloyd also kept them for the intervening years.

44   LP 261: 9–10 August 1894; 262: 16–28 August 1895; 263: 12 August 1896; 265: 11, 20 August 1898; 273: 24 August–11 September 1906; 274: 2–14 September 1907; 276: 3–4 August 1909; 277: 8–20 September 1910; 329; 345, pp. 33–6, 61–7.

45   LP 273: 12 February, 28 June, 25 July 1906; 274: 17 December 1907; 276: 27 March 1909; 341 (tennis netting: 1896–7 accounts), 342 (golf club: 1910–11 accounts).

46   LP 264: 16 May 1897; 276: 9, 23 May 1909; *UCNW Mag.*, 14, 1 (December 1904), 52; ibid., 18, 1 (December 1908), 59; ibid., 19, 1 (December 1909), 56; J. Glyn Davies to Lloyd, asking him to set out 'Why am I a Total Abstainer?', 4 January 1911, LP 314, no. 59.

47   *UCNW Mag.*, 9, 2 (March 1900), 48; 12, 1 (December 1902), 48; 13, 1 (December 1903), 46; 15, 1 (December 1905), 43; 18, 1 (December 1908), 57; LP 271: 11 January 1904; 272: 24 November 1905; David Jenkins, *Thomas Gwynn Jones: Cofiant* (2nd edn, Denbigh, 1994), pp. 100–1, 124– 30. The Students' Welsh National Society, founded in 1897, was

renamed the Cymric Society in 1899: *UCNW Mag.*, 7, 1 (December 1897), 61; 9, 1 (December 1899), 51.
48 J. E. L[loyd], 'St. David's Day', *UCNW Mag.*, 11, 1 (March 1902), 34–5.
49 For the date, see LP 268: 26 January 1901; 212 (a detailed chronology of progress on the book extending to ch. XX, §2, 5 March 1909); and the manuscript copy of *HW* in NLW MS 15701, fol. 1v.
50 Anon, 'Cymry'r colegau', *Cymru Fydd*, 1 (1888), 309; W. Warde Fowler to Lloyd, 3 June 1888, 8 May 1893, LP 314 nos 171, 174; H. W. C. Davis to Lloyd, 25 March 1899, ibid., no. 67.
51 *UCNW Mag.*, 9, 1 (December 1899), 37–8; Lloyd, 'Sir Harry Reichel', p. 16.
52 Lloyd was still open to new opportunities, though, as in October 1901 he made an unsuccessful application to be principal of the university college in Cardiff: LP 234.
53 [O. M. Edwards], 'Patriotism and pedantry', *Wales*, 2 (1895), 55.
54 *UCNW Cal. 1895–6*, pp. 68–9, 71–2. Later it was usually called 'History of Wales to the Act of Union': e.g., *UCNW Cal. 1897–8*, pp. 68–9; *UCNW Cal. 1901–2*, pp. 83–4.
55 Edwards to Lloyd, 26 October 1896, LP 314 no. 77.
56 *UCNW Cal. 1895–6*, p. 72; *UCNW Cal. 1929–30*, p. 130.
57 For the latter, see above, pp. 40 and 219, n. 73.
58 Rees was appointed in December 1909: *UCNW Mag.*, 19, 2 (March 1910), 47. Lloyd sang his praises in a letter to Tout, 17 December 1909, Tout Papers 1/721/8.
59 *UCNW Cal. 1910–11*, pp. 152–4; *UCNW Cal. 1911–12*, pp. 155–7; *UCNW Cal. 1913–14*, pp. 158–60.
60 Thomas Richards, 'Syr John Lloyd: atgofion amdano', *Y Llenor*, 25 (1947), 67–8 (my translation).
61 *UCNW Cal. 1901–2*, pp. 83–4.
62 Lloyd to O. M. Edwards, 29 March 1904, NLW, Sir O. M. Edwards Papers AG1/23/69.
63 Ibid.
64 Williams, *UCNW*, pp. 120–1; Peter R. H. Slee, *Learning and a Liberal Education: The Study of Modern History in the Universities of Oxford, Cambridge and Manchester, 1800–1914* (Manchester, 1986), pp. 128–49.
65 F. York Powell, *The Study of History in Universities: An Address Delivered at the Closing Ceremony of the Session 1901–2, June 20th, 1902* (Bangor, n.d.), p. 7; LP 269: 20 June 1902.
66 T. F. Tout, 'Schools of history', in *The Collected Papers of Thomas Frederick Tout*, vol. I (Manchester, 1932), pp. 93–109, esp. pp. 101–2; Lloyd to Tout, 2 June 1906, Tout Papers 1/721/3. See also Slee, *Learning and a Liberal Education*, pp. 141–2, 153–64.
67 Although Hubert Hall, at the Public Record Office, associated the universities of London, Manchester and Wales with training in historical research, including palaeography and diplomatic, it is unclear how far

this applied to Bangor, where only twenty students took the University of Wales MA between 1893 and 1907: Hall to Lloyd, 28 January 1909, LP 314 no. 210; Williams, *UCNW*, pp. 121–2. See also Williams, *Univ. Wales*, p. 46 and, for later developments, below, pp. 69–71.

68 Thomas to Lloyd, 27 August 1892, LP 314 no. 534. For further correspondence, with Thomas and also the *DNB*'s editor Sidney Lee, see ibid., nos 266, 535–7.

69 'List', 104–5. He published a further ten articles in the *DNB*'s second supplement (1912): ibid., 105.

70 LP 221, pp. 2, 31; 258: 7 August 1891; 259: 20 July 1892; W. Roberts to Lloyd, 26 February, 8 March 1894 (with enclosure), LP 314 nos 502–4.

71 Lloyd, *Llyfr Cyntaf*; idem, *Ail Lyfr*; idem, *Trydydd Llyfr*; English text of all three volumes reprinted as idem, *Outlines of the History of Wales for the Use of Schools and Colleges* (Caernarfon, 1906). Contracts: NLW MS 8843E, nos 4, 7.

72 LP 358. See also Edwards, 'Lloyd', 320, n. 2.

73 Cf. James Tait, 'Thomas Frederick Tout', *EHR*, 45 (1930), 79, 81. In 1896–7 Lloyd made £35 from the first two textbooks as well as £12 from the *DNB*, and in 1900 he was contracted to receive £45 for the third textbook: LP 341; NLW MS 8843E, no. 4.

74 Robert Smith, *Schools, Politics and Society: Elementary Education in Wales, 1870–1902* (Cardiff, 1999), p. 204.

75 LP 234; Lloyd, 'Cymdeithas yr Iaith', 209–11; Smith, *Schools, Politics and Society*, chapter 6.

76 Lloyd, 'Cymdeithas yr Iaith', 210; Morris Jones to Lloyd, 3 November [1896], LP 314 no. 253.

77 Lloyd, 'Cymdeithas yr Iaith', 211–14; LP 41A nos 1, 8.

78 T. E. Ellis, 'The duty of the Guild towards the literature and records of Wales', *Transactions of the Guild of Graduates of the University of Wales* (Second Annual Collegiate Meeting, UCNW, 17 October 1896), pp. 3–10; J. E. Lloyd, 'Proposals for the organization of the work of the Guild of Graduates of the University of Wales', ibid., pp. 11–14.

79 NLW MS 4498C; T. I. Ellis Papers F29.

80 Williams, *University Movement in Wales*, p. 412.

81 LP 264: 10, 15 March 1897. LP 91, 359 (manuscript and slides of the lecture).

82 Ellis to Lloyd, 13 May 1892, 24 November, 11 December 1893, LP 314 nos 116, 118–19.

83 J. E. Lloyd, 'Introduction', in Cambrian Archaeological Association, *A Hundred Years of Welsh Archaeology: Centenary Volume, 1846–1946*, ed. V. E. Nash-Williams (Gloucester, n.d.), pp. 18–23. Lloyd also adjudicated written competitions for the National Eisteddfod: Lloyd to O. M. Edwards, 20, 31 July, 10 August 1901, NLW, Sir O. M. Edwards Papers AG1/18/6, 16, 36; Lloyd to Edward Owen, 16, 24 August, 1 September 1910, NLW 18099C.

84   J. E. Lloyd, 'Wales and the coming of the Normans', *THSC*, 1899–1900, 122–79.

85   'List', 98; John Edward Lloyd, *Trem ar Hanes yr Anibynwyr yng Nghymru* (Cardiff [1909]); idem, *Carnarvonshire* (Cambridge, 1911). On the latter, see Huw Pryce, 'From the neolithic to nonconformity: J. E. Lloyd and the history of Caernarfonshire', *TCHS*, 66 (2005), 14–37.

86   R. T. Jenkins, 'Lloyd, Sir John Edward (1861–1947)', in idem, E. D. Jones and Brynley F. Roberts (eds), *The Dictionary of Welsh Biography, 1941–1970* (London, 2001), p. 172.

87   The multifarious duties of the Bangor secretary and registrar are listed in the conditions of appointment for the post, 17 February 1892: LP 233.

88   LP 269: 4 July, 5 November 1902; Williams, *UCNW*, pp. 263, 285.

89   LP 269: 30 April 1902; 212; *HW*, I, chapters II–III.

90   LP 212; *HW*, II, pp. 564–72; Williams, *UCNW*, pp. 259–60.

91   Lloyd to Tout, 14 December 1909, Tout Papers 1/721/7; Lloyd to his parents, 14 December 1909, LP 353; LP 277: 9 January 1910.

92   Lloyd to Tout, 25 February 1911, Tout Papers, 1/721/9.

93   LP 278: 2 February 1911; Lloyd to his parents, 25 February 1911, LP 354 (quotation). See also Lloyd, 'Sir Harry Reichel', p. 19.

94   Williams, *UCNW*, pp. 275–6, 281–5; John S. Ellis, *Investiture: Royal Ceremony and National Identity in Wales, 1911–1969* (Cardiff, 2008), pp. 3–5, 35, 111–13.

4 Historian of Wales, 1911–1947

1   Little to Lloyd, 28 May 1911, LP 314 no. 281. Little's lectures were published as *Mediaeval Wales* (London, 1902).

2   LP 287: 7 February 1920 ('Last day as Registrar'). Lloyd submitted his resignation as registrar in 1919, perhaps because of dissatisfaction with his salary; earlier that year he had unsuccessfully applied for the principalships of the university colleges of Cardiff and Aberystwyth: Williams, *UCNW*, p. 430, n. 25; LP 235–6; *University College of South Wales and Monmouthshire Calendar 1919–20*, pp. 26, 151, 168; Ellis, *UCW*, pp. 206–9.

3   The locations of these meetings from 1902 onwards are listed at the back of LP 302–8 (1935–41 diaries).

4   LP 247; 301: 16 August, September–December 1934; 302: 1935 *passim*.

5   LP 358 (reviews); 287, 294–6, 301, 307 (notes at back of 1920, 1927–9, 1934, 1939 diaries); 32–7 *passim*; BU, Bangor MSS 13933–4 (Lloyd's copies of two volumes of 1912 edition of *HW* with list of additions and corrections, noting sources). The 1,000 copies of the first edition sold out within a year, and a second edition of 1,000 copies was published in 1912; the normal print-run for such a work at this period was 500: J. Goronwy Edwards, 'Hanesyddiaeth Gymreig yn yr ugeinfed ganrif', *THSC*, 1953 (1955), 24 and n. 2.

6 *HW* (1939), pp. xxix–lv; University of Reading, Special Collections, Longman Papers; Lloyd, note of reply to Rex Beckett, 6 November 1942, LP 318 no. 4 (550 copies destroyed 1941).

7 The nearest he came to extending his geographical range were his contributions, covering Britain and Ireland before 1066, to *Hutchinson's Story of the British Nation* (London [1922]), a popular work first issued as a magazine series.

8 Edward Anwyl, review of *HW*, *Revue Celtique*, 32 (1911), 361; Isambard Owen to Lloyd, 18 March 1920, LP 315 no. 323; Decima Douie to Lloyd, 18 February 1945, LP 319 no. 31; Jenkins, 'Lloyd', 86–7.

9 Lloyd, *OG*.

10 Ibid., p. [vii]; Thomas Richards, 'Sir John Lloyd', *TCHS*, 8 (1947), 2. Regarding the Glyndŵr book, Lloyd confessed to D. L. Evans, 28 September 1935, BU, Bangor MS 26017: 'There are some very provoking gaps in the evidence and I had often to rely on conjecture.' See also Lloyd, note of reply to T. A. Williams, 12 March 1945, LP 319 no. 182: 'Hist. W. ended at 1282 for special reason. O. Gl. took yrs.'

11 *History* (1930); below, pp. 76–7.

12 Davies, 'Lloyd'; E. Vincent Evans, 'The Cymmrodorion Medal', *THSC*, 1912–13, 190; *Univ. Ct Minutes*, pp. 61–2; LP 242; 358 (note by his daughter of Lloyd's conversation, 25 January 1940). Students at Bangor seem to have thought that Lloyd was disappointed not to have been knighted in 1911: Williams, *UCNW*, pp. 284–5 and plate 53.

13 'Welsh statesmen in English history', *The Times*, 19 December 1916. For Lloyd's authorship, see J. Webb to Lloyd, 8, 13 December 1916, LP 315 nos 518–19.

14 Williams, *UCNW*, plate 52; see also ibid., plate 53.

15 J. L. Wheatley to Lloyd, 31 October, 4 November 1912, 11 March 1916, LP 314 nos 562–3; 315 no. 523 (cf. Angela Gaffney, '"A national Valhalla for Wales": D. A. Thomas and the Welsh historical sculpture scheme, 1910–1916', *THSC*, new ser., 5 (1999), 131–44); E. Madoc-Jones to Lloyd, 9, 24 May 1939, LP 318 nos 165–6; A. P. Graves to Lloyd, 29 March 1929, BU, Bangor MS 26647. See also Ernest Rhys, 'Owain Glyndwr's Parliament', in *The Pageant of Harlech Castle: Book of the Words by Alfred Perceval Graves and Ernest Rhys; Adapted for the Pageant Stage by Patrick Kirwan. (August 23rd. to 25th. 1922)* (London, 1922), pp. 17–20; and, for the wider context, Hywel Teifi Edwards, *The National Pageant of Wales* (Llandysul, 2009). Lloyd answered queries regarding other pageants from Gwyneddon Davies, 15 January 1911, LP 314 no. 60; W. T. Davies, 12 May 1914, ibid. no. 53; Ethel J. Beckett, 4 May 1924, LP 315 no. 21.

16 LP 292: November–December 1925 *passim* (presumably Gertrude Coventry: BU); 298: January–February *passim*, 14 March, 22 April, 12 October 1931; 299: 15 February, 13 July 1932; 241 (Raeburn Dobson:

private collection); 303: 16 December 1936; cf. L. Twiston Davies to Lloyd, 14 August 1936, LP 317 no. 292 (Evan Walters: National Museum Wales, A 5106); LP 305: October 1938 *passim* (Ivor Williams: NLW (W1AbNL) 003381769). Lloyd was also photographed for the National Portrait Gallery, London: ibid. 299: 14 October 1932 (fig. 6).

17 Beth Thomas kindly provided me with a videotaped copy of the film, and John Kenyon a copy of the associated booklet: Amgueddfa Genedlaethol Cymru/National Museum of Wales, *A Matter of Great Interest to Welsh-Americans* ([Cardiff] 1937). See also Cyril Fox to Lloyd, 7 September, 21 October 1937, LP 317 nos 105–6.

18 Lloyd, note of reply to Alfred T. Davies, 24 July 1946, LP 319 no. 17; R. T. Jenkins, 'Gwerthfawrogiad', *Y Cymro*, 27 June 1947, 6.

19 LP 280: 13 December 1913; 281: 4 April 1914; 285: 30 November 1918; 301: 11 January 1934.

20 LP 297: 15 January, 26 November 1930; 299: 13 January, 10 February 1932; 302: 16 January, 29 November 1935; 308: 12 February, 28 November 1941; 312: 9 February, 30 November 1945.

21 Radio: LP 301: 25 December 1933, 24 March 1934; 306: 25–6 December 1938; 307: 9 January 1940; 310: 11 April, 8 May 1943. Films: LP 290: 18 September 1923; 298: 11 April 1931; 305: 19 July 1938.

22 Whist: LP 286: 3 December 1919; 289: 18, 28 October 1922; 294: 1 January 1927; 297: 29 January, 25 October 1930; 303: 18 January 1936. Crib: LP 293: 16 December 1926; 302: 13, 16 December 1935 (Crib disappears for several days); 307: 29 April 1940 ('Crib put away').

23 LP 279: 9–16 September 1912; 289: 22 August–6 September 1922; 291: 3–18 July 1924; 292: 14 August–1 September 1925; 293: 13–31 August 1926; 294: 13 August–2 September 1927; 295: 19 August–4 September 1928; 297: 13 August–1 September 1930; 313: 7–17 September 1946.

24 LP 282: 24 July, 13 December 1915; 283: 21 March 1916; 284: 17 March, 8 December 1917; 288: 9, 14 June 1921; 295: 19 June, 16, 20 July 1928; Oxford, Lincoln College Archives, Lincoln College Matriculations 1919–1952, p. 8 (13 October 1925).

25 BU, Bangor MS 20176 ('Family Register' in Bible). Anne's visits to Bangor: LP 309: 2 November 1942; 310: 3 April, 13–14 June, 22 September 1943; 311: 28 January, 18 August 1944; 312: 19 April 1945; personal communication Mary Dodd, 11 April 2010. Cf. R. T. Jenkins, 'Lloyd, Sir John Edward (1861–1947)', in idem, E. D. Jones and Brynley F. Roberts (eds), *The Dictionary of Welsh Biography, 1941–1970* (London, 2001), p. 173.

26 LP 301: 29 March 1934; BU, Bangor MS 20176.

27 LP 284: 7 January 1917; D. Adams, 'Yn llefaru eto: marwolaeth a chladdedigaeth y diweddar Thomas Arthur Lloyd', *Y Dysgedydd*, 96 (1917), 82–6.

28 LP 284: 7 March 1917; 288: 6 December 1921; D. Adams, 'Edward Lloyd, Y.H., Lerpwl', *Y Dysgedydd*, 96 (1917), 216–18; John Felix, 'Y wraig

rinweddol', *Yr Eurgrawn Wesleyaidd*, 114 (1922), 54–9. Lloyd's sister, Maggie Alice, also predeceased him: LP 307: 26 May 1940.

29   LP 290: 11 July 1923; 297: 16 October 1930; 311 (1944 diary: Eluned's address in Birkenhead); 312: 16 March, 3 September 1945; A. S. Turberville to Lloyd [April 1945], ibid. 319 no. 159.

30   LP 2; 319 no. 155 (draft of Lloyd to J. Lloyd Thomas, 20 May 1947); see above, pp. 23–4.

31   Jenkins, 'Gwerthfawrogiad'.

32   The names and dates of Lloyd's wife, son and daughter-in-law were added later. Lloyd's obituary in *The Times*, 21 June 1947, likewise bore the heading 'Historian of Wales'.

33   See above, p. 57; Thomas Richards, 'Syr John Lloyd: atgofion amdano', *Y Llenor*, 25 (1947), 73; see also idem, BU, Bangor MS 16876.

34   Tout to Lloyd, 9 November 1918, LP 315 no. 503. For Manchester, see Peter R. H. Slee, *Learning and a Liberal Education: The Study of Modern History in the Universities of Oxford, Cambridge and Manchester, 1800–1914* (Manchester, 1986), pp. 153–64.

35   Williams, *UCNW*, pp. 327–8, 371; NLW, Edward Owen Papers, Lloyd to Owen, 18 June 1916.

36   Williams, *UCNW*, pp. 371, 397, 465.

37   See above, pp. 55–6; *UCNW Cal. 1921–2*, p. 100; *UCNW Cal. 1922–3 and 1923–4*, pp. 99–101; *UCNW Cal. 1929–30*, pp. 129–31. In 1928 the terminus of the modern European course was extended to 1914: *UCNW Cal. 1928–9*, p. 116.

38   Williams, *UCNW*, p. 371; Slee, *Learning and a Liberal Education*, pp. 155–9.

39   Most of the 170 Ph.D. graduates in the University of Wales 1923–39 were scientists: Williams, *Univ. Wales*, pp. 425–6.

40   *UCNW Cal. 1926–7*, pp. 110–11. For the thesis topics, which remained unaltered from 1898 until at least 1915 (after which university calendars cease to provide detailed MA syllabuses), see, for example, *UW Cal. 1911–12*, App. II, pp. xix–xx; and, for successful theses, NLW, *A List of Dissertations Submitted and Accepted for Higher Degrees in the University of Wales 1899–1949* (Aberystwyth, 1950).

41   NLW, *List of Dissertations*.

42   Lloyd to Richards, 2 July, 8 September 1903, BU, Bangor MSS 16716–17; Richards to Lloyd, 7 July 1914, LP 315 no. 402; Geraint H. Jenkins, *'Doc Tom': Thomas Richards* (Cardiff, 1999), pp. 83–9.

43   J. R. Gabriel had already completed an MA thesis on the clergy and the Glyndŵr movement in 1906: NLW, *List of Dissertations*.

44   Ruth Clarke Easterling, 'The friars in Wales' (unpublished MA thesis, University of Wales, 1913) (listed in NLW, *List of Dissertations*); LP 280 (1913 diary), *passim*; R. C. Easterling, 'The friars in Wales', *Arch. Camb.*, 6th ser., 14 (1914), 323–56. See also eadem, 'Anian of Nanneu', *Journal*

of the Flintshire Historical Society, 5 (1914–15), 9–30 (including warm acknowledgement of Lloyd's help at 29, n. 1).

45 Dora Ward, 'The mediaeval lordship of Montgomery' (unpublished MA thesis, University of Wales, 1924).

46 *UCNW Cal. 1922–23 and 1923–24*, p. 101.

47 NLW, *List of Dissertations*. The number of Welsh history theses from Cardiff was only slightly higher than that from Bangor.

48 Edward Arthur Lewis, *The Mediaeval Boroughs of Snowdonia* (London, 1912), esp. p. [v]; Ellis, *UCW*, pp. 167, 235. It is suggestive that eight of the Aberystwyth MA history theses from 1911 to 1928 were on individual Welsh boroughs: NLW, *List of Dissertations*. Lewis subsequently held the newly created Sir John Williams Chair of Welsh History at Aberystwyth (1931–42). See also Charles Johnson, revised G. H. Martin, 'Hall, Hubert (1857–1944)', *ODNB*.

49 See below, pp. 104–8.

50 Easterling, 'Friars in Wales' (1914), 323.

51 Ward, 'Mediaeval lordship of Montgomery'. Ward to the registrar of the University of Wales, 24 April 1924, enclosed in the copy of the thesis deposited at Bangor, acknowledges the help she had received in transcribing and translating 'unpublished documents' (at the Public Record Office).

52 It does not appear that Lloyd actively discouraged new work on Welsh history before 1300. Apart from the MA theses mentioned above, see also note of his reply to Miss E. J. Rees, 10 March 1930, LP 316 no. 309, regarding whether any primary sources had been published since *HW* for her proposed research on Anglo-Welsh relations in the thirteenth century: 'Hist W. covers ground generally but fresh details' available in several works which he listed. That prospective researchers may, nevertheless, have been discouraged is suggested by Frank R. Lewis to Lloyd, 20 February 1938, LP 317 no. 182: 'I am continuing my work on Welsh history. I am concentrating on the fourteenth and fifteenth centuries, for you yourself have deprived the historian of the chance of saying anything new about the earlier period.'

53 LP 283: 1–7 October 1916; 284: 4, 20–30 June, 25 September–6 October 1917; 285: 3–5 October 1918; 286: 1, 13–15 July, 25–7 September 1919; Lloyd to Tout, 3 December 1915, Tout Papers 1/721/13; Tout to Lloyd, 9 November 1918, LP 315 no. 503. Cf. F. X. Martin, 'Appendix 3: The vacant chair at University College, Dublin, 24 May 1916–24 May 1918', in idem and F. J. Byrne (eds), *The Scholar Revolutionary: Eoin MacNeill, 1867–1945, and the Making of the New Ireland* (Shannon, 1973), pp. 385–90.

54 Doris S. Goldstein, 'The organizational development of the British historical profession, 1884–1921', *Bulletin of the Institute of Historical Research*, 55 (1982), 191, 192. See also eadem, 'The professionalization of history in Britain in the late nineteenth and early twentieth centuries', *Storia della Storiografia*, 3 (1983), 3–27.

55 Lloyd was invited to support the *EHR* prior to its launch and was certainly a subscriber by 1894: R. L. Poole to Lloyd, 24 October 1885, LP 23; LP 341. Royal Historical Society: Lloyd, note of reply to H. E. Malden, 8 April 1911: LP 314 no. 298; Lloyd, note of reply to M. B. Curran, 14 January 1933, accepting an invitation to be an honorary vice-president of the society, ibid., 316 no. 57. Historical Association: Lloyd to Tout, 14 December 1911, Tout Papers 1/721/10; *1914 North Wales and Chester Year Book* (Liverpool, n.d.), p. 465; LP 282: 8–9 January 1915; 287: 14 February 1920; and regular entries in diaries thereafter. Conferences: LP 280: 2–5 April 1913; 288: 11–13 July 1921; 290: 8–14 April 1923; 298: 13–18 July 1931; 303: 6–7 July 1936.

56 Lloyd, speaking in the ecclesiastical history section, drew an audience of only six, whereas thirty-six heard Bloch in the medieval history section: G. des Marez and F.-L. Ganshof (eds), *Compte rendu du Ve Congrès International des Sciences Historiques, Bruxelles, 1923* (Brussels, 1923), pp. 101–4, 221–2. See also Lloyd, *OG*, pp. 112–18; Lloyd to Tout, 27 November 1922, Tout Papers 1/721/14; Bryce Lyon, *Henri Pirenne: A Biographical and Intellectual Study* (Ghent, 1974), pp. 292–7; Karl Dietrich Erdmann, *Toward a Global Community of Historians: The International Historical Congresses and the International Committee of Historical Sciences, 1898–2000* (New York/Oxford, 2005), chapter 7 (with discussion of Bloch's paper at pp. 91–2).

57 Peter Burke, *The French Historical Revolution: The Annales School, 1929–89* (Cambridge, 1990), chapter 2.

58 LP 280: 4–5 April 1913.

59 Doris Stenton to Lloyd, 1929–33, 1939, LP 316 nos 348–60; 318 nos 243–4; Curtis to Lloyd, 31 August 1921, ibid. 315 no. 59 (also ibid. nos 60–3); Morey to Lloyd, 18 July 1936, ibid. 317 no. 204.

60 See above, p. 59; below, p. 97.

61 'The future of Welsh literary and historical research' (8 November 1918), LP 93.

62 For the Haldane Commission, see Williams, *Univ. Wales*, chapter IV.

63 Prys Morgan, 'The creation of the National Museum and National Library', in John Osmond (ed.), *Myths, Memories and Futures: The National Library and National Museum in the Story of Wales* (Cardiff, 2007), pp. 13–22, quotation at p. 21. For the foundation of the National Museum, see also Rhiannon Mason, *Museums, Nations, Identities: Wales and its National Museums* (Cardiff, 2007), chapter 2; Bill Jones, 'Rooms at the top: Cardiff's municipal museum, 1862–1912', *Llafur*, 9, 4 (2007), 27, 44–5.

64 Cf. Goldstein, 'Organizational development', 189–90.

65 *Second Report of the Royal Commission on University Education in Wales: Evidence, Appendices, and Index* (London, 1917), Cd. 8699, pp. 169–72 (with ensuing questioning at pp. 172–80); *Final Report of*

the *Royal Commission on University Education in Wales: Evidence, Appendices, and Index* (London, 1918), Cd. 8993, p. 210.

66 For a brief history of the board in Lloyd's day, see Henry Lewis, 'Preface', in Elwyn Davies (ed.), *Celtic Studies in Wales: A Survey* (Cardiff, 1963), pp. v–xii. Lloyd's annual reports as chairman: *Univ. Ct Minutes*, 23 November 1921, pp. 36–7; ibid. 29 November 1922, App. III (also in *Acad. Bd Minutes*, 28–9 September 1922, App. IV); thereafter in *Acad. Bd Minutes*. Board's minutes during Lloyd's chairmanship: NLW, University of Wales, LJA 2/1–4.

67 *Final Report*, p. 210.

68 *UW Cal. 1921–2*, p. 21; *Second Report*, p. 170. The board was instrumental in organizing a national celebration of Hywel Dda, traditionally regarded as having codified medieval Welsh law, in 1928 to coincide with the millenary of the king's journey to Rome: NLW, University of Wales, LJA 4/3; J. E. Lloyd, *Hywel Dda, 928–1928* (Cardiff, 1928).

69 *UW Cal. 1921–2*, p. 21.

70 *Acad. Bd Minutes*, 28–9 September 1922, p. 2; ibid. 1 October 1937, p. 99; ibid., 29 September 1938, p. 84.

71 *Acad. Bd Minutes*, 21 November 1941, p. 79.

72 John Edward Lloyd, *Wales and the Past – Two Voices* (Cardiff, 1932).

73 LP 281: 2 April 1914; NLW, E. Vincent Evans Papers, K1.

74 Lloyd to E. Vincent Evans, 30 March 1916, E. Vincent Evans Papers, K11.

75 Royal Commission on the Ancient and Historical Monuments of Wales, *An Inventory of the Ancient Monuments in Anglesey* (HMSO, 1937), p. xviii; Peter Wakelin and Ralph A. Griffiths (eds), *Hidden Histories: Discovering the Heritage of Wales* (Aberystwyth, 2008), p. 307.

76 Lloyd, notes of replies to Watson Kirkconnell, 12, 19 October 1926, LP 315 no. 238–9; to R. B. Marston, 31 May 1921, ibid. no. 286; to V. E. Nash-Williams, 12 October 1927, ibid. no. 305; to Cyril Fox, 5 May 1930, ibid. 316, no. 139; to S. O'Dwyer, 13 February 1941, LP 318 no. 179.

77 Plans for what was eventually the eleventh volume in the series were in hand by 1926 and the first volume was published three years later: *Acad. Bd Minutes*, 30 September–1 October 1926, p. 59; Ifan ab Owen Edwards (comp.), *A Catalogue of Star Chamber Proceedings relating to Wales* (BCS, Hist. & Law Ser., no. 1; Cardiff, 1929); J. Goronwy Edwards, *Calendar of Ancient Correspondence concerning Wales* (BCS, Hist. & Law Ser., no. 11; Cardiff, 1935). One of the board's first tasks was to survey the sources available for Welsh history in all periods: NLW, University of Wales, LJA 2/1, pp. 16–18, 23–6, 29–33 (23 May 1919, 11 March, 7 May 1920).

78 Hall to Lloyd, 21 November 1928, LP 316 no. 152.

79 Progress on the dictionary and grants for archaeological fieldwork feature regularly in the board's reports. Orthography: *Acad. Bd Minutes*, 15 October 1925, p. 503; ibid., 29–30 September 1927, p. 50; ibid.

26–7 September 1929, p. 90; BCS, *Orgraff yr Iaith Gymraeg* (Cardiff, 1928); see above, p. 58. Dialects: *Acad. Bd Minutes*, 15 October 1925, p. 503; ibid. 26–7 September 1929, p. 91. Place-names: ibid., 27 September 1934, p. 70; ibid., 26 September 1935, pp. 119–20.

80   John E. Lloyd (ed.), *A History of Carmarthenshire*, 2 vols (Cardiff, 1935–9); 'Olwyn yr awr' (script of radio broadcast, 15 May 1939), LP 228.

81   R. B. Pugh, '*The Victoria County History*: its origin and progress', in idem (ed.), *The Victoria History of the Counties of England: General Introduction* (London, 1970), pp. 5–6.

82   LP 228: 'Ychydig a wyddwn y pryd hwnnw mai dyma a fyddai fy mhrif ofal a thestun pryder nos a dydd am yn agos i naw mlynedd.' Lloyd later held that the experience of editing the work had demonstrated the need for '(1) money (2) editor in sole authority (3) firm financial control': note of reply to T. B. Stephens, 15 October 1942, LP 318 no. 248. Lloyd's conscientious, courteous but firm approach to his editorial duties is revealed in his letters to D. L. Evans, one of the contributors, in 1935: BU, Bangor MSS 26010–18.

83   John Edward Lloyd and R. T. Jenkins (eds), *Y Bywgraffiadur Cymreig hyd 1940* (London, 1953); English version published as *DWB*. In 1937 Lloyd also delivered four lectures at Aberystwyth published as *The Story of Ceredigion (400–1277)* (Cardiff, 1937).

84   *DWB*, pp. xiii–xv. Lloyd gave his rationale for the project to a meeting at the National Eisteddfod in Cardiff in August 1938: John Edward Lloyd, 'A dictionary of Welsh biography', *THSC*, 1938, 67–75. He was closely involved in preparing the dictionary almost until his death: LP 68–71.

85   *DWB*, p. 5; cf. Allen to Lloyd, 11 September 1902, 25 January 1905, LP 314, nos 7–8. See also *DWB*, pp. 45, 50, 59.

86   J. E. Lloyd, 'A retrospect (1877–1881)', in Iwan Morgan (ed.), *The College by the Sea* (Aberystwyth, 1928), pp. 70–2; idem, 'Cymdeithas yr Iaith Gymraeg: trem ar hanes y mudiad', *Y Llenor*, 10 (1931), 207–14; idem, 'Hiraethog a'i gyfnod', *Adroddiad Cyfarfodydd yr Undeb*, new ser., 10, 4 (Undeb yr Annibynwyr Cymraeg; Swansea, 1932), pp. 21–4.

87   John Edward Lloyd, 'Early days of the University College of North Wales, Bangor', unpublished script, in Welsh, for broadcast on 19 September 1941, LP 230; idem, 'Tom Ellis', *Yr Eurgrawn*, 132 (1942), 20–5; idem, 'Cymry yn Rhydychen – atgofion o'r blynyddoedd 1881–1885', *Yr Eurgrawn*, 135 (1943), 13–18. See also idem, 'Introduction', in Cambrian Archaeological Association, *A Hundred Years of Welsh Archaeology: Centenary Volume, 1846–1946*, ed. V. E. Nash-Williams (Gloucester, n.d.), pp. 11–23.

88   LP 1, 2, 17.

89   As well as wedding anniversaries, Lloyd noted, for example, the twenty-fifth anniversary and jubilee of his arrival in Bangor and his jubilee as university teacher: LP 284: 20 April 1917; 302: 14 September 1935; 309: 20 April 1942. He also recorded 'Family notes' in some later diaries (e.g.

LP 303: 1936) and key events in his life on a sheet headed 'Adgofion' ('Recollections'; LP 25).

90 Jenkins, 'Gwerthfawrogiad'; Davies, 'Lloyd'.

91 Quotation from Saunders Lewis, 'Marwnad Syr John Edward Lloyd', in his *Siwan a Cherddi Eraill* (Llandybïe [1955]), p. 15 ('lusernwr y canrifoedd coll').

5 A Nation Revived: Lloyd and Modern Wales

1 'Anerchiad i Gymmrodorion Caerdydd, Chwefr. 27, 1937', LP 227; *Western Mail*, 1 March 1937, 13. Lloyd had previously criticized those 'sentimentalists who would take us back to the economic and ecclesiastical Paradise of the days before Luther': review of R. T. Jenkins, *Yr Apêl at Hanes*, *The Welsh Outlook*, 17 (1930), 227. As in 1937, his target was evidently the idealization of a nationally diverse medieval civilization, united under the authority of a supranational Church, presented in Saunders Lewis, *Egwyddorion Cenedlaetholdeb* (Machynlleth [1926]), which (p. 4) explicitly defined the new nationalism of Plaid Genedlaethol Cymru (The Welsh Nationalist Party) as 'going back to the principle of the Middle Ages'. That vision in turn emphatically rejected prevailing progressionist notions of Welsh history favoured by Welsh Liberal nationalists, notably O. M. Edwards and Lloyd himself. See D. Hywel Davies, *The Welsh Nationalist Party 1925–1945: A Call to Nationhood* (Cardiff, 1983), pp. 80–2; Richard Wyn Jones, *Rhoi Cymru'n Gyntaf: Syniadaeth Plaid Cymru*, vol. I (Cardiff, 2007), pp. 66–76.

2 Neil Evans, 'Casting nets: modern Wales', in Geraint H. Jenkins and Gareth Elwyn Jones (eds), *Degrees of Influence: A Memorial Volume for Glanmor Williams* (Cardiff, 2008), pp. 85–100, esp. pp. 85–6; Kenneth O. Morgan, 'Renaissance man', ibid., pp. 183–4.

3 Georg G. Iggers, 'Changing conceptions of national history since the French Revolution. A critical comparative perspective', in Erik Lönnroth, Karl Molin and Ragnar Björk (eds), *Conceptions of National History: Proceedings of Nobel Symposium 78* (Berlin/New York, 1994), pp. 132–50, esp. pp. 143–4; Michael Bentley, 'Introduction: approaches to modernity: western historiography since the enlightenment', in idem (ed.), *Companion to Historiography* (London, 1997), pp. 411–42.

4 Glanmor Williams, 'Local and national history in Wales', in D. Huw Owen (ed.), *Settlement and Society in Wales* (Cardiff, 1989), p. 10; Stefan Berger and Neil Evans, 'Two faces of King Coal: the impact of historiographical traditions on comparative history in the Ruhr and south Wales', in Stefan Berger, Andy Croll and Norman Laporte (eds), *Towards a Comparative History of Coalfield Societies* (Aldershot, 2005), pp. 35–7.

5 Humphrey Llwyd, *Cronica Walliae*, ed. Ieuan M. Williams (Cardiff, 2002), p. 224.

6 Price, *Hanes Cymru*.

7 Thus about 7.5 per cent and 2.5 per cent of the total respectively. Treatment of the period from the late seventeenth century onwards was particularly patchy, jumping ahead to the French invasion of Pembrokeshire in 1797 and thence proceeding to Welsh settlement in the United States via the Merthyr rising (1831), the Chartist attack on Newport (1839), the abolition of the courts of great sessions (1830) and the baptism of Albert Edward, prince of Wales (1842): Price, *Hanes Cymru*, pp. 792–4. Likewise only thirty-six of the 591 pages (about 6 per cent of the total) of B. B. Woodward, *The History of Wales* (London/New York, 1853) deal with the period from 1282 to the mid-nineteenth century, though their coverage is heavily weighted towards the later Middle Ages.

8 Williams, *History of Wales* allocates about eighty of its almost five hundred pages (about 16 per cent of the total) to the centuries from 1282 to the end of the Tudor period; *HBC*, though extending from 'the earliest times' to the age of Queen Victoria, still devotes about 75 per cent of its coverage to the period down to 1282.

9 John Rhys and David Brynmor-Jones, *The Welsh People* (London, 1900), p. [vii].

10 Ibid., p. xxvi.

11 Ibid., pp. 473–6 (quotation at p. 474).

12 Ibid., p. 485.

13 Edwards, 'Lloyd', 321.

14 The variants on Edwards's periodization of Welsh history in *Wales* and his earlier historical writings are examined in Manon Jones, '"I godi'r hen wlad yn ei hôl": arolwg o weithiau O. M. Edwards ar hanes Cymru' (unpublished MA thesis, Cardiff University, 2006), 37–8. For other recent analysis of Edwards as a historian, see Evans, 'Men and mountains', 223–8; idem, 'Finding a new story: the search for a usable past in Wales, 1869–1930', *THSC*, new ser., 10 (2004), 150–2; Lowri Angharad Hughes, 'Writing the Welsh people: O. M. Edwards and the shaping of Welsh identity' (unpublished D.Phil. thesis, University of Oxford, 2007), chapter 6.

15 Edwards, *Wales*, pp. 386–93. The period from 1730 onwards had already been characterized as 'The Awakening' ('Y Deffro'), resulting from religious revival, educational improvements and the discovery of natural resources, in Owen M. Edwards, *Holi ac Ateb ar Hanes Cymru* (Llanuwchllyn, 1892), p. 22.

16 Edwards, *Wales*, p. 397.

17 Ibid., p. 399.

18 Ibid., p. 400.

19 Jenkins, 'Lloyd', 87.

20 John Edward Lloyd, 'Thomas Ellis', *UCW Mag.*, 21 (1898–9), 331–2; idem, 'A retrospect (1877–1881)', in Iwan Morgan (ed.), *The College by the Sea* (Aberystwyth, 1928), pp. 70–2; idem, 'Cymdeithas yr Iaith Gymraeg – trem ar hanes y mudiad', *Y Llenor*, 10 (1931), 207–14; idem, 'Hiraethog a'i gyfnod', *Adroddiad Cyfarfodydd yr Undeb*, new ser. 10, 4 (Undeb yr Annibynwyr Cymraeg; Swansea, 1932), p. 21; above, pp. 36–7.

21 One demonstration of this engagement is a notebook, begun in December 1889, on 'Welsh History, Literature and Religion since 1485': LP 63.

22 'List', 104–5; see above, p. 57.

23 *History* (1930), pp. 40–78. Compare how Lloyd divided his model syllabus for the teaching of history in secondary schools equally between the periods before and after 1450: idem, 'A history course for secondary schools in Wales', *The Welsh Outlook*, 15 (1928), 5.

24 In addition, Lloyd encouraged the study of modern Welsh history as chairman of the History and Law Committee of the Board of Celtic Studies, one of whose first tasks was to commission reports on sources and topics requiring research in Welsh history from 1536 onwards: NLW, University of Wales, LJA 2/1, 11 March 1920, pp. 25–6; 7 May 1920, pp. 29–32.

25 R. T. Jenkins, *Hanes Cymru yn y Ddeunawfed Ganrif* (Cardiff, 1928). *History* (1930), 64, 75–6, 80; Lloyd to Jenkins, 9 January 1930, BU, Bangor MS 31110.

26 Evans, 'Men and mountains', 236. Compare *History* (1930), pp. 56–7, with Lloyd, 'Rowlands, Daniel (1713–1790)', in *DNB*, XLIX (London, 1897), pp. 350–1; idem, 'Williams, William (1717–1791)', in *DNB*, LXI (London, 1900), pp. 462–4.

27 *History* (1930), chap. VIII, esp. p. 40; J. E. Lloyd, 'How England and Wales became united', *TLWNS*, 1886–7, 83–99; [idem], 'Welsh statesmen in English history. Some memorable names', *The Times*, 19 December 1916. Positive assessments of Henry VII and the Tudor dynasty by other Welsh scholars in Lloyd's lifetime: *HBC*, II, pp. 400, 407–9; Edwards, *Wales*, p. 303; Rhys and Brynmor-Jones, *Welsh People*, pp. 395, 478–9; W. Llewelyn Williams, *The Making of Modern Wales: Studies in the Tudor Settlement of Wales* (London, 1919), esp. pp. 6–15. See also Peter Roberts, 'The "Act of Union" in Welsh history', *THSC*, 1972–3, 55–8; Glanmor Williams, 'Haneswyr a'r Deddfau Uno', in Geraint H. Jenkins (ed.), *Cof Cenedl X* (Llandysul, 1995), pp. 42–8.

28 *History* (1930), pp. 44, 47, 49–50. As a student Lloyd identified printing as a key change in sixteenth-century Wales, but by 1930 his emphasis had shifted away from the technology itself to the authors of the works printed: compare ibid., pp. 45–6, with J. E. L[loyd], 'Passages in the history of the Welsh Bible', *UCW Mag.*, 2 (1879–80), 24; idem, 'A word about prose-writing', *UCW Mag.*, 4 (1881–2), 266–7. The muted impact of the reformation is also stressed in Rhys and Brynmor-Jones, *Welsh People*, pp. 460–1; Edwards, *Wales*, chapter XXII.

29   *History* (1930), pp. 52–3. Shortly afterwards David Williams, *History of Wales 1485–1931, For School Certificate* (London, 1934), pp. 37, 49, likewise located the birth of modern Wales in the eighteenth century, but attributed this to a combination of Methodist revival, literary renaissance and Industrial Revolution.

30   *History* (1930), pp. 59–78. The relative importance Lloyd accorded to the modern period is also pointed up by his coverage of the eighteenth and nineteenth centuries, which occupy 23 per cent of the total text, compared with only 4 per cent in O. M. Edwards's *Wales*: cf. above, p. 84.

31   J. E. Lloyd, 'The rise of periodical literature in Wales', *UCW Mag.*, 1 (1878–9), 33. Admittedly, Lloyd believed there had been some decline in standards towards the end of the century: idem, 'A word about prose-writing', 267–8; idem, 'Some characteristics of modern Welsh poetry', *UCW Mag.*, 11 (1888–9), 241–9.

32   Lloyd, 'Taith archesgobol drwy Gymru', *Y Geninen*, 4 (1886), 56: 'Y meusydd ffrwythlon, y glofeydd a'r ffwrneisiau tanllyd, y rheilffyrdd, y capelau, y milldiroedd o dai! Nis gallwn, fel rhai yn caru ein cenedl, fod yn ddigon diolchgar am y cyfnewidiad.' See also idem, 'Ffurfiad y genedl Gymreig', ibid., 265–6.

33   In 1933 Saunders Lewis called for the deindustrialization of south Wales and for agriculture to be the foundation of Welsh civilization: 'Deg pwynt polisi', in idem, *Canlyn Arthur* (Aberystwyth, 1938), p. 12; see Jones, *Rhoi Cymru'n Gyntaf*, pp. 94–6.

34   *History* (1930), pp. 43, 47, 59. See also Lloyd, 'Wales: the land and its people', *Wales*, 2 (1912), 362.

35   *History* (1930), pp. 71–8. Cf. how Lloyd merely alluded to the recent Penrhyn quarry strike of 1900–3 in a circumspect reference to 'labour conflicts, some of which have been protracted', in idem, *Carnarvonshire* (Cambridge, 1911), p. 81.

36   The importance of establishing the university is also stressed in Rhys and Brynmor-Jones, *Welsh People*, pp. 488–500; Edwards, *Wales*, pp. 400–1.

37   Cf. R. J. W. Evans, review of Geraint H. Jenkins, *A Concise History of Wales*, *WHR*, 24, 4 (2009), 188. Note also the territorial and cultural definitions of Wales developed by educationalists and geographers in the first half of the twentieth century: W. T. R. Pryce, 'Region or national territory? Regionalism and the idea of the country of Wales, *c*.1927–1998', *WHR*, 23, 2 (2006), 120–6.

38   See, for instance, the characterization of his work on the history of Wales as an attempt 'to delineate the course of events which has created the Welsh people': J. E. Lloyd, *Wales and the Past – Two Voices* (Cardiff, 1932), p. 9; see also below, p. 166.

39   Among the earliest examples, see Lloyd, 'Rise of periodical literature'; idem, 'Two Welsh prose authors of the XVIIIth century', *UCW Mag.*, 1 (1878–9), 246–52; idem, 'Passages in the history of the Welsh Bible';

idem, 'A word about prose-writing'; idem, 'A volume of old letters', *UCW Mag.*, 9 (1886–7), 113–17; idem, 'Some characteristics of modern Welsh poetry'.

40 *History* (1930), pp. 31–4, 45–6. See also Lloyd's comment, '"Gradual Anglicisation", beginning with Tud[o]rs', referring to a draft memorandum on Welsh history in secondary schools: note of reply, A. G. Prys-Jones to Lloyd, 10 July 1939, LP 318 no. 214.

41 *History* (1930), p. 60. For an earlier positive assessment of quarrying in north Wales, see Lloyd, *Carnarvonshire*, pp. 5, 78–84, discussed in Huw Pryce, 'From the neolithic to nonconformity: J. E. Lloyd and the history of Caernarfonshire', *TCHS*, 66 (2005), 23, 26–8. Contrast the much less sanguine view of mass anglophone immigration into Wales from the eighteenth century onwards in Williams, *History of Wales 1485–1931*, p. 73.

42 Cf. above, pp. 6, 73.

43 *History* (1930), p. 77.

44 Cf. Evans, 'Men and mountains', 236–7.

45 O. M. Edwards, 'Editor's notes', *Wales*, 2 (1895), 473; Heinrich Zimmer, 'Der Pan-Keltismus in Grossbritannien und Irland. I. Die heutige nationale Bewegung in Wales in ihrer geschichtlichen Entwickelung', *Preussische Jahrbücher*, 92 (1898), 428–9. Compare, for instance, Roumen Daskalov, *The Making of a Nation in the Balkans: Historiography of the Bulgarian Revival* (Budapest/New York, 2004), esp. pp. 1–2; Derek Fewster, *Visions of Past Glory: Nationalism and the Construction of Early Finnish History* (Studia Fennica Historica, 11; Helsinki, 2006), pp. 156, 185–6.

46 Lloyd, 'A word about prose-writing', 265.

47 Lloyd, 'Ffurfiad y genedl Gymreig', 264: 'Y genedl sydd yn ymddeffroi, yn bwrw ymaith lyffetheiriau cwsg a difrawder, yn ymarfogi erbyn cyfnod newydd o weithgarwch. Nis gall unrhyw adeg, felly, fod yn fwy amserol at droi golwg yn ol ar ddechreuad y genedl . . .'

48 Lloyd, *Early Welsh Agriculture* (Bangor, 1894), 14; see below, pp. 135, 163–4. See also the (rather impractical) appeal to medieval precedent in idem, 'The geographical limits of Welsh home rule', *The Welsh Outlook*, 8 (1921), 247–8 (and, for the wider context, Gwyn Jenkins, 'The Welsh Outlook 1914–33', *NLWJ*, 24 (1985–6), 480–1; Andrew Edwards and Wil Griffith, 'Welsh national identity and governance, 1918–45', in Duncan Tanner et al. (eds), *Debating Nationhood and Governance in Britain, 1885–1945: Perspectives from the 'Four Nations'* (Manchester, 2006), pp. 118–27).

49 Lloyd, 'Yr iaith Gymraeg', *Y Dysgedydd*, 59 (1880), 117; idem, 'The future of Welsh literary and historical research. Nov. 8th 1918', LP 93, pp. 1–3; see above, p. 7.

50 Lloyd, 'The future of Welsh literary and historical research', p. 3. For the support given by Lloyd and his wife to the Serbian cause during the war,

see M. Curcin to Lloyd, 27 October 1917, 8, 29 May 1918, LP 315, nos 56–8.

51 Lloyd, 'History course', 5, evidently referring to Ernest Barker, *National Character and the Factors in its Formation* (London, 1927), based on lectures given at Glasgow whose substance was later repeated at Bangor (ibid., p. v; LP 294: 31 January, 1, 7–9 February 1927). Lloyd had come to know Barker personally by 1918 (LP 285: 10 June, 5 July 1918), and, as well as valuing the latter's great classical learning, seems to have shared some of his political views, notably a rejection of Prussian authoritarian nationalism, support for the right of small nations to self-determination and characterization of the United Kingdom as a multinational nation whose people were equally both British and English, Scottish or Welsh. Cf. Barker, *National Character*, pp. 9, 16–17; Julia Stapleton, *Englishness and the Study of Politics: The Social and Political Thought of Ernest Barker* (Cambridge, 1994), pp. 92–9, 120–7.

52 Lloyd, 'History course', 5.

53 Ibid.

54 Cf. John Burrow, 'Historicism and social evolution', in Benedikt Stuchtey and Peter Wende (eds), *British and German Historiography 1750–1950* (Oxford, 2000), pp. 250–64. See further below, chapter 7.

6 Assumptions and Methods

1 LP 358 (notes dated 9 March 1941). Ellipsis in original. Shortly after his appointment to the new lectureship in Welsh history at Bangor, R. T. Jenkins wrote to Lloyd hoping he could say 'how thankful I am to you for the great work you have done in the field of Welsh History? I simply cannot tell you how I admire the History of Wales, so I shall leave it at that.' Jenkins to Lloyd, 27 June 1930, LP 316 no. 178.

2 *HW*, I, p. v.

3 Ibid., p. vi. It is telling that, in his copy of an anonymous review of *HW*, *Educational Times*, October 1912, Lloyd marked the following sentence in blue pencil: 'The volumes constitute one of the weightiest works of the modern historical school.' LP 358.

4 Unlike Lloyd, none of the four was appointed to a university position in history, although Rhys held the chair of Celtic at Oxford and Williams spent most of his career teaching at the Calvinist Methodist college in Bala, where he was eventually appointed professor of church history. By contrast, Palmer worked in industry for a considerable period and Phillimore, a qualified barrister, was a scholar of independent means. Their work concentrated mainly on linguistic evidence, including inscriptions (Rhys), place-names, topography and early Welsh annals and genealogies (Phillimore), land tenure and local history (Palmer, whose

works on Wrexham were later praised as being 'unique in their full and scholarly treatment of Welsh local history': J. E. Lloyd, *A Brief Bibliography of Welsh History for the Use of Teachers*, Historical Association Leaflet no. 49 ([London] 1921), p. 7), and the early British church (Williams). See *DWB*; Christopher J. Williams, 'A. N. Palmer, historian of Wrexham', *Denbighshire Historical Society Transactions*, 46 (1997), 109–36; and see below, pp. 124–6.

5   T. F. Tout, review of *HW*, *EHR*, 27 (1912), 131.

6   Ibid., 132.

7   LP 254: 8 October 1887, 256: 2 November 1889; Lloyd to Tout, 27 November 1889, Tout Papers 1/721/1.

8   J. E. Lloyd, 'The organization of Welsh historical and archaeological research', *THSC*, 1910–11, 116.

9   Ibid.

10   Peter H. Slee, *Learning and a Liberal Education: The Study of Modern History in the Universities of Oxford, Cambridge and Manchester, 1800–1914* (Manchester, 1986), pp. 130–3 (quotations at pp. 131, 133). See also Rosemary Jann, *The Art and Science of Victorian History* (Columbus, OH, 1985), pp. xii–xiii, xxiii–xxvii.

11   Cf. the prescription for training undergraduates in historical method in T. F. Tout, 'Schools of history' [1906], in idem, *The Collected Papers of Thomas Frederick Tout*, vol. I (Manchester, 1932), p. 104: 'Biography is the easiest, and one of the best of trainings in the collection of facts . . . What should be left behind by such a bit of work ought to be some knowledge of method and criticism, an insight into the handling of books, in weighing of evidence, and some familiarity with medieval Latin and old French.' See also Thomas Hodgkin, *The History of England from the Earliest Times to the Norman Conquest* (London, 1906), p. 506: 'It is to be wished that some scholar would carefully sift the Welsh chronicles and poems, and tell us what are the *solid historical facts* that may be gathered from their pages' (emphasis added).

12   Lloyd to Edward Owen, 18 June 1916, NLW, Edward Owen Papers 18099C, evidently referring to Royal Commission on the Ancient and Historical Monuments and Constructions in Wales and Monmouthshire, *An Inventory of the Ancient Monuments in Wales and Monmouthshire, V, County of Carmarthen* (London, 1917).

13   *HW*, I, pp. [v], ix; BU, Bangor MSS 13933–4 (Lloyd's annotated copy of *HW* (2nd edn, London, 1912)), first flyleaf of each volume and pp. 208, 429, 508, 599, 687.

14   See above, pp. 4–8, and cf. Jann, *Art and Science of Victorian History*, pp. xxvii, 213–14.

15   *HW*, II, p. 379. Lloyd had already noticed the significance of the reference to *Porthlarg* (Waterford) for the dating of the Life: J. E. Lloyd, 'Wales and the coming of the Normans', *THSC*, 1899–1900, 152, n. 1; cf. Arthur

Jones (ed.), *The History of Gruffydd ap Cynan* (Manchester, 1910), pp. [v], 18–19.

[16] *HW*, I, p. 327, n. 27.

[17] J. E. Lloyd, *The Welsh Chronicles* (London, 1928); quotation at p. 4.

[18] *HW*, I, p. vi.

[19] LP 41A, no. 8 (6 August 1903), referring to Edward Hyde, earl of Clarendon (1609–74), *The History of the Rebellion and Civil Wars in England Begun in the Year 1641* (1703); David Hume, *The History of England, from the Invasion of Julius Caesar to the Revolution in 1688* (1754–62); Sharon Turner, *The History of the Anglo-Saxons* (1799–1805). Cf. also n. 21 below.

[20] LP 41A, no. 1 (7 August 1905; repeated 1907). For Lingard, see also below, p. 219, n.15. Cf. the rationale for 'standard histories' in C. Oman, 'Introductory note', in H. W. C. Davis, *England under the Normans and Angevins 1066–1272* (London, 1905), p. vi.

[21] T. F. Tout, *The History of England from the Accession of Henry III. to the Death of Edward III. (1216–1377)* (London, 1905), p. 462, which adds that Pauli's coverage of the period in vols III and IV of J. M. Lappenberg et al., *Geschichte von England* (1834–98) 'remains . . . the fullest and most satisfactory *working up* in detail of these reigns' (emphasis added).

[22] Before obtaining (with Tout's help) a contract with Longmans, Lloyd had unsuccessfully approached both Constable and Blackie: Lloyd to Tout, 23 October, 17 November, 14 December 1909, Tout Papers 1/721/5–7. Longmans was a major publisher of history, including the *English Historical Review*: Asa Briggs, *A History of Longmans and their Books 1724–1990* (London/New Castle, DE, 2008), pp. 317–20. There were no similar publishing houses to these in Wales before the establishment of the University of Wales Press Board in 1922, the nearest potential equivalents being the Honourable Society of Cymmrodorion and the University of Wales Guild of Graduates: cf. Brynley F. Roberts, 'Scholarly publishing 1820–1922', in Philip Henry Jones and Eiluned Rees (eds), *A Nation and its Books: A History of the Book in Wales* ([Aberystwyth] 1998), pp. 221–35.

[23] Thomas Stephens, *The Literature of the Kymry* (Merthyr Tydfil, 1849), p. vii. Cf. above, pp. 5–7.

[24] See Geraint H. Jenkins, '"Wales, the Welsh and the Welsh language": introduction', in idem (ed.), *The Welsh Language and its Social Domains 1801–1911* (Cardiff, 2000), pp. 6–10, 17–19, 23–7, 34–5.

[25] John Rhys, *Lectures on Welsh Philology* (London, 1877); J. Morris-Jones, *A Welsh Grammar, Historical and Comparative* (Oxford, 1913). Cf. Hywel Teifi Edwards, 'John Rhŷs yn achos trafferth', *Y Traethodydd*, 161 (2006), 162–86.

[26] John Edward Lloyd, 'A dictionary of Welsh biography', *THSC*, 1938, 74–5. By contrast, W. J. Gruffydd argued forcefully for publishing the

dictionary first in Welsh, a view which prevailed by 1944: LP 68 nos 22, 24.
27 Lloyd, *Brief Bibliography*, p. 2. For Lloyd's early familiarity with these Welsh-language works, see above, p. 24.
28 John E. Lloyd, 'Taliesin Ben Beirdd', *Y Geninen*, 2 (1884), 145, 148.
29 Jenkins, 'Lloyd', 84–5; Thomas Richards, 'Sir John Lloyd', *TCHS*, 8 (1947), 1–2.
30 Lloyd, *Llyfr Cyntaf*, p. [3]:

> yr ydys wedi gwneud pob ymdrech i sicrhau cywirdeb yn y ffeithiau. Mae gwir hanes Cymru wedi gorwedd mor hir dan bentwr o chwedlau fel mai prin, fe allai, yr adnebydd ambell i Gymro ei wlad yn y tudalennau a ganlyn; ond teimlwyd bod dechreuad cyfnod newydd ar addysg yng Nghymru yn gofyn am gyfnewidiad yn y mater hwn hefyd, ac y dylai y llyfrau hanes hyn fod yn wir hanesyddol, hyd yn oed ar draul esgeuluso llawer o draddodiadau difyr a hynafol. Gwir y dylai'r to sydd yn codi fod yn hyddysg yn chwedloniaeth y tadau, ond ni ddylent ei derbyn yn lle hanesiaeth.

Thomas Stephens, *Welshmen: A Sketch of their History, from the Earliest Times to the Death of Llywelyn, the Last Welsh Prince* (London/Cardiff, 1901), pp. 3–4, similarly presents itself as an attempt to satisfy a 'growing demand' for knowledge about the early Welsh past resulting from changes in education.
31 Lloyd, *Ail Lyfr*, p. 3: 'am fod cymaint o wir yn y chwedlau, a neb, serch hynny, yn medru dweyd yn benderfynol pa faint'. The same point is made in *HW*, I, pp. 124–5.
32 *HW*, I, pp. 2–3. Lloyd dismissed the authenticity of the collection of triads to which this example belongs, and in the third edition of the *History* accepted G. J. Williams's argument that these had been fabricated by Iolo Morganwg: *HW* (1939), I, p. 123.
33 *HW*, I, pp. 11–12.
34 Ibid., pp. 43–6 (quotation at p. 46, referring to John Morris-Jones, 'Gorsedd Beirdd Ynys Prydain', *Cymru*, 10 (1896), 21–9, 133–40, 153–61, 198–204, 293–9). See further Marion Löffler, *The Literary and Historical Legacy of Iolo Morganwg, 1826–1926* (Cardiff, 2007), pp. 139–43. Lloyd had earlier criticized Davies for bringing Welsh literature into disrepute with outsiders: 'Taliesin Ben Beirdd. II', *Y Geninen*, 3 (1885), 65–9.
35 *HW*, I, p. 46.
36 Lloyd, 'Taliesin Ben Beirdd. II', esp. 69 ('pe dibynu a wnelsem yn hollol ar lais awdurdodol Hanesyddiaeth').
37 *HW*, I, p. 5.
38 Ibid., pp. 25–6. For an earlier discussion of the legend, described as 'a bit, not of Welsh history . . . but of old Welsh mythology', see J. E. Lloyd, 'The buried hundred', *UCW Mag.*, 13 (1890–1), 261–6 (quotation at 264).
39 *HW*, I, p. 116.

40 *HW*, I, pp. 116–20. See also the note on BL, Harleian MS 3859: ibid., pp. 159–60.

41 *HW*, I, p. 338. Cf. *HW*, II, p. 587, which states that 'there is good reason for thinking' that, after his father's death, the young Llywelyn ap Iorwerth (d.1240) 'was taken for safety from his first home at Dolwyddelan or its neighbourhood' to Powys, while noting (ibid., n. 63), with reference to antiquarian sources, that the tradition he was born at Dolwyddelan 'is merely a conjecture'. However, Lloyd, note of reply to letter from J. Davies, 2 April 1936, LP 317 no. 53, was less cautious: 'Trad[ition] only as to birth of Ll[ywely]n: prob[ably] sound.'

42 *HW*, I, pp. 341–2, 354–6.

43 The principal primary and secondary sources used are listed in *HW*, I, pp. xiii–xxiv, reflecting the thorough preparation shown by his notebooks, e.g. LP 32–7.

44 Cf. Edwards, 'Lloyd', 322; A. D. Carr, *Medieval Wales* (Houndmills, 1995), p. 14.

45 *HW*, I, pp. vi, 27, 43, 280; II, pp. 379, 487, 537, n. 2. Cf. Hodgkin, *History of England*, p. 493; Tout, *History of England*, p. 443; see above, pp. 42–3.

46 Cf. the lengthy list of archival sources in a celebrated French work published in the same year as *HW*: Lucien Febvre, *Philippe II et la Franche-Comté* (Paris, 1911), pp. xvi–xxvii. See also Anthony Grafton, *The Footnote: A Curious History* (London, 1997), chapter 2.

47 LP 41A, no. 1.

48 Glanmor Williams, 'Preface', in Sir J. E. Lloyd, *A History of Wales*, vol. I (facsimile repr. of 3rd edn; Carmarthen, 1988), p. xv.

49 John E. Morris, *The Welsh Wars of Edward I: A Contribution to Mediaeval Military History, Based on Original Documents* (Oxford, 1901); Edward Arthur Lewis, *The Mediaeval Boroughs of Snowdonia* (London, 1912). See also Alfred Neobard Palmer and Edward Owen, *A History of Ancient Tenures in North Wales and the Marches* (2nd edn, n.p., 1910), and, for the use of sources by MA students at Bangor, above, p. 71.

50 For 'the cult of original research', see Jann, *Art and Science of Victorian History*, pp. 216–18. See also Michael Bentley, *Modernizing England's Past: English Historiography in the Age of Modernism 1870–1970* (Cambridge, 2005), pp. 202–3.

51 Lewis, *Mediaeval Boroughs*, title page and p. v; Morris, *Welsh Wars*, p. viii. Caroline A. J. Skeel, *The Council in the Marches of Wales: A Study in Local Government during the Sixteenth and Seventeenth Centuries* (London, 1903; reissued 1904), which made extensive use of unpublished sources (listed at pp. ix–xii), also secured its author a London doctorate; see further Neil Evans, 'Finding a new story: the search for a usable past in Wales, 1869–1930', *THSC*, new ser., 10 (2004), 160.

52 See above, pp. 95–6.

53 *HW*, I, p. 229. This is borne out by the detailed preparatory notebooks for this chapter and related topics: LP 42–9.

54 J. E. Lloyd, 'Adjudication', in E. Vincent Evans (ed.), *The Thirty-Eighth Annual Report of the National Eisteddfod Association . . . National Eisteddfod (Neath), 1918* (Cardiff, 1919), pp. 77–8.

55 Ibid., p. 81. The essay, by Lloyd's former pupil Thomas Richards, was published as *The History of the Puritan Movement in Wales* (London, 1920), with a preface by Lloyd praising the author as 'the first who has examined and collated the MS. evidence' (ibid., p. viii).

56 David Knowles, *Great Historical Enterprises and Problems in Monastic History* (London, 1963), pp. 65–134; Patrick J. Geary, *The Myth of Nations: The Medieval Origins of Europe* (Princeton, NJ/Oxford, 2002), pp. 26–9; Joep Leerssen, *National Thought in Europe: A Cultural History* (Amsterdam, 2006), pp. 191, 199–200. In addition, some earlier national collections of sources were republished in the nineteenth century, e.g. Dugdale's *Monasticon Anglicanum* and Bouquet's *Recueil des historiens des Gaules et de la France*.

57 See above, pp. 75–6.

58 *HW*, I, pp. xv–xxvi; II, p. 612; J. Gwenogvryn Evans, *Report on Manuscripts in the Welsh Language*, 2 vols (London, 1898–1910).

59 *HW*, I, p. 159, referring to John Williams (Ab Ithel) (ed.), *Annales Cambriae* (Rolls Series, London, 1860); Egerton Phillimore, 'The *Annales Cambriae* and Old-Welsh genealogies from Harleian MS. 3859', *Y Cymmrodor*, 9 (1888), 141–83. See also Lloyd, 'Wales and the coming of the Normans', 165.

60 Lloyd, 'Organization', 120.

61 Lloyd, 'Wales and the coming of the Normans', 165–79; BU, Bangor MS 8716 (Lloyd's annotated copy of John Williams (Ab Ithel) (ed.), *Brut y Tywysogion* (Rolls Series, London, 1860)); see above, pp. 64–5. See also BU, Bangor MS 8717 (Lloyd's annotated copy of Ab Ithel (ed.), *Annales Cambriae*); Lloyd, *Welsh Chronicles*, p. 10.

62 A. L. Smith, *Church and State in the Middle Ages: The Ford Lectures Delivered at Oxford in 1905* (Oxford, 1913), p. 1 (emphasis added).

63 Ibid., pp. 33, 36, n. 1 *et passim*.

64 Tout, *History of England*, p. 443.

65 Tout, 'Schools of history', pp. 106–7; idem, *Chapters in the Administrative History of Mediaeval England*, 6 vols (Manchester, 1920–33) (with list of sources in I, pp. ix–xiv).

66 Tout, 'Schools of history', p. 96.

67 Tout, *History of England*, esp. pp. 443–62; idem, 'Wales and the march during the barons' wars' [1902], *Collected Papers*, vol. II (Manchester, 1934), p. 48: 'The present paper attempts to recast the facts that can be gathered from printed sources'. See also a 'standard history' by another Oxford historian and friend of Lloyd's: Davis, *England under the Normans and Angevins*, which refers extensively to printed sources (listed at pp. 534–41), and declares (p. xi) that 'the book is based throughout on the original authorities'.

68   Leopold von Ranke, *A History of England Principally in the Seventeenth Century*, 6 vols (Oxford, 1875), I, p. v. For Lloyd's familiarity with this work, see above, p. 42, and cf. Jenkins, 'Lloyd', 81.

69   For Ranke's approach, see Hayden White, *Metahistory: The Historical Imagination in Nineteenth-Century Europe* (Baltimore, MD/London, 1973), chapter 4; Peter Gay, *Style in History* (London, 1975), chapter 2.

70   LP 41A, no. 1 (1907).

71   *HW*, I, p. 227.

72   See above, pp. 95–6.

73   See above, p. 95; Lloyd, *Llyfr Cyntaf*; idem, *Ail Lyfr*; idem, *Trydydd Llyfr*.

74   Cf. Tout, review of *HW*, 132, 133, 134–5. The three divisions occupy approximately 200, 160 and 400 pages respectively.

75   Cf. Edwards, 'Lloyd', 322–3, and see also below, pp. 135, 151–3.

76   See below, chapter 7, esp. p. 133, and, for the sidelining of the Normans in Lloyd's account, Huw Pryce, 'The Normans in Welsh history', in C. P. Lewis (ed.), *Anglo-Norman Studies XXX* (Woodbridge, 2008), pp. 13–15.

77   *HBC*.

78   This may be contrasted with the work Lloyd effectively claimed to supersede (*HW*, I, p. v), namely Williams, *History of Wales*, chapters XIII–XVI, which cover 1039–1137 in chronological succession; as throughout the book, each chapter provides a continuous narrative subdivided only by six to eight short numbered, but untitled, sections. Likewise *HBC*, II, section I, chapters I–VI, provides a chronological narrative of political history from 1066 to 1137, without any subdivisions.

79   IV. 3; VI. 2; VII. 2–3; XII. 4; XIII. 3; XVI. 3; XVII. 2. See also below, pp. 146–9.

80   *HW*, II, pp. 462–86.

81   *HW*, II, p. 462.

82   Ibid., p. 469.

83   Ibid.

84   Ibid., p. 480.

85   Ibid.

86   Ibid., p. 485.

87   *HW*, I, pp. 81 (cited below, p. 129), 235, 236, 245, 249; II, p. 399.

88   Ranke, *History of England*, vol. I, p. vi.

89   Jenkins, 'Lloyd', 81: 'fe fedrai sgrifennu – sgrifennu'n gain, weithiau'n lliwgar, yn aml iawn yn arddunol'.

90   Cf. Grafton, *Footnote*, pp. 15, 232–3.

91   For example, *HW*, II, p. 555, cited in Williams, 'Preface', p. xii, which notes that Lloyd's 'jokes were mostly at the expense of saints or religious figures'.

92   *HW*, I, pp. 236, 245, 263, 270 (and, for post-Roman Wales as a 'romantic' period, ibid., pp. 124, 134); Lloyd, 'Buried hundred', 266; idem, 'Wales: the land and its people', *Wales*, 2 (1912), 360, 361; Elfed, 'Dewisol lyfrau yr oes hon', *Cyfaill yr Aelwyd a'r Frythones*, new ser., 1 (1892), 162.

Contrast Stubbs's skilful use of organic and mechanical metaphors noticed in J. W. Burrow, *A Liberal Descent: Victorian Historians and the English Past* (Cambridge, 1981), pp. 145–7.

93   Jenkins, 'Lloyd', 81–2.

94   *HW*, II, 522, 623; see also ibid., pp. 478 ('the tide of revolt'), 694 ('Between two tides'), and below, p. 166.

95   *HW*, II, p. 764; see below, pp. 167–8.

7 Origins: From Prehistoric to Post-Roman Wales

1   James Harvey Robinson, 'The new allies of history', in idem, *The New History: Essays Illustrating the Modern Historical Outlook* (New York, 1912), pp. 70–100, esp. pp. 84–7; for the date, see ibid., p. v.

2   Daniel Lord Smail, *On Deep History and the Brain* (Berkeley/Los Angeles/London, 2008), pp. 31–3. See also Doris Goldstein, 'Confronting time: the Oxford school of history and the non-Darwinian revolution', *Storia della Storiografia*, 45 (2004), 3–27.

3   See, for instance, Susan Reynolds, 'Medieval *origines gentium* and the community of the realm', *History*, 68 (1983), 375–90; Andrew Hadfield, 'Briton and Scythian: Tudor representations of Irish origins', *Irish Historical Studies*, 28 (1993), 390–408; Thomas Nicklas, 'Gallier, Germanen, Trojaner. Zur Geschichtspolitik im Frankreich des 16. Jahrhunderts', *Francia*, 32, 2 (2005), 145–58; Hugh A. MacDougall, *Racial Myth in English History: Trojans, Teutons, and Anglo-Saxons* (Montreal/Hanover, NH, 1982); Colin Kidd, *British Identities before Nationalism: Ethnicity and Nationhood in the Atlantic World 1600–1800* (Cambridge, 1999), pp. 59–72.

4   *Historia Brittonum*, cc. 10–11, 17–18, ed. and trans. John Morris, *Nennius: British History and the Welsh Annals* (London/Chichester, 1980), pp. 19–20, 22, 60–1, 63.

5   Geoffrey of Monmouth, *The History of the Kings of Britain*, ed. Michael D. Reeve and trans. Neil Wright (Woodbridge, 2007), pp. 26–31.

6   Brynley F. Roberts, 'The *Historia Regum Britanniae* in Wales', in idem (ed.), *Brut y Brenhinedd: Llanstephan MS. 1 Version* (Dublin, 1971), pp. 55–74; Ceri Davies, *Welsh Literature and the Classical Tradition* (Cardiff, 1995), pp. 60–3.

7   Glyn E. Daniel, 'Who are the Welsh?', *Proceedings of the British Academy*, 40 (1954), 148; Timothy Champion, 'The appropriation of the Phoenicians in British imperial ideology', *Nations and Nationalism*, 7 (2001), 451–65.

8   Geraint H. Jenkins, 'Evans, Theophilus (1693–1767)', *ODNB*.

9   For Pezron and his influence, see Kidd, *British Identities*, pp. 66–70.

10   Theophilus Evans, *Drych y Prif Oesoedd. Yn ôl yr Argraffiad Cyntaf: 1716*, ed. Garfield H. Hughes (Cardiff, 1961), pp. 18–19, 22–4.

11 Marion Löffler, *The Literary and Historical Legacy of Iolo Morganwg, 1826–1926* (Cardiff, 2007).

12 R. W. Morgan, *The British Kymry, or Britons of Cambria: Outlines of their History and Institutions, from the Earliest to the Present Times* (Ruthin/ London [1857]).

13 John Rhys and David Brynmor-Jones, *The Welsh People* (London, 1900), p. xxii.

14 T. D. Kendrick, *British Antiquity* (London, 1950), chapters VI–VII; May McKisack, *Medieval History in the Tudor Age* (Oxford, 1971), pp. 98–103; Davies, *Welsh Literature and the Classical Tradition*, p. 60.

15 A periodization still commonplace in the later nineteenth century according to Lloyd, *Wales and the Past – Two Voices* (Cardiff, 1932), p. 8. For an influential example, see John Lingard, *A History of England from the First Invasion of the Romans (to the Revolution of 1688)*, 8 vols (London, 1819–30), of which new editions continued to be published into the early twentieth century. Cf. T. F. Tout, *The History of England from the Accession of Henry III. to the Death of Edward III. (1216–1377)* (London, 1905), p. [i].

16 William Coxe, *An Historical Tour in Monmouthshire*, 2 vols (London, 1801), vol. I, pp. 3, 6.

17 Rice Rees, *An Essay on the Welsh Saints or the Primitive Christians usually considered to have been the Founders of Churches in Wales* (London, 1836), esp. pp. vi–viii, x; Thomas Stephens, *The Literature of the Kymry* (Llandovery, 1849). For Stephens, see Löffler, *Literary and Historical Legacy*, pp. 32–3, 56–7, 134–7.

18 Ben Bowen Thomas, 'The Cambrians and the nineteenth-century crisis in Welsh studies, 1847–70', *Arch. Camb.*, 127 (1978), 1–15.

19 Thomas Price, *Hanes Cymru, a Chenedl y Cymry, o'r Cynoesoedd hyd at Farwolaeth Llewelyn ap Gruffydd; ynghyd a Rhai Cofiaint Perthynol i'r Amseroedd o'r Pryd Hynny i Waered* (Crickhowell, 1842), pp. 1–12.

20 For a recent overview, see Graham Parry, 'Edward Lhuyd: from formed stones to standing stones', *WHR*, 25, 1 (2010), 7–17.

21 B. B. Woodward, *The History of Wales, from the Earliest Times, to its Final Incorporation with the Kingdom of England* (London/New York, 1853), p. iv. Cf. ibid., p. v, where Woodward admits to having erred in the early parts of the work by narrating legends as 'genuine history'.

22 Ibid., p. 21. For Prichard, see George W. Stocking, 'From chronology to ethnology: James Cowles Prichard and British anthropology 1800–1850', in idem (ed.), James Cowles Prichard, *Researches into the Physical History of Man* (Chicago, IL/London, 1973), pp. ix–cx; H. F. Augstein, *James Cowles Prichard's Anthropology: Remaking the Science of Man in Early Nineteenth-Century Britain* (Amsterdam/Atlanta, GA, 1999).

23 Woodward, *History of Wales*, pp. 21–4.

24 Peter Rowley-Conwy, *From Genesis to Prehistory: The Archaeological Three Age System and its Contested Reception in Denmark, Britain, and*

Ireland (Oxford, 2007), chapters 2–4, esp. pp. 89–99. The new periodization was accepted earlier in Scotland, however, thanks to Daniel Wilson, whose *The Archaeology and Prehistoric Annals of Scotland* appeared in 1851: ibid., chapter 5.

25 Woodward, *History of Wales*, p. 25.

26 Ibid., p. 31.

27 Williams, *History of Wales*, pp. 9–10, 16, 17.

28 *HBC*, I, pp. 46–7, 54 (quotation), 66–73.

29 Ibid., pp. 2–3, 14, 16, 20–2, 83–5.

30 For recent discussion of Teutonism and its critics in the nineteenth and early twentieth centuries, see Robert J. C. Young, *The Idea of English Ethnicity* (Malden, MA, 2008).

31 Reginald Horsman, 'Origins of racial Anglo-Saxonism in Great Britain before 1850', *Journal of the History of Ideas*, 37 (1976), 387–410; Michael Banton, *The Idea of Race* (London, 1977), pp. 23–6; J. W. Burrow, *A Liberal Descent: Victorian Historians and the English Past* (Cambridge, 1981), pp. 188–92; George W. Stocking, *Victorian Anthropology* (New York, 1987), pp. 62–3; Peter J. Bowler, *The Invention of Progress: The Victorians and the Past* (Oxford, 1989), pp. 55–6, 59–66.

32 Richard Hingley, *The Recovery of Roman Britain 1586–1906: A Colony So Fertile* (Oxford, 2008), pp. 275–8, 291, 299.

33 Luke Owen Pike, *The English and their Origin: A Prologue to Authentic English History* (London, 1866), esp. pp. 106–29, 150–8, 171–8, 183–237, 242–3.

34 Bruce G. Trigger, *A History of Archaeological Thought* (Cambridge, 1989), pp. 87–102; Rowley-Conwy, *From Genesis to Prehistory*, chapter 7.

35 Trigger, *History of Archaeological Thought*, pp. 110–18. For racial continuity between prehistoric and modern populations in works used by Lloyd, see W. Boyd Dawkins, *Early Man in Britain and his Place in the Tertiary Period* (London, 1880), chapter IX, esp. pp. 309–16, 330–1; Isaac Taylor, *The Origin of the Aryans: An Account of the Prehistoric Ethnology and Civilisation of Europe* (London, 1889), pp. 63–81.

36 Taylor, *Origin of the Aryans*, esp. pp. 5, 204–13, 273–81; Stocking, *Victorian Anthropology*, pp. 65–8.

37 Nancy Stepan, *The Idea of Race in Science: Great Britain 1800–1960* (London, 1982), pp. 93–110 (quotation at p. 93).

38 For the need to distinguish between race and nation, see Isambard Owen, 'Race and nationality', *Y Cymmrodor*, 8 (1887), 1–24, esp. 11; William Z. Ripley, *The Races of Europe: A Sociological Study* (London/New York, 1899), pp. 15–16, 17, 32, 56. For contrary views, see the arguments against home rule in John Lubbock, 'The nationalities of the United Kingdom: extracts from letters to the "Times"', *Journal of the Anthropological Institute of Great Britain and Ireland*, 16 (1887), 418–22; Boyd Dawkins, *The Place of the Welsh in the History of Britain* (London/Manchester, 1889), esp. pp. 5–6, 14–15, 45–8. In addition, 'race' still continued to be

used with the general meaning of 'nation' or 'people'; new scholarly definitions were no guarantee of terminological consistency: see below, n. 75.

39   Thomas Henry Huxley, 'On the methods and results of ethnology', in
     idem, *Critiques and Addresses* (London, 1873), p. 140. See also idem, 'On
     some fixed points in British ethnology' [1870], ibid., pp. 167–80; Stepan,
     Idea of Race, pp. 78–82; and, for other mid-nineteenth-century views
     favouring a hybrid ancestry for the English, Tony Ballantyne, *Orientalism
     and Race: Aryanism in the British Empire* (Houndmills/New York, 2002),
     pp. 41, 206, n. 119. For hostility to the idea of racial hybridity, though,
     see Young, *Idea of English Ethnicity*, pp. 153–5.
40   John Beddoe, *The Races of Britain: A Contribution to the Anthropology
     of Western Europe* (Bristol/London, 1885), p. 269, n. *.
41   Grant Allen, *Anglo-Saxon Britain* (London [1881]), pp. vi, 70.
42   Ibid., pp. 226, 229.
43   Charles Elton, *Origins of English History* (London, 1882), pp. 2, 232. For
     further evidence of Arnold's influence in this context, see Dawkins, *Place
     of the Welsh*, p. 42; John Williams, 'Influence of the Welsh on the form-
     ation of the British constitution', in *Transactions of the Royal National
     Eisteddfod of Wales, Liverpool, 1884* (Liverpool, 1885), pp. 482–5;
     Bertram C. A. Windle, *Life in Early Britain* (London, 1897), p. 219.
44   Elton, *Origins of English History*, p. 142. See also ibid., pp. vi–vii: 'The
     men of the long heads . . . and the men of the round skulls . . . have left
     abiding influences on the population of Britain.' The prevalence of such
     views in the late nineteenth and early twentieth centuries is emphasized
     in Stepan, *Idea of Race*, p. 103.
45   Windle, *Life in Early Britain*, pp. 1–10, 215–19; 'General advertisement',
     in *The Victoria History of the Counties of England. Hampshire and the
     Isle of Wight. Volume One* (Westminster, 1900), p. vii; Thomas Hodgkin,
     The History of England from the Earliest Times to the Norman Conquest
     (London, 1906), pp. 1–7; Charles Oman, *England before the Norman
     Conquest, being a History of the Celtic, Roman and Anglo-Saxon Periods
     down to the Year A.D. 1066* (London, 1910), pp. 1–10.
46   J. B. Bury, 'The science of history' [1902], in Fritz Stern (ed.), *The
     Varieties of History from Voltaire to the Present* (2nd edn, London/
     Basingstoke, 1970), pp. 222–3.
47   Contrast nineteenth- and early twentieth-century Norwegian and
     Finnish attempts to claim radically different racial origins from dom-
     inant neighbours: Knut Kjeldstadli, 'History as science', in William H.
     Hubbard et al. (eds), *Making a Historical Culture: Historiography in
     Norway* (Oslo, 1995), pp. 53–4; Derek Fewster, *Visions of Past Glory:
     Nationalism and the Construction of Early Finnish History* (Studia Fennica
     Historica, 11; Helsinki, 2006), pp. 117–18, 299–300.
48   Dawkins, *Place of the Welsh*, pp. 45–8, even argued that from the late
     thirteenth century onwards the English and Welsh had been gradually
     fused into one nation.

[49] Elton, *Origins of English History*, pp. vii, 102, also acknowledged a debt to Rhys, but, unlike Lloyd, did not try to synthesize the conclusions of the latter's *Celtic Britain* with those of prehistoric archaeology.

[50] See above, p. 44. Debt to Rhys: Lloyd, 'History', pp. 354, 359; idem, *Llyfr Cyntaf*, p. 3; *HW*, I, p. viii.

[51] Lloyd, *Wales and the Past*, pp. 8–9.

[52] Dawkins, *Early Man in Britain*, p. 340.

[53] Ibid., pp. 7–8, 486–7. For the views of Dawkins and others on racial invasions, see Bowler, *Invention of Progress*, pp. 115–28.

[54] John Rhys, *Celtic Britain* (London, 1882), pp. 2–4, 52–3, 80, 215, 242–4, 257–8, 262–3, 270–1. For the description of the Silures in Tacitus' *Agricola*, see *HW*, I, p. 15 and n. 48. The Goidelic theory was first developed by Edward Lhuyd: Daniel, 'Who are the Welsh?', 150–1.

[55] Rhys and Brynmor-Jones, *Welsh People*, pp. 10–13.

[56] Ibid., p. 13.

[57] Rhys, *Celtic Britain*, p. 272.

[58] Ibid., chapter IV, esp. pp. 138–9; Rhys and Brynmor-Jones, *Welsh People*, pp. xxiii, 118–20.

[59] Rhys, *Celtic Britain*, pp. 245–7, 255–6, 272. Cf. Rhys and Brynmor-Jones, *Welsh People*, pp. 1, 4–5.

[60] Lloyd, *Wales and the Past*, p. 8, observed, with only slight exaggeration, that it was 'remarkable' that Rhys's *Celtic Britain* 'gathers together . . . every scrap of evidence to be drawn from the philological, literary and ethnological sources, but appears to know nothing of the bearing upon his subject of the conclusions of prehistoric archaeology. The gap between arts and science was as yet too wide . . .' Owen, 'Race and nationality', 3–4, 6, is another early, but very sketchy, attempt to correlate Rhys's picture of racial invasions with archaeological evidence. For a fuller attempt, comparable in detail to that in O. M. Edwards's *Wales*, see Thomas Stephens, *Welshmen: A Sketch of their History, from the Earliest Times to the Death of Llywelyn, the Last Welsh Prince* (London/Cardiff, 1901), pp. 1–28.

[61] LP 212 (26 January 1901–30 July 1902).

[62] *HW*, I, p. 1.

[63] Ibid., p. 3. This break was argued, with respect to Europe as a whole, in Dawkins, *Early Man*, pp. 242–3, 265–6, and also followed by Elton, *Origins of the English*, p. 128; Hodgkin, *History of England*, p. 3. However, the point was controversial: Beddoe, *Races of Britain*, p. 9; Windle, *Life in Early Britain*, pp. 8, 207.

[64] *HW*, I, p. 4. Cf. Hodgkin, *History of England*, p. 5: 'the age of iron may be said to have lasted through Roman, Saxon and Norman domination down to our own day'.

[65] A classification also accepted in John Evans, *A Popular History of the Ancient Britons or the Welsh People* (London, 1901), p. 13; Edwards, *Wales*, pp. 10–15.

[66] *HW*, I, pp. 30, 54, 58, 110–22; see below, pp. 132–3.

⁶⁷   *History of Wales* (1930), pp. 7–8; *HW* (1939), I, pp. xxxi–xxxvii (which also refines the earlier chronology by referring, p. xxxi, to the Mesolithic period, drawn to Lloyd's attention in Cyril Fox, 'Presidential address', *Arch. Camb.*, 88 (1933), 156; see LP 32, p. 32; Trigger, *History of Archaeological Thought*, p. 155. Lloyd was also influenced by criticism of Rhys's hypothesis of a Goidelic invasion (*History of Wales* (1930), p. 9; *HW* (1939), I, p. xxxix; cf. LP 33, fol. 58v), and was familiar with the revised interpretation of Welsh racial origins advanced by H. J. Fleure, whose *The Races of England and Wales* (London, 1923) was added to the list of 'authorities' for prehistoric Britain in LP 32, p. 4.

⁶⁸   Cf. also Lloyd, *Llyfr Cyntaf*, p. 11: 'Thus, though ancestors of ours have for many centuries lived among the hills of Wales, we should not recognize one of them, if he were to come to life again, but should certainly believe him to be some wild savage.'

⁶⁹   *HW*, I, p. 13. For other examples of racial thinking applied to Wales see F. W. Rudler, 'Welsh anthropology', *Y Cymmrodor*, 4 (1881), 70–89; Dawkins, *Early Man in Britain*, p. 330; idem, 'The ancient ethnology of Wales', *Y Cymmrodor*, 5 (1882), 209–23; idem, *Place of the Welsh*.

⁷⁰   *HW*, I, p. 15 and n. 47.

⁷¹   This is true, for example, of two of the works cited in *HW*, I, p. 1, n. 1: Taylor, *Origin of the Aryans*, pp. 244–50; Ripley, *Races of Europe*, pp. 332–4. See also [William] Geddes, *Historical Characteristics of the Celtic Race* (Aberdeen, 1885).

⁷²   *HW*, I, p. 15. For other racial explanations of Welsh religious history, see *History of Wales* (1930), pp. 52 (Quakers), 55–6 (Methodist revival).

⁷³   See below, pp. 137–8.

⁷⁴   See below, p. 158.

⁷⁵   Contrast Rhys, *Celtic Britain*, p. 64, for the alleged survival of Goidelic beliefs 'among the descendants of the ancient Silures' in the twelfth century, though *HW*, I, p. 274, suggests that the 'old Silurian traditions' may have contributed to the separate identity of Morgannwg in south-east Wales. Note also J. E. Lloyd, 'The preparation for the Norman conquest', in *Hutchinson's Story of the British Nation* (London [1922]), p. 202: Canute 'was of Polish ancestry on his mother's side and it cannot be doubted that the Slavonic blood he inherited tempered in him the fierce and reckless daring of the Scandinavian chief'. In common with many other writers well into the twentieth century, later in the *History* Lloyd uses the term 'race' in the general sense of 'people' or 'nation', rather than with specific reference to early racial groups: *HW*, I, p. 182; II, pp. 462, 740, 763.

⁷⁶   *HW*, I, p. 30. Lloyd had earlier stated that the Bronze Age Goidels had introduced 'tribal life': *HW*, I, p. 23.

⁷⁷   *HW*, I, pp. 47–90 ('Wales under Roman Rule'); LP 212 (14 May–30 July 1902).

78 The relevance of the survey is made explicit in Lloyd, *Llyfr Cyntaf*, p. 85: 'since they are *our ancestors* and from them *springs the Welsh nation*, it is right that we should scan them more closely than their neighbours.' (Emphasis added.)

79 *HW*, I, p. 81.

80 Ibid., p. 59; quotation: Hingley, *Recovery of Roman Britain*, p. 313.

81 Lloyd, *Llyfr Cyntaf*, p. 104: 'It was in Wales as it is in India at present.' See also Hingley, *Recovery of Roman Britain*, pp. 238, 240–1, 308.

82 *HW*, I, pp. 59–61. Cf. Lloyd, 'History of Wales', p. 373.

83 *HW*, I, pp. 81–2.

84 Ibid., pp. 84–7, citing Joseph Marie Loth, *Les mots Latins dans les langues Brittoniques (gallois, armoricain, cornique), phonetique et commentaire, avec une introduction sur la romanization de l'île de Bretagne* (Paris, 1892). This seems also to have influenced Lloyd, *Llyfr Cyntaf*, pp. 105–6. For the concept of Romanization and its development by Haverfield, see Hingley, *Recovery of Roman Britain*, pp. 315–19.

85 *HW*, I, p. 84.

86 Ibid., p. 89. For the advent of Christianity, see chapter 8 below.

87 Lloyd, 'History of Wales', p. 365. Cf. Stubbs, *CH*, I, p. 12.

88 *HW*, I, p. 51. See also ibid., p. 82: 'It would, indeed, be not at all wonderful, but in conformity with the earlier and the later history of Britain, if it should ultimately appear that during the Roman period the corn-lands of the East went a different way from the rough hill-pastures of the West.'

89 Lloyd, *Ail Lyfr*, p. 83; *History of Wales* (1930), p. 5.

90 J. E. Lloyd, 'Wales: the land and its people', *Wales*, 2 (1912), 359–68.

91 Lloyd, 'Wales: the land and its people', 359.

92 Ibid.

93 Ibid., 360.

94 Edwards, *Wales*, p. 1. See Evans, 'Men and mountains', 224–7.

95 *HW*, I, p. 37. Lloyd explicitly drew a comparison with the pastoral society of the Old Testament patriarchs of Palestine, which, according to Henry Sumner Maine, *Ancient Law* (London, 1861), pp. 122–4, represented the first stage of society among *all* races: Lloyd, 'Wales', 361; *History of Wales* (1930), p. 5; Stocking, *Victorian Anthropology*, pp. 125–6. However, in his later account of bond vills Lloyd seems to contradict himself by making the Iberians agriculturalists: see below, p. 138.

96 *HW*, I, pp. 36–7, 51.

97 Lloyd, 'Wales', 362–3. *History of Wales* (1930), p. 5, is very similar.

98 *HW*, I, pp. 110–22.

99 *HW*, I, p. 191. For the term 'Cymry', see ibid., pp. 164, 191–2. The importance of 655 in defining Wales is already emphasized in Lloyd, 'History of Wales', pp. 381, 382 ('Period III. Mediaeval Wales. From 655 to 1282.'); idem, *Ail Lyfr Hanes*, pp. 79–83; and evidently derives from Rhys, *Celtic Britain*, p. 138. Cf. Rhys and Brynmor-Jones, *Welsh People*, p. 121.

[100] See above, p. 102.

8 Tribal Wales: Society and the Church

[1] Cf. Clive Dewey, 'Celtic agrarian legislation and the Celtic revival: historicist implications of Gladstone's Irish and Scottish land acts 1870–1886', *Past & Present*, 64 (1974), 30–70; John Shaw, 'Land, people and nation: historicist voices in the Highland land campaign, *c*.1850–1883', in Eugenio F. Biagini (ed.), *Citizenship and Community: Liberals, Radicals and Collective Identitties in the British Isles, 1865–1932* (Cambridge, 1996), pp. 305–24. True, J. E. Lloyd, *Early Welsh Agriculture* (Bangor, 1894), p. 14, observes that the study of medieval landholding could be relevant to the solution of contemporary agrarian problems, and that John Rhys and Frederic Seebohm were members of the Welsh Land Commission of 1893–6 (for which, see Morgan, *WBP*, pp. 123–9, 176–8). However, neither that lecture nor the *History* suggests that Lloyd was inspired to study these issues because of their potential bearing on modern economics and politics, in contrast to the motives declared in Frederic Seebohm, *The English Village Community Examined in its Relations to the Manorial and Tribal Systems and to the Common or Open Field System of Husbandry: An Essay in Economic History* (London, 1883), pp. vii–ix, 179–80, 439–41. Lloyd also differed from E. A. Lewis, who argued that both the Normans and Edward I had helped to lay the foundations of the modern Welsh economy: Huw Pryce, 'The Normans in Welsh history', in C. P. Lewis (ed.), *Anglo-Norman Studies XXX* (Woodbridge, 2008), pp. 15–16 and nn. 87–8.

[2] For comparison of Lloyd's interpretation of medieval Welsh society with that of other historians in his lifetime and later, see Huw Pryce, 'Cenedligrwydd a chymdeithas: dehongli oes y tywysogion', *TCHS*, 67 (2006), 12–29, esp. 17–20.

[3] Cf. Frederic Seebohm, *The Tribal System in Wales* (London, 1895), p. 172: the Church 'strikes from outside like a wedge into the Welsh Tribal system'.

[4] *HW*, I, chapters VIII–IX; II, pp. 604–11; written respectively November 1904–March 1905, April–May 1905; June 1908: LP 212.

[5] *HW*, I, pp. 291–2. See also above, pp. 131–2.

[6] LP 35, fol. 1v. Fuller exposition in LP 210 (draft introduction to abortive book on the laws *c*.1898: see below, p. 142); *HW*, II, pp. 606–11; Lloyd, 'Wales', 363–6.

[7] *HW*, II, p. 611. See also ibid., pp. 528–35, and Lloyd, 'Wales', 366. The point had already been made in Lloyd, 'History of Wales', p. 406: 'even though the Welsh tribesmen were but just emerging from the tribal mode of living . . . the age that produced the Bruts, the romantic tales, the poetry of Cynddelw . . . can scarcely be considered destitute of civilisation'.

8 *HW*, I, p. 284.

9 Ibid., p. 291.

10 Ibid., p. 297. Ibid., n. 97, cites Hubert Lewis, *The Ancient Laws of Wales, Viewed Especially in Regard to the Light They Throw upon the Origin of Some English Institutions*, ed. J. E. Lloyd (London, 1889), p. 47; John Rhys and David Brynmor-Jones, *The Welsh People* (London, 1900), p. 251; Paul Vinogradoff, *The Growth of the Manor* (London, 1905), p. 25. Cf. Seebohm, *Tribal System*, pp. 105–6, 142, 147.

11 *HW*, I, p. 304. Despite the implication in ibid., n. 92, the connection with ancestor worship is lacking in Seebohm, *Tribal System*, pp. 81–3, and thus seems to have been deduced by Lloyd himself.

12 *HW*, I, p. 308 (citing Romans 13:4); see also ibid., p. 309.

13 Ibid., p. 291.

14 Ibid., II, p. 605. The idea already appears in Lloyd, 'History of Wales', p. 342: 'we see the tribal system, the earliest form of civilised organization, survive for many centuries after the manorial system had become firmly established in Europe and in England'. See also ibid., p. 365, cited above, pp. 130–1.

15 J. E. Lloyd, 'Wales: the land and its people', *Wales*, 2 (1912), 359–68, esp. 365.

16 *History* (1930), p. 31. Lloyd accepted, though, that conquest could make a difference in *HW*, I, p. 264: 'In the three southern cantrefs of Dyfed the traces of the ancient Welsh life have been almost entirely obliterated by the Norman Conquest and the Flemish and English settlements.'

17 Lloyd, 'Wales', 361–2.

18 *HW*, I, p. 302. For the equivalence of the cantref and tribe, see also ibid., p. 283.

19 Ibid., p. 243. See also ibid., p. 234.

20 One theme in the topographical survey is the reduction in the number of smaller dynasties by the tenth century as the result of conquest, usually by the rulers of Gwynedd: *HW*, I, pp. 237–8, 239, 257, 271.

21 Ibid., p. 303.

22 See ibid., p. 291, for '[t]he structure of Welsh society as an aggregation of kins'.

23 Ibid., p. 283.

24 Ibid., pp. 284–5.

25 Ibid., pp. 285–6, 297–9, 302.

26 Ibid., pp. 299–300.

27 Ibid., pp. 283–4. See also ibid., p. 308: 'From the earliest period at which it is possible to study the organisation of the Welsh tribes, they were under the rule of chiefs or kings.' Although some early kings, most notably Cunedda, established their authority over particular territories through conquest, Lloyd does not suggest that conquest was itself sufficient to endow the conqueror with royal status.

28 Ibid., pp. 293–7, 302–3, 308, 311–17.

29   Ibid., p. 317.
30   Ibid., p. 310. Cf. Edwards, 'Lloyd', 323–4.
31   Price, *Hanes Cymru*, pp. 637–48; *HBC*, II, pp. 158–65 (quotation at
     p. 158: 'gellir casglu i arferion teuluaidd a chymdeithasol y Cymry bara'n
     hynod ddigyfnewid dros lawer o oesau hirion'). For other accounts of
     twelfth-century Welsh society based mainly on Giraldus, see B. B.
     Woodward, *The History of Wales* (London/New York, 1853), pp. 316–21;
     Williams, *History of Wales*, pp. 288–91.
32   For the medieval sections, see *HBC*, I, pp. 481–6; II, pp. 158–73.
33   In England, this owed much to the influence of German legal history:
     J. W. Burrow, *A Liberal Descent: Victorian Historians and the English Past*
     (Cambridge, 1981), pp. 119–25; Adam Kuper, 'The rise and fall of Maine's
     patriarchal society', in Alan Diamond (ed.), *The Victorian Achievement
     of Sir Henry Maine: A Centennial Appraisal* (Cambridge, 1991), pp. 104–5.
34   Lewis, *Ancient Laws*; LP 210 ('Ancient Welsh Laws', which is presumably
     related to LP 52 ('The Ancient Laws of Wales. Notes, etc.'), also dating
     from after Lloyd's move to Bangor); 'Cyfreithiau'r Hen Gymry' (1938),
     LP 211, p. 6. The texts had been made more accessible, and understanding
     of them considerably advanced, by the publication of Aneurin Owen (ed.
     and trans.), *Ancient Laws and Institutes of Wales* (Record Commission,
     London, 1841), on whose genesis and significance see Hywel D. Emanuel,
     'Studies in the Welsh laws', in Elwyn Davies (ed.), *Celtic Studies in Wales:
     A Survey* (Cardiff, 1963), pp. 76–8; Glenda Carr, *William Owen Pughe*
     (Cardiff, 1983), pp. 247–50.
35   For a critical analysis of these prologues in a lecture at Bangor attended
     by Lloyd, see J. Goronwy Edwards, *Hywel Dda and the Welsh Lawbooks*
     (Hywel Dda Millenary Lecture, 9 May 1928; Bangor, 1929). Cf. LP 295:
     9 May 1928.
36   Cf. above, p. 104. *HW*, I, pp. 284, 338–42, 354–6. See also Lloyd, 'History
     of Wales', p. 385, which, while noting that the earliest surviving law texts
     date from *c*.1200, asserts that 'no doubt they depict a state of society
     which is in its main features as old as the tenth century, and is nothing
     less than the tribal system of pre-Roman times, developed considerably
     under the pressure of circumstances, yet substantially the same in its
     groundwork and main principles'.
37   *HBC*, I, pp. 466–79, 481–6; Lewis, *Ancient Laws*, pp. 79, 102–4 (the
     argument that the Anglo-Saxons had borrowed institutions such as com-
     purgation from the Britons also implied that some features of Welsh law
     already existed in the post-Roman period: cf. ibid., pp. vi, 410–11). The
     brief treatment in Price, *Hanes Cymru*, pp. 407–9, accepts that the law
     books contain some later material but regards them as largely reflecting
     the law in Hywel Dda's time, as does Ferdinand Walter, *Das alte Wales.
     Ein Beitrag zur Völker-, Rechts- und Kirchen-geschichte* (Bonn, 1859),
     pp. 356–7.
38   Woodward, *History of Wales*, pp. 174, 179–94.

³⁹ Seebohm, *Tribal System*, p. 52; F. W. Maitland, 'The tribal system in Wales' [1895], in H. A. L. Fisher (ed.), *The Collected Papers of Frederic William Maitland*, 3 vols (Cambridge, 1911), III, p. 3. Maitland had already recognized the challenges of interpreting the law texts in 'The laws of Wales – the kindred and the blood feud' [1881], in ibid., I, pp. 202–21. (Lloyd seems to have read these articles only after they were reprinted in 1911: LP 52, fols 8r, 91r, 117v.)

⁴⁰ For the tribe as an extension of the family in patriarchal society, which in turn was conceived of as the earliest form of social organization, see Henry Sumner Maine, *Ancient Law* (London, 1861), pp. 128–35, with discussion in Kuper, 'Rise and fall', pp. 99–110. See also Glanville R. J. Jones, 'The tribal system in Wales: a re-assessment in the light of settlement studies', *WHR*, 1, 2 (1961), 111–13; R. R. Davies, *Historical Perception: Celts and Saxons* (Cardiff, 1979), pp. 21–3; Wendy Davies, 'Looking backwards to the early medieval past: Wales and England, a contrast in approaches', *WHR*, 22 (2004–5), 206–9.

⁴¹ Seebohm, *Tribal System*, p. ix. This point had already been emphasized in idem, *English Village Community*, p. 244.

⁴² Seebohm, *English Village Community*, pp. 179, 412; J. W. Burrow, '"The village community" and the uses of history in late nineteenth-century England', in Neil McKendrick (ed.), *Historical Perspectives: Studies in English Thought and Society in Honour of J. H. Plumb* (London, 1974), pp. 255–84, esp. pp. 257–60, 273–5.

⁴³ Seebohm, *Tribal System*, chapters I–II and pp. 89–92, 94–7, 110–14 *et passim*. For early charters, see ibid., chapter VII.

⁴⁴ Ibid., p. 53.

⁴⁵ Walter, *Das alte Wales*, pp. 207–14; Lewis, *Ancient Laws*, pp. 43, 110–11, 142–50, 166–7, 178–91. It is worth noting that – like Seebohm, though in different ways from him – both these authors emphasized the wider comparative significance of medieval Wales, Walter presenting the Welsh as a people subject to Rome which had uniquely preserved its distinctive law and language in the post-Roman period, Lewis asserting that Welsh law provided parallels with many early English institutions and that the latter, therefore, had a common British origin with those of medieval Wales: Walter, *Das alte Wales*, p. vi; Lewis, *Ancient Laws*, pp. 201–543 (part II, 'The British element in English institutions', which occupies over 60 per cent of the book). For Walter, a product of German Romanticism whose interest in Welsh law had first been awakened in 1823, see Stefan Zimmer, 'Julius Rodenberg und Ferdinand Walter – deutsche Annäherungen an Wales im 19. Jahrhundert', in Bernhard Maier and Stefan Zimmer with Christiane Batke (eds), *150 Jahre 'Mabinogion' – deutsch-walisische Kulturbeziehungen* (Tübingen, 2001), pp. 258–63.

⁴⁶ *HW*, I, p. 283. The validity of combining the laws with the surveys is also accepted, albeit cautiously, in another work used by Lloyd: Vinogradoff, *Growth of the Manor*, pp. 3–4, 8–13. See also idem and Frank Morgan

(eds), *The Survey of the Honour of Denbigh 1334* (London, 1914), esp. pp. [v], xv–xxxv.

47 *HW*, I, pp. 231–2, 235, 236, 245, 250, 255, 281.

48 Why this was the case is unclear; possibly Lloyd was less confident than Seebohm and others that the social organization revealed by the extents could illuminate that of the early Middle Ages.

49 However, see *HW*, I, pp. 285, 286, 304, for references to Aryan customs; see above, n. 11, for Irish parallels; and, for comparisons with England, *HW*, I, pp. 298, 300, 317; Lloyd, *Early Welsh Agriculture*, pp. 5–6.

50 See above, pp. 87, 125.

51 *HW*, I, pp. 289–91. Cf. Seebohm, *Tribal System*, pp. 95–6 (citing Maine), criticized in Maitland, 'Tribal system', pp. 7–8.

52 *HW*, I, p. 297. Cf. Seebohm, *English Village Community*, pp. xiv, 179, 214, 437–8. Vinogradoff, *Growth of the Manor*, pp. 15, 19, refers to Welsh settlements as villages.

53 *HW*, I, pp. 292, 298. Cf. Maine, *Ancient Law*, p. 170; Alan D. J. Macfarlane, 'Some contributions of Maine to history and anthropology', in Diamond (ed.), *Victorian Achievement*, pp. 132–6.

54 Macfarlane, 'Some contributions', pp. 129–32.

55 See above, p. 138. The association of feudalism with foreign tyranny draws on the well-established notion of the 'Norman yoke' oppressing England; this was popularized by Walter Scott and thence promoted by Augustin Thierry's *Histoire de la conquête de l'Angleterre par les Normands* (1825), the English translation of which influenced the juxtaposition of Norman feudalism and Welsh freedom in Williams, *History of Wales*, pp. 205, 255. Cf. Marjorie Chibnall, *The Debate on the Norman Conquest* (Manchester/New York, 1999), pp. 53–5. Feudalism is likewise condemned as oppressive, though not exclusively alien, in *HBC*, II, p. 158, here perhaps echoing radical Liberal rhetoric against the political dominance of English or anglicized landlords in Victorian Wales: cf. Henry Richard, *Letters on the Social and Political Condition of the Principality of Wales* (London [1884]), p. 106. See also Rhys and Brynmor-Jones, *Welsh People*, pp. 438–52. Feudalism has different negative connotations, i.e. aristocratic independence from royal authority, in Stubbs, *CH*, I, pp. 374, 504, 538, 583, 596.

56 Seebohm, *Tribal System*, chapter VII; Alfred Neobard Palmer, 'The portionary churches of mediaeval north Wales', *Arch. Camb.*, 5th ser., 3 (1886), 175–209; J. W. Willis Bund, *The Celtic Church of Wales* (London, 1897).

57 For a criticism of Palmer, 'Portionary churches', an article that Lloyd otherwise admired, see *HW*, I, p. 205, n. 45. He later described Willis Bund, *Celtic Church*, as '[a] book of original, but highly disputable views': J. E. Lloyd, *A Brief Bibliography of Welsh History for the Use of Teachers*, Historical Association Leaflet no. 49 ([London] 1921), p. 4. Seebohm's reliance on early Welsh charter evidence was criticized in Maitland, 'Tribal system', pp. 8–9.

58 A feature praised in L. Gougaud, review of *HW, Revue d'histoire ecclésiastique*, 12, 1 (1911), 811: 'Souhaitons de voir ses conclusions judicieuses et exemptes de parti-pris s'imposer à tous les esprits sérieux' ('Let us hope to see his judicious and unbiased conclusions accepted by all serious minds').

59 *HW*, I, p. 173. For attempts to invoke medieval Welsh ecclesiastical history to argue for and against disestablishment, see respectively David Davies, *The Ancient Celtic Church of Wales: Where is It?* (London, 1910), and T. J. Jones, *The Church in Wales not Alien: A Reply to Mr. J. W. Willis Bund* (Cardiff, 1906).

60 See Glanmor Williams, 'Some protestant views of early British Church history', in idem, *Welsh Reformation Essays* (Cardiff, 1967), pp. 207–19, esp. pp. 215–16; Rice Rees, *An Essay on the Welsh Saints or the Primitive Christians usually considered to have been the Founders of Churches in Wales* (London, 1836), pp. 313–14.

61 LP 325 no. 1 (1 January 1879); 79 (11 October 1882); also LP 80 (25 November 1882). Cf. Williams, *History of Wales*, pp. 206, 225, 308 (and Neil Evans, 'Finding a new story: the search for a usable past in Wales, 1869–1930', *THSC*, new ser., 10 (2004), 147–8; *HBC*, I, pp. 495–508; II, pp. 6, 33, 240–3; E. J. Newell, *A History of the Welsh Church to the Dissolution of the Monasteries* (London, 1895), p. 274. For the softening of Welsh hostility towards Catholicism between the mid- and late Victorian periods, see R. Tudur Jones, *Faith and the Crisis of a Nation: Wales, 1890–1914* (Cardiff, 2004), pp. 147–8; Aled Gruffydd Jones and Bill Jones, 'Empire and the Welsh press', in Simon J. Potter (ed.), *Newspapers and Empire: Ireland and Britain, c.1857–1921* (Dublin, 2004), pp. 78–9. Although in his school textbooks Lloyd occasionally states that, when viewed from a modern perspective, aspects of medieval Welsh religion might appear irrational and superstitious, he takes care to emphasize their virtues in the circumstances of the time: *Ail Lyfr*, pp. 94–5; *Trydydd Llyfr*, p. 149.

62 F. E. Warren, *The Liturgy and Ritual of the Celtic Church* (Oxford, 1881), pp. 12–26; Hugh Williams, 'Some aspects of the Christian church in Wales during the fifth and sixth centuries', *THSC*, 1893–4, 107–20; Willis Bund, *Celtic Church*, chapter IV; Heinrich Zimmer, *The Celtic Church in Britain and Ireland* (London, 1902), pp. 58–9.

63 *HW*, I, pp. 102–10, 124, 143–59. Lloyd followed Williams, 'Some aspects', notwithstanding the criticisms in F. Haverfield, 'Early British Christianity', *EHR*, 11 (1896), 417–30, esp. 428ff. (one of whose arguments is, indeed, used in *HW*, I, p. 105 and n. 51, to suggest that Welsh tribes were unlikely to have been exposed to Romano-British Christianity before *c*.400), and Zimmer, *Celtic Church*, pp. 56–7 (reviewed critically in Hugh Williams, 'Heinrich Zimmer on the history of the Celtic church', *Zeitschrift für celtische Philologie*, 4 (1903), 527–74). See also Hugh Williams, *Christianity in Early Britain* (Oxford, 1912). The influence of

the Romano-British Church is likewise minimized in Alfred Plummer, *The Churches in Britain before A.D. 1000*, 2 vols (London, 1911), I, pp. 9–16. Willis Bund, *Celtic Church*, pp. 204–5, proposes monastic decline from *c*.600 onwards.

64   *HW*, I, pp. 202–28; II, pp. 591–3. For examples of churches designated by the term *clas*, see ibid., pp. 232, 235, 237, 247, 250, 254, 258, 263, 268, 272, 276. As the designation is lacking in Lloyd's earlier writings (or, as far as I can see, other earlier works), he seems to have devised it in the *History*, probably by adapting usage in the Welsh law books: cf. Lloyd, 'History of Wales', pp. 379–80; idem, *Ail Lyfr*, pp. 94–5; idem, *Trydydd Llyfr*, pp. 149–50. Laws: LP 52, fol. 64r.

65   *HW*, II, p. 591.

66   Ibid., pp. 595, 596. For a similar characterization of the Benedictines, see Newell, *History*, p. 301 (a work noticed in *HW*, II, p. 447). Cf. A. G. Little, *Mediaeval Wales* (London, 1902), pp. 105–7.

67   *HW*, II, p. 596.

68   Ibid., pp. 596–604. Lloyd's view of the Cistercians is clearly indebted to Newell, *History*, chapter X (including comparison with early saints at pp. 301–2). His assertion that their popularity among the Welsh 'was very largely due to the enlightened policy of the Lord Rhys' echoes the praise for 'the enlightened ecclesiastical policy of Rhys ap Gruffudd' in Edward Owen, review of Emily M. Pritchard, *Cardigan Priory in the Olden Days*, in *Arch. Camb.*, 6th ser., 5 (1905), 323. Cf. also Willis Bund, *Celtic Church*, pp. 484–6; Little, *Mediaeval Wales*, pp. 109–10.

69   Cf. Alice M. Cooke, 'The settlement of the Cistercians in England', *EHR*, 8 (1893), 648, 667–8 (referred to in *HW*, II, p. 590), which attributes the success of the order in northern England and Wales to a combination of geographical conditions and the impulse given by Clairvaux.

70   Quotation: *HW*, II, p. 595. Previous writers: Price, *Hanes Cymru*, pp. 605–8, 757–8; Williams, *History of Wales*, pp. 205–7; *HBC*, II, pp. 240–3; Henry William Clarke, *A History of the Church of Wales* (London, 1896), chapters VIII–X; Paul Barbier, *The Age of Owain Gwynedd* (London/Newport, 1908), pp. 26–32, 45–6, 124–7.

71   *HW*, I, p. 177. See also Newell, *History*, p. 115.

72   *HW*, II, pp. 447–59, 480–5 (discussed above, pp. 111–12). The echo of the 'Norman yoke' (see above, n. 55) is probably not coincidental. Newell, *History*, p. ix, emphasized 'the nationality of the Welsh Church' and defended the usage 'the Church *of* Wales'.

73   *HW*, II, pp. 623–4.

74   Cf. Price, *Hanes Cymru*, pp. 756–61; Newell, *History*, chapter IX.

75   *HW*, II, pp. 556–9, 611 (quotation).

76   Ibid., p. 611. However, elsewhere comments on some individual bishops are positive: ibid., pp. 453–4, 563, 688–9.

77   *History* (1930), pp. 55–6. For the link between race, emotion and Protestantism, see Isaac Taylor, *The Origin of the Aryans: An Account of*

the Prehistoric Ethnology and Civilisation of Europe (London, 1889), pp. 248–9.

9 Princely Wales: Rulers as Nation Builders

1 J. Beverley Smith and Llinos Beverley Smith, 'Wales: politics, government and law', in S. H. Rigby (ed.), *A Companion to Britain in the Later Middle Ages* (Malden, MA/Oxford, 2003), p. 311.

2 See, for example, *HW*, II, pp. 536, 650; J. E. Lloyd, 'Wales: the land and its people', *Wales*, 2 (1912), 364; Edwards, 'Lloyd', 323. For the difference a leader could make, see *HW*, I, pp. 49–50, which argues that the death of Cunobelinus triggered the Claudian conquest of Britain in AD 43. In later life Lloyd stressed the importance of the individual in history with reference to leaders such as Lenin, Hitler, Roosevelt and Gandhi: 'A dictionary of Welsh biography', *THSC*, 1938, 67–75; 'Arwyr ein cenedl' (1940), LP 229.

3 J. E. Lloyd, 'The teaching of history', *UCW Mag.*, 10 (1887–8), 105.

4 Glanmor Williams, 'Preface', in Sir J. E. Lloyd, *A History of Wales*, vol. I (facsimile repr. of 3rd edn, Carmarthen, 1988), pp. xii–xiii; Evans, 'Men and mountains', 229–30, 234.

5 Robert Harrison, Aled Jones and Peter Lambert, 'The primacy of political history', in Peter Lambert and Phillipp Schofield (eds), *Making History: An Introduction to the History and Practices of a Discipline* (London/New York, 2004), pp. 38–54.

6 The exceptions are 'Maelgwn Gwynedd and his contemporaries' in chapter V and 'The House of Rhodri the Great' and 'Hywel the Good' in chapter X.

7 Chapters XIV, XV, XVII, XVIII, XX. Sections as indicated in chapters XI (1, 4), XVI (2), XIX (1).

8 *HW*, I, pp. 182, 188.

9 Ibid., p. 324.

10 Ibid., pp. 342–3.

11 Ibid., p. 343.

12 Ibid., II, p. 371. The assessment was essentially the same as that of Gruffudd in Lloyd, 'Wales and the coming of the Normans', *THSC*, 1899–1900, 123:

> It cannot be doubted that his vigorous personality and independent attitude did much to infuse into his fellow countrymen a greater confidence in themselves, and so helped them after his death to offer a united resistance to the invader. His successes fired them, as the Elizabethans were fired by the triumphs of Drake and the sea-dogs.

13 *HW*, II, p. 487.

14 Ibid., p. 706.
15 See J. E. Lloyd, 'Hiraethog a'i gyfnod', *Adroddiad Cyfarfodydd yr Undeb*, new ser. 10, 4 (Swansea, 1932), p. 23; idem, 'Thomas Ellis', *UCW Mag.*, 21 (1898–9), 331, which states that Ellis's contribution to 'the making and guiding of the Welsh national revival of our day' remained 'a great inspiration'.
16 Lloyd, 'Teaching of history', 106.
17 Stubbs, *CH*, II, p. 107; Edward A. Freeman, *The History of the Norman Conquest of England, its Causes and its Results*, vol. I (Oxford, 1867), p. 51. True, Lloyd called John a tyrant, and also praised Alfred, but never as extravagantly as Freeman: Lloyd, *Trydydd Llyfr*, p. 183; *HW*, I, pp. 334–8; II, p. 650; J. E. Lloyd, 'Wessex and the Danes', in *Hutchinson's Story of the British Nation* (London [1922]), pp. 161, 169.
18 *HW*, I, p. 128. Cf. the description of Gruffudd ap Llywelyn in Lloyd, 'Wales and the coming of the Normans', 127, 129.
19 For a rare exception, see the criticism of Owain Gwynedd in John H. Parry, *The Cambrian Plutarch* (London, 1834), p. 143. Gweirydd ap Rhys also condemned Owain for the 'foul deed' of blinding and castrating his nephew, Cunedda, though he added that this was 'consistent enough with the barbaric customs of the age': *HBC*, II, p. 47.
20 See above, p. 38; Lloyd, 'Thomas Ellis', 331; Neville Masterman, *The Forerunner: The Dilemmas of Tom Ellis 1859–1899* (Swansea/Llandybïe, 1972), pp. 47–8. Compare also the positive connotations Matthew Arnold gave to 'national' and 'public' as opposed to 'provincial' or 'sectarian' with respect to the provision of public education: Stefan Collini, *Matthew Arnold: A Critical Portrait* (paperback edn, Oxford, 1994), p. 72.
21 Cf. Slee, *Learning and a Liberal Education: The Study of Modern History in the Universities of Oxford, Cambridge and Manchester, 1800–1914* (Manchester, 1986), pp. 90–1, 109; Reba N. Soffer, *Discipline and Power: The University, History, and the Making of an English Elite, 1870–1930* (Stanford, CA, 1994), pp. 140–2.
22 Cited in Slee, *Learning and a Liberal Education*, p. 109. Here Boase quite possibly followed a work he had helped to translate and edit: Leopold von Ranke, *A History of England Principally in the Seventeenth Century* (Oxford, 1875), I, pp. xvi, 472–3.
23 *HW*, II, p. 417.
24 For the cultivation of heroes in nineteenth-century Wales, see Hywel Teifi Edwards, '"Gosodir ni yn îs na phawb": Cymru Victoria ar drywydd enwogrwydd', in Jason Walford Davies (ed.), *Gweledigaethau: Cyfrol Deyrnged Yr Athro Gwyn Thomas* (Llandybïe, 2007), pp. 159–72; Marion Löffler, *The Literary and Historical Legacy of Iolo Morganwg, 1826–1926* (Cardiff, 2007), chapter 2; and, more generally, Geoffrey Cubitt, 'Introduction: heroic reputations and exemplary lives', in idem and Allen Warren (eds), *Heroic Reputations and Exemplary Lives* (Manchester/New York, 2000), pp. 1–26.

25   John E. Lloyd, 'Taliesin Ben Beirdd', *Y Geninen*, 2 (1884), 147.

26   *HW*, I, p. 55; II, pp. 582, 587. The description in ibid., p. 686, of Gruffudd ap Llywelyn (d.1244) as 'a popular hero' refers to contemporaneous perceptions rather than Lloyd's own judgement. In the eisteddfod essay Lloyd reserved the term 'heroic' for Owain Gwynedd: 'History of Wales', p. 401. See also Lloyd, *Trydydd Llyfr*, p. 135 (Rhys ap Gruffudd).

27   *HW*, II, pp. 417–18.

28   Ibid., pp. 488–9. Likewise the 'fiery and headstrong' Gwenwynwyn (d.1216) of southern Powys is contrasted unfavourably with his 'cool, sagacious' father Owain Cyfeiliog and 'the more wary and cautious' Llywelyn ap Iorwerth: ibid., pp. 583, 587.

29   Cf. above, p. 6. For an earlier depiction of a medieval Welsh ruler intended to give the lie to Arnoldian notions of impetuous, impractical Celts, see W.W., 'Gruffydd ap Cynan', *The University College of North Wales Magazine*, 1, 1 [1888], 10–18, which maintains (at 18) that the ruler it describes was 'not a mere free-booter and adventurer, but an enlightened and cultivated prince who possessed considerable administrative power, and who distinguished himself as statesman, reformer, and scholar so far as those terms are applicable to the circumstances of his times'. That exceptional personal qualities enabled princes to rise above an unfavourable inheritance is also stated without racial connotations, for example, with respect to the Lord Rhys's success in overcoming the constraints imposed by the geography of south-west Wales and to Llywelyn the Great's defeat of dynastic rivals: *HW*, II, pp. 536, 587 (cited below, p. 166).

30   Cf. above, p. 29.

31   *HW*, I, pp. 334–8; II, p. 542.

32   Cf. Cubitt, 'Introduction', pp. 9–10.

33   Lloyd, *OG*, p. [vii].

34   R. R. Davies, *The Revolt of Owain Glyn Dŵr* (Oxford, 1995), p. 332.

35   See above, pp. 154–5.

36   See [Johann Gottlieb] Fichte, *Addresses to the German Nation* [1807–8], ed. Gregory Moore (Cambridge, 2008), p. 103; Joep Leerssen, *National Thought in Europe: A Cultural History* (Amsterdam, 2006), pp. 112–14. Other parallels include nineteenth- and early twentieth-century attempts to formulate and mobilize a primordial Finnish spirit and differing evocations of a unique Magyar 'spirit' or 'soul' as a motor of Hungarian history: Derek Fewster, *Visions of Past Glory: Nationalism and the Construction of Early Finnish History* (Studia Fennica Historica, 11; Helsinki, 2006), pp. 116–20, 158–9, 299; Steven Bela Vardy, *Modern Hungarian Historiography* (East European Monographs, 17; Boulder, CO, 1976), pp. 44–9, 66–71, 102–20.

37   *HBC*, II, p. 399: 'wedi cadw ei hyspryd cenedlaethol yn fyw, yr hwn y methodd canrifoedd o lywodraethiad estronol ei ddiffodd na'i wanhau'.

This view also appears in Machreth, 'Y goresgyniad olaf', *Y Beirniad*, 1 (1911), 39.

38 *HBC*, II, pp. 299–300.
39 See above, pp. 90–1, 153–5; *HW*, I, p. 182; II, pp. 470, 682, 692; cf. *HW*, I, pp. 334–5.
40 Stubbs, *CH*, I, p. 1. See also ibid., pp. 197, 244, 538.
41 T. F. Tout, 'The Welsh shires: a study in constitutional history' [1888], in idem, *Collected Papers*, vol. II (Manchester, 1934), p. 20; idem, 'Wales and the march during the barons' wars' [1902], in ibid., p. 49; idem, review of *HW*, *EHR*, 27 (1912), 135.
42 Stubbs, *CH*, I, p. 597.
43 *HW*, II, pp. 587–90, 612–93 (XVI. 2; XVII–XVIII).
44 Lloyd, 'History of Wales', pp. 407, 408.
45 T. E. Ellis, 'The memory of the Kymric dead' [1892], in his *Speeches and Addresses* (Wrexham, 1912), p. 11.
46 See above, p. 113.
47 *North Wales Chronicle*, 10 December 1887. The prince's greatness and unifying achievements were likewise praised in Lloyd, *Trydydd Llyfr*, pp. 159, 181, 184, 193, 204, 209.
48 O. M. Edwards, 'Editor's notes', *Wales*, 2 (1895), 473–4; see above, p. 25.
49 'If other Welsh kings were equally warlike, the son of Iorwerth was by far the most politic of them': T. F. T[out], 'Llywelyn ab Iorwerth, called Llywelyn the Great (d.1240)', *DNB*, XXXIV, p. 12. Views earlier in the nineteenth century: Price, *Hanes Cymru*, pp. 611, 662; Williams, *History of Wales*, p. 336; *HBC*, II, pp. 88–90. See also Llinos Beverley Smith, 'Llywelyn ap Gruffudd and the Welsh historical consciousness', *WHR*, 12 (1984–5), 16.
50 *North Wales Chronicle*, 10 December 1887.
51 Tout, 'Llywelyn ab Iorwerth', p. 12.
52 T. F. Tout, *The History of England from the Accession of Henry III. to the Death of Edward III. (1216–1377)* (London, 1905), p. 155. Cf. idem, 'Llywelyn ab Gruffydd (d.1282), prince of Wales', *DNB*, XXXIV, pp. 13–21, esp. p. 21; idem, 'Wales and the march', p. 82.
53 A. G. Little, *Mediaeval Wales* (London, 1902), p. 23.
54 Edwards, *Wales*, p. 127.
55 Ibid., pp. 127, 141–50.
56 Ibid., p. 148. Cf. above, pp. 131–2.
57 Edwards, *Wales*, pp. 149–50.
58 *Western Mail*, 22 April 1895. For political context, see Morgan, *WBP*, pp. 160–5.
59 Edwards, *Wales*, pp. 150–1.
60 Price, *Hanes Cymru*, pp. 630–7; Tout, 'Llywelyn ab Iorwerth', p. 8; *Western Mail*, 22 April, 25 November 1895. See also Little, *Mediaeval Wales*, pp. 4–5; Tout, 'Wales and the march', p. 48.

61   For a different argument, based on the Celtic elements in English nation-
ality, see John Williams, 'Influence of the Welsh on the formation of the
British constitution', in *Transactions of the Royal National Eisteddfod of
Wales, Liverpool, 1884* (Liverpool, 1885), pp. 455–518. Cf. Wendy Davies,
'Looking backwards to the early medieval past: Wales and England, a
contrast in approaches', *WHR*, 22 (2004–5), 219.

62   Owen Rhoscomyl, *Flame-Bearers of Welsh History* (Merthyr Tydfil, 1905),
p. 172 (original emphasis). See also ibid., p. 256, n. 9.

63   *HW*, II, chapters XVII–XVIII (written in 1908: LP 212).

64   *HW*, II, pp. 642–6.

65   Ibid., p. 682.

66   Ibid., pp. 689, 691. Cf. ibid., p. 596; Lloyd, *Trydydd Llyfr*, p. 193. Llywelyn's
role in fostering literature had been stressed in Thomas Stephens, *The
Literature of the Kymry* (Llandovery, 1849), p. 349.

67   Qualities praised by Lloyd partly, perhaps, because they reflected aspects
of his own character: Jenkins, 'Lloyd', 85.

68   *HW*, II, p. 587.

69   Ibid., p. 623. Owain Gwynedd, ibid., p. 522: 'the trusty pilot, whose
steady hand and watchful eye had guided the ship of state through
foaming rapids and whirling eddies into the full, smooth current of
freedom and prosperity'.

70   Ibid., p. 654.

71   Ibid., pp. 655 (quotation), 662–4, 669.

72   Ibid., p. 693.

73   See above, p. 161. Lloyd sometimes uses the term 'state', but merely as a
synonym for a Welsh principality: *HW*, I, p. 324; II, pp. 467–8, 522, 647.

74   *HW*, II, pp. 684–5. Cf. Evans, 'Men and mountains', 234.

75   Above, pp. 138, 161; *HW*, II, pp. 683, 684; cf. p. 686.

76   *HW*, II, p. 648.

77   For early criticism of Lloyd's treatment of the two Llywelyns, see W. H.
Jones, 'Llywelyn ap Gruffudd', *Y Beirniad*, 1 (1911), 123–7.

78   *HW*, II, p. 612. Lloyd recommended the inclusion of both Llywelyns
among the statues of prominent figures in Welsh history in Cardiff City
Hall: Lloyd, note of reply to letter from J. L. Wheatley, 31 October 1912,
LP 314 no. 562.

79   Smith, 'Llywelyn', 22. Lloyd devoted only one chapter, of almost fifty
pages, to the last Llywelyn and explained that its final section on 1277–82
was deliberately concise as Edward I's conquest fell outside the scope of
his study: *HW*, II, p. 754.

80   Cf. Cubitt, 'Introduction', p. 20.

81   *HW*, II, p. 716.

82   Ibid., p. 741, and cf. p. 612. Fate is also evoked in ibid., pp. 417, 469, 572,
650.

83   Ibid., p. 764. The eisteddfod essay concluded that the defeat of Llywelyn
was 'to the ruin of Welsh independence, but not of Welsh nationality,

which with surprising tenacity has survived this as it has survived the Roman and the Norman Conquests', while, in 1900, Lloyd declared that the struggle with Edward I 'enabled the Welsh to maintain their place as a distinct nation and their national characteristics': Lloyd, 'History of Wales', p. 408; idem, *Trydydd Llyfr*, p. 13. See also above, p. 161.

10. Conclusion: Creating Welsh History?

1   *The Times*, 21 June 1947.
2   See above, p. 95; J. Goronwy Edwards, 'Hanesyddiaeth Gymreig yn yr ugeinfed ganrif', *THSC*, 1953 (1955), 27; Davies, 'Lloyd'.
3   See above, pp. 42–3, 118, 120.
4   See above, pp. 120–3, 143–4.
5   Cf. R. D. Anderson, *European Universities from the Enlightenment to 1914* (Oxford, 2004), chapters 13, 15, esp. pp. 199, 204–5, 231–3.
6   A point emphasized in [T. C. Edwards], 'National colleges and a university for Wales', *UCW Mag.*, 3 (1880–1), 231–7.
7   See above, p. 44.
8   Jenkins, 'Lloyd', 79, 85.
9   Cf. H. S. Jones, *Intellect and Character in Victorian England: Mark Pattison and the Invention of the Don* (Cambridge, 2007), pp. 5, 187–92; see above, pp. 36, 43–4.
10   Michael Bentley, *Modernizing England's Past: English Historiography in the Age of Modernism 1870–1970* (Cambridge, 2005), p. 106.
11   Cf. ibid., esp. pp. 8–10.
12   See Hazel Davies, *O. M. Edwards* (Cardiff, 1988), pp. 75–6, which rightly warns against patronizing Edwards for his popularizing aims.
13   LP 41A, no. 1, p. [2] (1907); J. E. Lloyd, *A Brief Bibliography of Welsh History for the Use of Teachers*, Historical Association Leaflet no. 49 ([London] 1921), p. 2; *Y Cymro*, 26 May 1920, pp. 1–2.
14   J. F. A. Mason, 'Edwards, Sir (John) Goronwy (1891–1976)', *ODNB*.
15   Cf. Thomas Richards, 'Sir John Lloyd', *TCHS*, 8 (1947), 4.
16   Edwards, 'Lloyd', 325.
17   Thomas Richards, 'Syr John Lloyd: atgofion amdano', *Y Llenor*, 25 (1947), 75.
18   William Rees, *South Wales and the March 1284–1415: A Social and Agrarian Study* (Oxford, 1924); David Williams, *John Frost: A Study in Chartism* (Cardiff, 1939). For Lewis, Skeel and Richards, see above, pp. 70–1, 105, 215, n. 51. Examples of Lloyd's contacts with these historians: LP 314 no. 271 (Lewis); 315 no. 469 (Skeel); 317 nos 248–9 (Rees), 298 (Williams); see above, pp. 70, 106 (Richards).

Bibliography

Unpublished manuscripts

Aberystwyth
Aberystwyth University Archives
    A/D/M6/14 (Lloyd's Sanskrit notebook)
    C/MN/2 (Council minutes)
National Library of Wales
    NLW MSS 877 C (minutes of the ACC), 8843E (W. J. Parry
    MS 111: The Welsh National Press Co.), 15701–3 (Lloyd's
    manuscript copy of *HW*), 18099C (Edward Owen Papers)
    Sir O. M. Edwards Papers
    T. E. Ellis Papers
    T. I. Ellis Papers
    University of Wales Archive
    Vincent Evans Papers
    W. J. Gruffydd Papers

Bangor University, Archives and Special Collections
    Bangor MSS
    The Papers of Sir John Edward Lloyd

London, The National Archives
    HO107/2499 (1851 census)

RG10/3784 (1871 census)
RG11/3623 (1881 census)
RG13/5279 (1901 census)

Oxford
Bodleian Library
G. A. Oxon. b. 140 (4) ('Vivisection in Oxford. Convocation
of the University, 2 p.m., Tuesday, Feb. 5, 1884'; C. R. L.
F[letcher], 'Honour School of Modern History')
Lincoln College Archives
Lincoln College Matriculations 1919–1952
Mansfield College Library Archives
Minute Book of Oxford University Nonconformists'
Union

Reading
University of Reading, Special Collections
Longman Papers

Newspapers

Cambrian News
North Wales Chronicle
Western Mail
Y Cymro

Published writings of J. E. Lloyd

Note:
The following list contains only works referred to in this book.
For a fuller, though not complete, bibliography, see 'A list of the
published writings of the late Sir John Edward Lloyd', *Bulletin of
the Board of Celtic Studies*, 12 (1946–8), 96–105.

'Addysg uwchraddol yng Nghymru', *Y Traethodydd*, 55 (1900), 68–77.

'Adjudication', in E. Vincent Evans (ed.), *The Thirty-Eighth Annual Report of the National Eisteddfod Association . . . National Eisteddfod (Neath), 1918* (Cardiff, 1919), pp. 77–81.

Ail Lyfr Hanes (Caernarfon, 1896).

'Athrylith y Celt', *Cenad Hedd*, 1 (1881), 179–81, 335–9.

'Yr awyrgylch', *Y Beirniad*, 19 (1877), 61–7.

'"The Blind Harper," by Ceiriog, in English verse', *UCW Mag.*, 4 (1881–2), 122–4.

A Brief Bibliography of Welsh History for the Use of Teachers, Historical Association Leaflet no. 49 ([London] 1921).

'The buried hundred', *UCW Mag.*, 13 (1890–1), 261–6.

Carnarvonshire (Cambridge, 1911).

'Cymdeithas yr Iaith Gymraeg: trem ar hanes y mudiad', *Y Llenor*, 10 (1931), 207–14.

'Cymry yn Rhydychen – atgofion o'r blynyddoedd 1881–1885', *Yr Eurgrawn*, 135 (1943), 13–18.

'A dictionary of Welsh biography', *THSC*, 1938, 67–75.

Early Welsh Agriculture (Bangor, 1894).

'Ffurfiad y genedl Gymreig. (Cyfres o ddarlithiau ar hanes y Cymry, o'r bummed hyd y ddeuddegfed ganrif.)', *Y Geninen*, 4 (1886), 264–70.

(revised R. Rhys), 'Foulkes, Isaac [*pseud.* Llyfrbryf] (1836–1904)', *ODNB.*

'The geographical limits of Welsh home rule', *The Welsh Outlook*, 8 (1921), 247–8.

'Hiraethog a'i gyfnod', *Adroddiad Cyfarfodydd yr Undeb*, new ser., 10, 4 (Undeb yr Annibynwyr Cymraeg; Swansea, 1932).

'A history course for secondary schools in Wales', *The Welsh Outlook*, 15 (1928), 4–7.

'History of Wales', *Transactions of the Royal National Eisteddfod of Wales, Liverpool, 1884* (Liverpool, 1885), pp. 341–408.

A History of Wales, Benn's Sixpenny Library no. 119 (London, 1930).

A History of Wales from the Earliest Times to the Edwardian Conquest, 2 vols (London, 1911; 2nd edn, London, 1912; 3rd edn, London, 1939).

'How England and Wales became united', *TLWNS*, 1886–7, 83–99.

Hywel Dda, 928–1928 (Cardiff, 1928).

'Yr iaith Gymraeg', *Y Dysgedydd*, 59 (1880), 114–17.

'Introduction', in Cambrian Archaeological Association, *A Hundred Years of Welsh Archaeology: Centenary Volume, 1846–1946*, ed. V. E. Nash-Williams (Gloucester, n.d.), pp. 11–23.

'Law and lawyers among the ancient Welsh', *TLWNS*, 1890–1, 96–113.

Llyfr Cyntaf Hanes (Caernarfon, 1893).

'Mendelssohn's "St. Paul."', *UCW Mag.*, 14 (1891–2), 219–21.

'The organization of Welsh historical and archaeological research', *THSC*, 1910–11, 115–24.

Outlines of the History of Wales for the Use of Schools and Colleges (Caernarfon, 1906).

'Oxford letter', *UCW Mag.*, 6 (1883–4), 269–72.

'Passages in the history of the Welsh Bible', *UCW Mag.*, 2 (1879–80), 23–9.

'The personal name-system in Old Welsh', *Y Cymmrodor*, 9 (1888), 39–55.

'The preparation for the Norman conquest', in *Hutchinson's Story of the British Nation* (London [1922]), pp. 197–217.

'Proposals for the organization of the work of the Guild of Graduates of the University of Wales', *Transactions of the Guild of Graduates of the University of Wales* (Second Annual Collegiate Meeting, UCNW, 17 October 1896), pp. 11–14.

'A retrospect (1877–1881)', in Iwan Morgan (ed.), *The College by the Sea* (Aberystwyth), pp. 70–2.

Review of R. T. Jenkins, *Yr Apêl at Hanes*, *The Welsh Outlook*, 17 (1930), 227.

'The rise of periodical literature in Wales', *UCW Mag.*, 1 (1878–9), 32–7.

'Rowlands, Daniel (1713–1790)', in *DNB*, XLIX (London, 1897), pp. 350–1.

'St. David's Day', *UCNW Mag.*, 11, 1 (March 1902), 34–5.

'Sir Harry Reichel 1856–1931', in idem (ed.), *Sir Harry Reichel 1856–1931: A Memorial Volume* (Cardiff, 1934), pp. 1–28.

'Some characteristics of modern Welsh poetry', *UCW Mag.*, 11 (1888–9), 241–9.

The Story of Ceredigion (400–1277) (Cardiff, 1937).

'Taith archesgobol drwy Gymru', *Y Geninen*, 4 (1886), 54–6.

'Taliesin Ben Beirdd', *Y Geninen*, 2 (1884), 145–8; 3 (1885), 65–9.

'The teaching of history', *UCW Mag.*, 10 (1887–8), 99–108.

'Thomas Ellis', *UCW Mag.*, 21 (1898–9), 331–2.

'Tom Ellis', *Yr Eurgrawn*, 132 (1942), 20–5.

Trem ar Hanes yr Anibynwyr yng Nghymru (Cardiff [1909]).

Trydydd Llyfr Hanes (Hanes Cymru o 1066 hyd 1282) (Caernarfon, 1900).

'Two Welsh prose authors of the XVIIIth century', *UCW Mag.*, 1 (1878–9), 246–52.

'A volume of old letters', *UCW Mag.*, 9 (1886–7), 113–17.

'Wales and the coming of the Normans', *THSC*, 1899–1900, 122–79.

Wales and the Past – Two Voices (Cardiff, 1932).

'Wales: the land and its people', *Wales*, 2 (1912), 359–68.

The Welsh Chronicles (London, 1928).

'Welsh place-names: a study of some common name-elements (with notes by the editor [Egerton Phillimore])', *Y Cymmrodor*, 11 (1892), 15–60.

'The Welsh romance', *UCW Mag.*, 3 (1880–1), 66–70.

'Welsh statesmen in English history. Some memorable names', *The Times*, 19 December 1916.

'Welsh words for three of Schubert's songs', *UCW Mag.*, 5 (1882–3), 66–8.

'Wessex and the Danes', in *Hutchinson's Story of the British Nation* (London [1922]), pp. 149–77.

'Williams, William (1717–1791)', in *DNB*, LXI (London, 1900), pp. 462–4.

'A word about prose-writing', *UCW Mag.*, 4 (1881–2), 265–8.

(ed.) *A History of Carmarthenshire*, 2 vols (Cardiff, 1935–9).

—— and R. T. Jenkins (eds), *Y Bywgraffiadur Cymreig hyd 1940* (London, 1953).

——, *The Dictionary of Welsh Biography down to 1940* (London, 1959).

Writings on Lloyd, including reviews and obituaries

Anon, review of *HW*, *Educational Times*, October 1912.

——, review of *HW*, *Guardian*, 30 September 1911.

——, review of *HW*, *Times Literary Supplement*, 20 April 1911, 158.

——, review of *HW*, *Western Mail*, 4 February 1911.

Anwyl, Edward, review of *HW*, *Y Brython*, 13 April 1911.

——, review of *HW*, *Revue Celtique*, 32 (1911), 357–61.

D[avies], R. H., 'Yr Athro J. E. Lloyd, M.A., D.Litt., Bangor', *Y Dysgedydd*, 113 (1933), 164–7.

Davies, R. R., 'Lloyd, Sir John Edward (1861–1947)', *ODNB*.

Edwards, J. G., 'Sir John Edward Lloyd 1861–1947', *Proceedings of the British Academy*, 41 (1955), 319–27.

Gougaud, L., review of *HW*, *Revue d'histoire ecclésiastique*, 12, 1 (1911), 811.

Jenkins, R. T., 'Gwerthfawrogiad', *Y Cymro*, 27 June 1947, 6.

——, 'Syr John Edward Lloyd', *Y Llenor*, 25 (1947), 77–87.

——, 'Lloyd, Sir John Edward (1861–1947)', in idem, E. D. Jones and Brynley F. Roberts (eds), *The Dictionary of Welsh Biography, 1941–1970* (London, 2001), pp. 172–3.

Lewis, Saunders, 'Marwnad Syr John Edward Lloyd', in idem, *Siwan a Cherddi Eraill* (Llandybïe [1955]), pp. 13–15.

Pryce, Huw, 'Modern nationality and the medieval past: the Wales of John Edward Lloyd', in R. R. Davies and Geraint H. Jenkins (eds),

From Medieval to Modern Wales: Historical Essays in Honour of Kenneth O. Morgan and Ralph A. Griffiths (Cardiff, 2004), pp. 14–29.

——, 'From the neolithic to nonconformity: J. E. Lloyd and the history of Caernarfonshire', *TCHS*, 66 (2005), 14–37.

Rhys, Ernest, review of *HW*, *Manchester Guardian* (Welsh edition), 4 March 1911.

Richards, Thomas, 'Sir John Lloyd', *TCHS*, 8 (1947), 1–4.

——, 'Syr John Lloyd: atgofion amdano', *Y Llenor*, 25 (1947), 67–76.

Thurneysen, R., review of *HW*, *Historische Zeitschrift*, 110 (1913), 405–8.

Tout, T. F., review of *HW*, *EHR*, 27 (1912), 131–5.

Williams, Glanmor, 'Preface', in Sir J. E. Lloyd, *A History of Wales*, vol. I (facsimile repr. of 3rd edn; Carmarthen, 1988), pp. ix–xviii.

Other printed primary sources

ab Owen Edwards, Ifan (comp.), *A Catalogue of Star Chamber Proceedings relating to Wales* (BCS, Hist. & Law Ser., no. 1; Cardiff, 1929).

Adams, David, 'Edward Lloyd, Y.H., Lerpwl', *Y Dysgedydd*, 96 (1917), 216–18.

——, 'Yn llefaru eto: marwolaeth a chladdedigaeth y diweddar Thomas Arthur Lloyd', *Y Dysgedydd*, 96 (1917), 82–6.

——, 'Y ddiweddar Mrs. Edward Lloyd, Falkner Square, Liverpool', *Y Dysgedydd*, 101 (1922), 64–5.

Allen, Grant, *Anglo-Saxon Britain* (London [1881]).

Amgueddfa Genedlaethol Cymru/National Museum of Wales, *A Matter of Great Interest to Welsh-Americans* ([Cardiff] 1937).

Anon, *1914 North Wales and Chester Year Book* (Liverpool, n.d.).

——, *Adroddiad Eglwys Gynulleidfaol Grove Street, Liverpool. 1876.* ([Liverpool, 1877]).

——, *Adroddiad Eglwys Gynulleidfaol Grove Street, Liverpool. 1877.* ([Liverpool, 1878]).

——, 'Cymry'r colegau', *Cymru Fydd*, 1 (1888), 305–9.

Arnold, Matthew, 'On the study of Celtic literature', in *The Complete Prose Works of Matthew Arnold*, vol. III, *Lectures and Essays in Criticism*, ed. R. H. Super (Ann Arbor, MI, 1962), pp. 291–395.

——, *Schools and Universities on the Continent* (1868), in *Complete Prose Works*, vol. IV, ed. R. H. Super (Ann Arbor, MI, 1964).

Barbier, Paul, *The Age of Owain Gwynedd* (London/Newport, 1908).

Barker, Ernest, *National Character and the Factors in its Formation* (London, 1927).

Beddoe, John, *The Races of Britain: A Contribution to the Anthropology of Western Europe* (Bristol/London, 1885).

Board of Celtic Studies, *Orgraff yr Iaith Gymraeg* (Cardiff, 1928).

Bury, J. B., 'The science of history' [1902], in Fritz Stern (ed.), *The Varieties of History from Voltaire to the Present* (2nd edn, London/Basingstoke, 1970), pp. 210–23.

The Calendar of the University College of Wales, Aberystwyth.

The Cambrian News Almanack for the Year 1878.

Census of England and Wales, 1871. (33 & 34 Vict. c. 107.) Population Tables. Area, Houses, and Inhabitants, vol. I, *Counties* (London, 1872), C. 676.

Clarke, Henry William, *A History of the Church of Wales* (London, 1896).

Cooke, Alice M., 'The settlement of the Cistercians in England', *EHR*, 8 (1893), 625–76.

Coxe, William, *An Historical Tour in Monmouthshire*, 2 vols (London, 1801).

Davies, David, *The Ancient Celtic Church of Wales: Where is It?* (London, 1910).

Davis, H. W. C., *England under the Normans and Angevins 1066–1272* (London, 1905).

Dawes, T. R., 'Aberystwyth in '85 – or life in the Queen's Hotel '85', in Iwan Morgan (ed.), *The College by the Sea* (Aberystwyth, 1928), pp. 82–7.

Dawkins, W. Boyd, *Early Man in Britain and his Place in the Tertiary Period* (London, 1880).

——, 'The ancient ethnology of Wales', *Y Cymmrodor*, 5 (1882), 209–23.

——, *The Place of the Welsh in the History of Britain* (London/Manchester, 1889).

des Marez, G. and F.-L. Ganshof (eds), *Compte rendu du Ve Congrès International des Sciences Historiques, Bruxelles, 1923* (Brussels, 1923).

Easterling, R. C., 'The friars in Wales', *Arch. Camb.*, 6th ser., 14 (1914), 323–56.

——, 'Anian of Nanneu', *Journal of the Flintshire Historical Society*, 5 (1914–15), 9–30.

Edwards, J. Goronwy, *Hywel Dda and the Welsh Lawbooks* (Hywel Dda Millenary Lecture, 9 May 1928; Bangor, 1929).

——, *Calendar of Ancient Correspondence concerning Wales* (BCS, Hist. & Law Ser., no. 11; Cardiff, 1935).

——, 'Hanesyddiaeth Gymreig yn yr ugeinfed ganrif', *THSC*, 1953 (1955), 21–31.

Edwards, J. Hugh, *The Life of David Lloyd George, with a Short History of the Welsh People*, vol. I (London [1913]).

Edwards, Owen M., 'An Oxford letter', *UCW Mag.*, 7 (1884–5), 269–72.

——, *Holi ac Ateb ar Hanes Cymru* (Llanuwchllyn, 1892).

——, 'Editor's notes', *Wales*, 2 (1895), 473–4.

[——], 'Patriotism and pedantry', *Wales*, 2 (1895), 53–5.

——, *Wales* (London, 1901).

E[dwards], T. C., 'Introductory', *UCW Mag.*, 1 (1878–9), 3–6.

——, 'A nation's wish', *UCW Mag.*, 3 (1880–1), 105–7.

——, 'National colleges and a university for Wales', *UCW Mag.*, 3 (1880–1), 231–7.

——, *Thomas Charles Edwards Letters*, ed. T. I. Ellis (Aberystwyth, 1952–3).

Elfed [Howell Elvet Lewis], 'Dewisol lyfrau yr oes hon', *Cyfaill yr Aelwyd a'r Frythones*, new ser., 1 (1892), 160–4, 190–4.

E[llis], T. E., 'The college calendar', *UCW Mag.*, 1 (1878–9), 170–4.

——, 'The duty of the Guild towards the literature and records of Wales', *Transactions of the Guild of Graduates of the University of Wales* (Second Annual Collegiate Meeting, UCNW, 17 October 1896), pp. 3–10.

——, 'The memory of the Kymric dead' [1892], in idem, *Speeches and Addresses* (Wrexham, 1912), pp. 3–26.

Ellis, T. I., 'Rhydychen yn yr wythdegau', *Y Llenor*, 21 (1942), 25–33.

Elton, Charles, *Origins of English History* (London, 1882).

Evans, E. Vincent, 'The Cymmrodorion Medal', *THSC*, 1912–13, 172–90.

Evans, J. Gwenogvryn, *Report on Manuscripts in the Welsh Language*, 2 vols (London, 1898–1910).

Evans, John, *A Popular History of the Ancient Britons or the Welsh People* (London, 1901).

Evans, T. Eli, *Hanes Cymanfaoedd Annibynwyr Lerpwl* (Liverpool, 1902).

Evans, Theophilus, *Drych y Prif Oesoedd. Yn ôl yr Argraffiad Cyntaf: 1716*, ed. Garfield H. Hughes (Cardiff, 1961).

The Examination Statutes . . . Revised to the End of Trinity Term, 1882 (Oxford, 1882).

The Examination Statutes . . . Revised to the End of Trinity Term, 1883 (Oxford, 1883).

The Examination Statutes . . . Revised to the End of Trinity Term, 1884 (Oxford, 1884).

Febvre, Lucien, *Philippe II et la Franche-Comté* (Paris, 1911).

Felix, John, 'Y wraig rinweddol', *Yr Eurgrawn Wesleyaidd*, 114 (1922), 54–9.

Fichte, [Johann Gottlieb], *Addresses to the German Nation* [1807–8], ed. Gregory Moore (Cambridge, 2008).

Final Report of the Royal Commission on University Education in Wales: Evidence, Appendices, and Index (London, 1918), Cd. 8993.

Fleure, H. J., *The Races of England and Wales* (London, 1923).

Fox, Cyril, 'Presidential address', *Arch. Camb.*, 88 (1933), 153–84.

Frédéricq, Paul, *The Study of History in England and Scotland*, trans. Henrietta Leonard, Johns Hopkins Studies in Historical and Political Science, 5th ser., 10 (Baltimore, MD, 1887).

Freeman, Edward A., *The History of the Norman Conquest of England, its Causes and its Results*, vol. I (Oxford, 1867).

Geddes, [William], *Historical Characteristics of the Celtic Race* (Aberdeen, 1885).

Genese, R. W., 'When the college was residential', in Iwan Morgan (ed.), *The College by the Sea* (Aberystwyth, 1928), pp. 73–6.

Geoffrey of Monmouth, *The History of the Kings of Britain*, ed. Michael D. Reeve and trans. Neil Wright (Woodbridge, 2007).

Glanystwyth, 'Mrs. Lloyd, Falkner Square, Liverpool', *Y Gymraes*, 3 (1899), 145–8.

Grimley, H. N., 'How to spend the vacation', *UCW Mag.*, 1 (1878–9), 184–9.

Gweirydd ap Rhys [R. J. Pryse], *Hanes y Brytaniaid a'r Cymry*, 2 vols (London, 1872–4).

Haverfield, F., 'Early British Christianity', *EHR*, 11 (1896), 417–30.

Herford, C. H., 'Impressions of Aberystwyth, 1887–1901', in Iwan Morgan (ed.), *The College by the Sea* (Aberystwyth, 1928), pp. 96–100.

Historia Brittonum, ed. and trans. John Morris, *Nennius: British History and the Welsh Annals* (London/Chichester, 1980).

Hodgkin, Thomas, *The History of England from the Earliest Times to the Norman Conquest* (London, 1906).

Huxley, Thomas Henry, 'On some fixed points in British ethnology' [1870], in idem, *Critiques and Addresses* (London, 1873), pp. 167–80.

——, 'On the methods and results of ethnology', in idem, *Critiques and Addresses*, pp. 134–66.

Jenkins, R. T., *Hanes Cymru yn y Ddeunawfed Ganrif* (Cardiff, 1928).

——, 'William Wynne and the *History of Wales*', *Bulletin of the Board of Celtic Studies*, 6 (1931–3), 153–9.

——, 'The development of nationalism in Wales', *Sociological Review*, 27 (1935), 163–82.

Jones, Arthur (ed.), *The History of Gruffydd ap Cynan* (Manchester, 1910).

Jones, D. Brynmor, 'Introduction', in J. Hugh Edwards, *The Life of David Lloyd George, with a Short History of the Welsh People*, vol. I (London [1913]), pp. xxi–xxxii.

Jones, T. J., *The Church in Wales not Alien: A Reply to Mr. J. W. Willis Bund* (Cardiff, 1906).

Jones, Thomas, 'College memories: Aberystwyth in the nineties', in idem, *Leeks and Daffodils* (Newtown, 1942), pp. 1–88.

Jones, W. H., 'Llywelyn ap Gruffudd', *Y Beirniad*, 1 (1911), 123–7.

Jones, W. Silvanus, 'Our Oxford letter', *UCW Mag.*, 5 (1882–3), 152–5.

——, 'Our Oxford letter', *UCW Mag.*, 6 (1883–4), 80–4.

Lewis, Edward Arthur, *The Mediaeval Boroughs of Snowdonia* (London, 1912).

Lewis, Hubert, *The Ancient Laws of Wales, Viewed Especially in Regard to the Light They Throw upon the Origin of Some English Institutions*, ed. J. E. Lloyd (London, 1889).

Lewis, Saunders, *Egwyddorion Cenedlaetholdeb* (Machynlleth [1926]).

——, 'Deg pwynt polisi', in idem, *Canlyn Arthur* (Aberystwyth, 1938), pp. 11–13.

Lingard, John, *A History of England from the First Invasion of the Romans (to the Revolution of 1688)*, 8 vols (London, 1819–30).

Little, A. G., *Mediaeval Wales* (London, 1902).

Llwyd, Humphrey, *Cronica Walliae*, ed. Ieuan M. Williams (Cardiff, 2002).

Loth, Joseph Marie, *Les mots Latins dans les langues Brittoniques (gallois, armoricain, cornique), phonetique et commentaire, avec une introduction sur la romanization de l'île de Bretagne* (Paris, 1892).

Lubbock, John, 'The nationalities of the United Kingdom: extracts from letters to the "Times"', *Journal of the Anthropological Institute of Great Britain and Ireland*, 16 (1887), 418–22.

Machreth, 'Y goresgyniad olaf', *Y Beirniad*, 1 (1911), 39–46.

The Magazine of the University College of North Wales.

Maine, Henry Sumner, *Ancient Law* (London, 1861).

Maitland, F. W., 'The laws of Wales – the kindred and the blood feud' [1881], in H. A. L. Fisher (ed.), *The Collected Papers of Frederic William Maitland* (Cambridge, 1911), I, pp. 202–21.

——, 'The tribal system in Wales' [1895], in Fisher (ed.), *Collected Papers*, III, pp. 1–10.

Morgan, Iwan (ed.), *The College by the Sea* (Aberystwyth, 1928).

Morgan, R. W., *The British Kymry, or Britons of Cambria: Outlines of their History and Institutions, from the Earliest to the Present Times* (Ruthin/London [1857]).

Morris, John E., *The Welsh Wars of Edward I: A Contribution to Mediaeval Military History, Based on Original Documents* (Oxford, 1901).

Morris, Lewis, 'The principle of national development in relation to Wales', *TLWNS*, 1 (1885–6), 1–15.

Morris-Jones, J., 'Gorsedd Beirdd Ynys Prydain', *Cymru*, 10 (1896), 21–9, 133–40, 153–61, 198–204, 293–9.

——, *A Welsh Grammar, Historical and Comparative* (Oxford, 1913).

Newell, E. J., *A History of the Welsh Church to the Dissolution of the Monasteries* (London, 1895).

Nicholson, W., 'Anerchiad', *Adroddiad Eglwys Gynulleidfaol Grove Street, Liverpool, am 1878* (n.p., n.d.).

'Official List of Subjects, Second Issue' (Liverpool, 1884).

Oman, Charles, *England before the Norman Conquest, being a History of the Celtic, Roman and Anglo-Saxon Periods down to the Year A.D. 1066* (London, 1910).

——, *Memories of Victorian Oxford and of Some Early Years* (London, 1941).

Owen, Aneurin (ed. and trans.), *Ancient Laws and Institutes of Wales* (Record Commission, London, 1841).

Owen, Edward, review of Emily M. Pritchard, *Cardigan Priory in the Olden Days*, in *Arch. Camb.*, 6th ser., 5 (1905), 322–8.

Owen, Isambard, 'Race and nationality', *Y Cymmrodor*, 8 (1887), 1–24.

Oxford University Calendar.

Oxford University Examination Papers. Second Public Examination. Honour School of Modern History. Trinity Term, 1885 (Oxford, 1885).

Palmer, Alfred Neobard, 'The portionary churches of mediaeval north Wales', *Arch. Camb.*, 5th ser., 3 (1886), 175–209.

—— and Edward Owen, *A History of Ancient Tenures in North Wales and the Marches* (2nd edn, n.p., 1910).

Parry, John H., *The Cambrian Plutarch* (London, 1834).

Pattison, Mark, 'An address to the students', *UCW Cal. 1877–8*, pp. 23–31.

Phillimore, Egerton, 'The *Annales Cambriae* and Old-Welsh genealogies from Harleian MS. 3859', *Y Cymmrodor*, 9 (1888), 141–83.

Pike, Luke Owen, *The English and their Origin: A Prologue to Authentic English History* (London, 1866).

Plummer, Alfred, *The Churches in Britain before A.D. 1000*, 2 vols (London, 1911).

Powel, David, *The Historie of Cambria, Now Called Wales* (London, 1584).

Powell, F. York, *The Study of History in Universities: An Address Delivered at the Closing Ceremony of the Session 1901–2, June 20th, 1902* (Bangor, n.d.).

Price, Thomas, *Hanes Cymru, a Chenedl y Cymry, o'r Cynoesoedd hyd at Farwolaeth Llewelyn ap Gruffydd; ynghyd a Rhai Cofiaint Perthynol i'r Amseroedd o'r Pryd Hynny i Waered* (Crickhowell, 1842).

Ranke, Leopold von, *A History of England Principally in the Seventeenth Century*, 6 vols (Oxford, 1875).

Rees, Rice, *An Essay on the Welsh Saints or the Primitive Christians usually considered to have been the Founders of Churches in Wales* (London, 1836).

Rees, T. and J. Thomas, *Hanes Eglwysi Annibynol Cymru*, vol. IV (Liverpool, 1875).

Rees, William, *South Wales and the March 1284–1415: A Social and Agrarian Study* (Oxford, 1924).

Rhoscomyl, Owen, *Flame-Bearers of Welsh History* (Merthyr Tydfil, 1905).

Rhys, Ernest, 'Owain Glyndwr's Parliament', in *The Pageant of Harlech Castle: Book of the Words by Alfred Perceval Graves and Ernest Rhys; Adapted for the Pageant Stage by Patrick Kirwan. (August 23rd. to 25th. 1922)* (London, 1922), pp. 17–20.

Rhys, John, *Lectures on Welsh Philology* (London, 1877).

——, *Celtic Britain* (London, 1882).

—— and David Brynmor-Jones, *The Welsh People* (London, 1900).

Richard, Henry, *Letters on the Social and Political Condition of the Principality of Wales* (London [1884]).

Richards, Robert, *Cymru'r Oesau Canol* (Wrexham, 1933).

Richards, Thomas, *The History of the Puritan Movement in Wales* (London, 1920).

Ripley, William Z., *The Races of Europe: A Sociological Study* (London/ New York, 1899).

Roberts, T. F., 'Gyrfa athrofaol y diweddar Mr. Thomas Ellis', *Y Traethodydd*, 54 (1899), 269–75.

Robinson, James Harvey, 'The new allies of history', in idem, *The New History: Essays Illustrating the Modern Historical Outlook* (New York, 1912), pp. 70–100.

Royal Commission on the Ancient and Historical Monuments and Constructions in Wales and Monmouthshire, *An Inventory of the Ancient Monuments in Wales and Monmouthshire. V, County of Carmarthen* (London, 1917).

Royal Commission on the Ancient and Historical Monuments of Wales, *An Inventory of the Ancient Monuments in Anglesey* (HMSO, 1937).

Rudler, F. W., 'Welsh anthropology', *Y Cymmrodor*, 4 (1881), 70–89.

Second Report of the Royal Commission on University Education in Wales: Evidence, Appendices, and Index (London, 1917), Cd. 8699.

Seebohm, Frederic, *The English Village Community Examined in its Relations to the Manorial and Tribal Systems and to the Common or Open Field System of Husbandry: An Essay in Economic History* (London, 1883).

——, *The Tribal System in Wales* (London, 1895).

Skeel, Caroline A. J., *The Council in the Marches of Wales: A Study in Local Government during the Sixteenth and Seventeenth Centuries* (London, 1903).

Smith, A. L., *Church and State in the Middle Ages: The Ford Lectures Delivered at Oxford in 1905* (Oxford, 1913).

Stephen, Leslie and Sidney Lee (eds), *Dictionary of National Biography*, 63 vols (London, 1885–1901).

Stephens, Thomas, *The Literature of the Kymry* (Llandovery, 1849).

Stephens, Thomas, *Welshmen: A Sketch of their History, from the Earliest Times to the Death of Llywelyn, the Last Welsh Prince* (London/Cardiff, 1901).

Tait, James, 'Thomas Frederick Tout', *EHR*, 45 (1930), 78–85.

Taylor, Isaac, *The Origin of the Aryans: An Account of the Prehistoric Ethnology and Civilisation of Europe* (London, 1889).

Thomas, John, *Hanes Eglwysi Annibynol Cymru*, vol. V (Dolgellau [1891]).

Tout, T. F., 'Llywelyn ab Iorwerth, called Llywelyn the Great (d.1240)', *DNB*, XXXIV, pp. 7–13.

——, 'Llywelyn ab Gruffydd (d.1282), prince of Wales', *DNB*, XXXIV, pp. 13–21.

——, 'The Welsh shires: a study in constitutional history' [1888], in idem, *Collected Papers*, II, pp. 1–20.

——, 'Wales and the march during the barons' wars' [1902], in idem, *Collected Papers*, II, pp. 47–100.

——, *The History of England from the Accession of Henry III. to the Death of Edward III. (1216–1377)* (London, 1905).

——, 'Schools of history' [1906], in idem, *Collected Papers*, I, pp. 93–109.

——, *Chapters in the Administrative History of Mediaeval England*, 6 vols (Manchester, 1920–33).

——, *The Collected Papers of Thomas Frederick Tout*, 2 vols (Manchester, 1932–4).

University College of North Wales Calendar.

University College of South Wales and Monmouthshire Calendar.

University of Wales, *Minutes of the Academic Board*.

——, *Minutes of the University Court*.

The Victoria History of the Counties of England. Hampshire and the Isle of Wight, Volume 1 (Westminster, 1900).

Vinogradoff, Paul, *The Growth of the Manor* (London, 1905).

—— and Frank Morgan (eds), *The Survey of the Honour of Denbigh 1334* (London, 1914).

W.W., 'Gruffydd ap Cynan', *The University College of North Wales Magazine*, 1, 1 [1888], 10–18.

Walter, Ferdinand, *Das alte Wales. Ein Beitrag zur Völker-, Rechts- und Kirchen-geschichte* (Bonn, 1859).

Warren, F. E., *The Liturgy and Ritual of the Celtic Church* (Oxford, 1881).

Williams, David, *History of Wales 1485–1931, For School Certificate* (London, 1934).

——, *John Frost: A Study in Chartism* (Cardiff, 1939).

Williams, Hugh, 'Some aspects of the Christian church in Wales during the fifth and sixth centuries', *THSC*, 1893–4, 55–132.

——, 'Heinrich Zimmer on the history of the Celtic church', *Zeitschrift für celtische Philologie*, 4 (1903), 527–74.

——, *Christianity in Early Britain* (Oxford, 1912).

Williams, Jane, *A History of Wales Derived from Authentic Sources* (London, 1869).

Williams, John, 'Influence of the Welsh on the formation of the British constitution', in *Transactions of the Royal National Eisteddfod of Wales, Liverpool, 1884* (Liverpool, 1885), pp. 455–518.

Williams, John (Ab Ithel) (ed.), *Annales Cambriae* (Rolls Series, London, 1860).

—— (ed.), *Brut y Tywysogion* (Rolls Series, London, 1860).

Williams, W. Llewelyn, *The Making of Modern Wales: Studies in the Tudor Settlement of Wales* (London, 1919).

Willis Bund, J. W., *The Celtic Church of Wales* (London, 1897).

Windle, Bertram C. A., *Life in Early Britain* (London, 1897).

Woodward, B. B., *The History of Wales, from the Earliest Times, to its Final Incorporation with the Kingdom of England* (London/New York, 1853).

Zimmer, Heinrich, 'Der Pan-Keltismus in Grossbritannien und Irland. I. Die heutige nationale Bewegung in Wales in ihrer geschichtlichen Entwickelung', *Preussische Jahrbücher*, 92 (1898), 426–94.

——, *The Celtic Church in Britain and Ireland* (London, 1902).

Zimmer, Stefan, 'Julius Rodenberg und Ferdinand Walter – deutsche Annäherungen an Wales im 19. Jahrhundert', in Bernhard Maier and Stefan Zimmer with Christiane Batke (eds), *150 Jahre 'Mabinogion' – deutsch-walisische Kulturbeziehungen* (Tübingen, 2001), pp. 253–64.

Secondary works

Anderson, R. D., *European Universities from the Enlightenment to 1914* (Oxford, 2004).

Augstein, H. F., *James Cowles Prichard's Anthropology: Remaking the Science of Man in Early Nineteenth-Century Britain* (Amsterdam/Atlanta, GA, 1999).

Ballantyne, Tony, *Orientalism and Race: Aryanism in the British Empire* (Houndmills/New York, 2002).

Banton, Michael, *The Idea of Race* (London, 1977).

Belchem, John and Donald M. MacRaild, 'Cosmopolitan Liverpool', in John Belchem (ed.), *Liverpool 800: Culture, Character and History* (Liverpool, 2006), pp. 311–91, 500–4.

Bentley, Michael, 'Introduction: approaches to modernity: western historiography since the enlightenment', in idem (ed.), *Companion to Historiography* (London, 1997), pp. 395–506.

——, *Modernizing England's Past: English Historiography in the Age of Modernism 1870–1970* (Cambridge, 2005).

Berger, Stefan (ed.), *Writing the Nation: A Global Perspective* (Houndmills, 2007).

——, Mark Donovan and Kevin Passmore (eds), *Writing National Histories: Western Europe since 1800* (London/New York, 1999).

—— and Neil Evans, 'Two faces of King Coal: the impact of historiographical traditions on comparative history in the Ruhr and south Wales', in Stefan Berger, Andy Croll and Norman Laporte (eds), *Towards a Comparative History of Coalfield Societies* (Aldershot, 2005), pp. 29–42.

—— and Chris Lorenz, 'Introduction: national history writing in Europe in a global age', in Berger and Lorenz (eds), *Contested Nation*, pp. 1–23.

—— and Chris Lorenz (eds), *The Contested Nation: Ethnicity, Class, Religion and Gender in National Histories* (Houndmills, 2008).

Beyen, Marnix and Benoît Majerus, 'Weak and strong nations in the Low Countries: national historiography and its "others" in Belgium, Luxembourg and the Netherlands in the nineteenth and twentieth centuries', in Stefan Berger and Chris Lorenz (eds), *The Contested Nation: Ethnicity, Class, Religion and Gender in National Histories* (Houndmills, 2008), pp. 283–310.

Bowler, Peter J., *The Invention of Progress: The Victorians and the Past* (Oxford, 1989).

Briggs, Asa, *A History of Longmans and their Books 1724–1990* (London/New Castle, DE, 2008).

Brock, M. G. and M. C. Curthoys (eds), *The History of the University of Oxford. Volume VII: Nineteenth-Century Oxford, Part 2* (Oxford, 2000).

Bromwich, Rachel, *Matthew Arnold and Celtic Literature: A Retrospect 1865–1965* (Oxford, 1965).

Burke, Peter, *The French Historical Revolution: The Annales School, 1929–89* (Cambridge, 1990).

Burrow, J. W., '"The village community" and the uses of history in late nineteenth-century England', in Neil McKendrick (ed.), *Historical Perspectives: Studies in English Thought and Society in Honour of J. H. Plumb* (London, 1974), pp. 255–84.

——, *A Liberal Descent: Victorian Historians and the English Past* (Cambridge, 1981).

——, 'Historicism and social evolution', in Benedikt Stuchtey and Peter Wende (eds), *British and German Historiography 1750–1950* (Oxford, 2000), pp. 250–64.

Carr, A. D., *Medieval Wales* (Houndmills, 1995).

Carr, Glenda, *William Owen Pughe* (Cardiff, 1983).

Champion, Timothy, 'The appropriation of the Phoenicians in British imperial ideology', *Nations and Nationalism*, 7 (2001), 451–65.

Chibnall, Marjorie, *The Debate on the Norman Conquest* (Manchester/New York, 1999).

Collini, Stefan, *Matthew Arnold: A Critical Portrait* (paperback edn, Oxford, 1994).

Cragoe, Matthew, 'Welsh electioneering and the purpose of parliament: "From radicalism to nationalism" reconsidered', *Parliamentary History*, 17 (1998), 113–30.

Cubitt, Geoffrey, 'Introduction: heroic reputations and exemplary lives', in idem and Allen Warren (eds), *Heroic Reputations and Exemplary Lives* (Manchester/New York, 2000), pp. 1–26.

Curthoys, M. C., 'The colleges in the new era', in M. G. Brock and M. C. Curthoys (eds), *The History of the University of Oxford. Volume VII: Nineteenth-Century Oxford, Part 2* (Oxford, 2000), pp. 115–57.

——, and Janet Howarth, 'Origins and destinations: the social mobility of Oxford men and women', in M. G. Brock and M. C. Curthoys (eds), *The History of the University of Oxford. Volume VII: Nineteenth-Century Oxford, Part 2* (Oxford, 2000), pp. 571–95.

Daniel, Glyn E., 'Who are the Welsh?', *Proceedings of the British Academy*, 40 (1954), 145–67.

Daskalov, Roumen, *The Making of a Nation in the Balkans: Historiography of the Bulgarian Revival* (Budapest/New York, 2004).

Davidoff, Leonore and Catherine Hall, *Family Fortunes* (revd edn, London/New York, 2002).

Davies, Ceri, *Welsh Literature and the Classical Tradition* (Cardiff, 1995).

Davies, D. Hywel, *The Welsh Nationalist Party 1925–1945: A Call to Nationhood* (Cardiff, 1983).

Davies, Hazel, *O. M. Edwards* (Cardiff, 1988).

Davies, J. Glyn, *Nationalism as a Social Phenomenon* (Liverpool, 1965).

Davies, R. R., *Historical Perception: Celts and Saxons* (Cardiff, 1979).
——, *The Revolt of Owain Glyn Dŵr* (Oxford, 1995).
Davies, Wendy, 'Looking backwards to the early medieval past: Wales and England, a contrast in approaches', *WHR*, 22 (2004–5), 197–221.
de S. Honey, J. R. and M. C. Curthoys, 'Oxford and schooling', in M. G. Brock and M. C. Curthoys (eds), *The History of the University of Oxford. Volume VII: Nineteenth-Century Oxford, Part 2* (Oxford, 2000), pp. 545–69.
Deneckere, Gita and Thomas Welskopp, 'The "nation" and "class": European national master narratives and their social "other"', in Stefan Berger and Chris Lorenz (eds), *The Contested Nation: Ethnicity, Class, Religion and Gender in National Histories* (Houndmills, 2008), pp. 135–70.
Dewey, Clive, 'Celtic agrarian legislation and the Celtic revival: historicist implications of Gladstone's Irish and Scottish land acts 1870–1886', *Past & Present*, 64 (1974), 30–70.
Edwards, Andrew and Wil Griffith, 'Welsh national identity and governance, 1918–45', in Duncan Tanner et al. (eds), *Debating Nationhood and Governance in Britain, 1885–1945: Perspectives from the 'Four Nations'* (Manchester, 2006), pp. 118–45.
Edwards, Hywel Teifi, *Coffáu Llywelyn 1856–1956* (Llandysul, 1983).
——, 'John Rhŷs yn achos trafferth', *Y Traethodydd*, 161 (2006), 162–86.
——, '"Gosodir ni yn îs na phawb": Cymru Victoria ar drywydd enwogrwydd', in Jason Walford Davies (ed.), *Gweledigaethau: Cyfrol Deyrnged Yr Athro Gwyn Thomas* (Llandybïe, 2007), pp. 159–72.
——, *The National Pageant of Wales* (Llandysul, 2009).
Ellis, E. L., *The University College of Wales, Aberystwyth, 1872–1972* (Cardiff, 1972).
Ellis, John S., *Investiture: Royal Ceremony and National Identity in Wales, 1911–1969* (Cardiff, 2008).
Emanuel, Hywel D., 'Studies in the Welsh laws', in Elwyn Davies (ed.), *Celtic Studies in Wales: A Survey* (Cardiff, 1963), pp. 71–100.
Engman, Max, 'National conceptions of history in Finland', in Erik Lönnroth, Karl Molin and Ragnar Björk (eds), *Conceptions of National History: Proceedings of Nobel Symposium 78* (Berlin/New York, 1994), pp. 49–63.
Erdmann, Karl Dietrich, *Toward a Global Community of Historians: The International Historical Congresses and the International Committee of Historical Sciences, 1898–2000* (New York/Oxford, 2005).
Evans, Neil,'Finding a new story: the search for a usable past in Wales, 1869–1930', *THSC*, new ser., 10 (2004), 144–62.

——, '"When men and mountains meet": historians' explanations of the history of Wales, 1890–1970', *WHR*, 22 (2004–5), 222–51.

——, 'Casting nets: modern Wales', in Geraint H. Jenkins and Gareth Elwyn Jones (eds), *Degrees of Influence: A Memorial Volume for Glanmor Williams* (Cardiff, 2008), pp. 85–100.

Evans, R. J. W., review of Geraint H. Jenkins, *A Concise History of Wales*, *WHR*, 24, 4 (2009), 187–9.

Fewster, Derek, *Visions of Past Glory: Nationalism and the Construction of Early Finnish History* (Studia Fennica Historica, 11; Helsinki, 2006).

Floud, Roderick, 'Britain, 1860–1914: a survey', in idem and Donald McCloskey (eds), *The Economic History of Britain since 1700*, vol. 2, *1860–1939* (2nd edn, Cambridge, 1994), pp. 1–28.

Foster, Idris, 'Sir John Rhŷs', in D. Ellis Evans, John G. Griffith and E. M. Jope (eds), *Proceedings of the Seventh International Congress of Celtic Studies, Oxford, 1983* (Oxford, 1986), pp. 10–14.

Fritzsche, Peter, *Stranded in the Present: Modern Time and the Melancholy of History* (Cambridge, MA/London, 2004).

Gaffney, Angela, '"A national Valhalla for Wales": D. A. Thomas and the Welsh historical sculpture scheme, 1910–1916', *THSC*, new ser., 5 (1999), 131–44.

Gay, Peter, *Style in History* (London, 1975).

Geary, Patrick J., *The Myth of Nations: The Medieval Origins of Europe* (Princeton, NJ/Oxford, 2002).

Goldstein, Doris S.,'The organizational development of the British historical profession, 1884–1921', *Bulletin of the Institute of Historical Research*, 55 (1982), 180–93.

——, 'The professionalization of history in Britain in the late nineteenth and early twentieth centuries', *Storia della Storiografia*, 3 (1983), 3–27.

——, 'Confronting time: the Oxford school of history and the non-Darwinian revolution', *Storia della Storiografia*, 45 (2004), 3–27.

Grafton, Anthony, *The Footnote: A Curious History* (London, 1997).

Green, Vivian, *The Commonwealth of Lincoln College, 1427–1977* (Oxford, 1979).

Griffith, Wil, 'Devolutionist tendencies in Wales, 1885–1914', in Duncan Tanner et al. (eds), *Debating Nationhood and Governance in Britain, 1885–1945: Perspectives from the 'Four Nations'* (Manchester/New York, 2006), pp. 89–117.

Griffiths, Gwyn, *Land of My Fathers: Evan, James, Their Lives and Times* (Llanrwst, 2006).

Hadfield, Andrew, 'Briton and Scythian: Tudor representations of Irish origins', *Irish Historical Studies*, 28 (1993), 390–408.

Harrison, Robert, Aled Jones and Peter Lambert, 'The primacy of polit-ical history', in Peter Lambert and Phillipp Schofield (eds), *Making History: An Introduction to the History and Practices of a Discipline* (London/New York, 2004), pp. 38–54.

Hilton, Tim, *John Ruskin: The Later Years* (New Haven, CT/London, 2000).

Hinchcliff, Peter, 'Religious issues, 1870–1914', in M. G. Brock and M. C. Curthoys (eds), *The History of the University of Oxford. Volume VII: Nineteenth-Century Oxford, Part 2* (Oxford, 2000), pp. 97–112.

—— and John Prest, 'Jowett, Benjamin (1817–1893)', *ODNB*.

Hingley, Richard, *The Recovery of Roman Britain 1586–1906: A Colony So Fertile* (Oxford, 2008).

Horsman, Reginald, 'Origins of racial Anglo-Saxonism in Great Britain before 1850', *Journal of the History of Ideas*, 37 (1976), 387–410.

Howarth, Janet, '"In Oxford but . . . not of Oxford": the women's colleges', in M. G. Brock and M. C. Curthoys (eds), *The History of the University of Oxford. Volume VII: Nineteenth-Century Oxford, Part 2* (Oxford, 2000), pp. 237–307.

Hughes, J. Elwyn, *Arloeswr Dwyieithedd: Dan Isaac Davies 1839–1887* (Cardiff, 1984).

Hughes, Lowri Angharad, 'O. M. Edwards: ei waith a'i weledigaeth', in Gerwyn Wiliams (ed.), *Ysgrifau Beirniadol XXIX* (Denbigh, 2010), pp. 51–77.

Humphreys, E. Morgan, *Gwŷr Enwog Gynt: Argraffiadau ac Atgofion Personol* (n.p., 1950).

Humphreys, Melvin et al., *Llanfyllin: Portrait of an Age* (Llanfyllin, 2002).

Iggers, Georg G., 'Changing conceptions of national history since the French Revolution: a critical comparative perspective', in Erik Lönnroth, Karl Molin and Ragnar Björk (eds), *Conceptions of National History: Proceedings of Nobel Symposium 78* (Berlin/New York, 1994), pp. 132–50.

Jann, Rosemary, *The Art and Science of Victorian History* (Columbus, OH, 1985).

Jenkins, David, *Thomas Gwynn Jones: Cofiant* (2nd edn, Denbigh, 1994).

Jenkins, Geraint H., *'Doc Tom': Thomas Richards* (Cardiff, 1999).

——, '"Wales, the Welsh and the Welsh language": introduction', in idem (ed.), *The Welsh Language and its Social Domains 1801–1911* (Cardiff, 2000), pp. 1–35.

——, 'Clio and Wales: Welsh remembrancers and historical writing, 1751–2001', *THSC*, new ser., 8 (2002), 119–36.

——, 'Evans, Theophilus (1693–1767)', *ODNB*.

Jenkins, Gwyn, 'The Welsh Outlook 1914–33', *NLWJ*, 24 (1985–6), 463–92.

Jenkyns, Richard, 'Classical studies, 1872–1914', in M. G. Brock and M. C. Curthoys, (eds), *The History of the University of Oxford. Volume VII: Nineteenth-Century Oxford, Part 2* (Oxford, 2000), pp. 327–31.

Johnson, Charles, revised G. H. Martin, 'Hall, Hubert (1857–1944)', *ODNB*.

Johnson, R. A., revised M. A. Williams, 'Rees, William [*pseud.* Gwilym Hiraethog] (1802–1833)', *ODNB*.

Jones, Aled Gruffydd, *Press, Politics and Society: A History of Journalism in Wales* (Cardiff, 1993).

—— and Bill Jones, 'The Welsh world and the British empire, *c.*1850–1939: an exploration', *Journal of Imperial and Commonwealth History*, 31 (2003), 57–81.

——, 'Empire and the Welsh press', in Simon J. Potter (ed.), *Newspapers and Empire: Ireland and Britain, c.1857–1921* (Dublin, 2004), pp. 75–91.

Jones, Bill, 'Rooms at the top: Cardiff's municipal museum, 1862–1912', *Llafur*, 9, 4 (2007), 26–46.

Jones, Dot, *Statistical Evidence relating to the Welsh Language 1801–1911 / Tystiolaeth Ystadegol yn ymwneud â'r Iaith Gymraeg 1801–1911* (Cardiff, 1998).

Jones, Glanville R. J., 'The tribal system in Wales: a re-assessment in the light of settlement studies', *WHR*, 1, 2 (1961), 111–32.

Jones, H. S., 'Pattison, Mark (1813–1884)', *ODNB*.

——, *Intellect and Character in Victorian England: Mark Pattison and the Invention of the Don* (Cambridge, 2007).

Jones, Ieuan Gwynedd, '1848 and 1868: "Brad y Llyfrau Gleision" and Welsh politics', in idem, *Mid-Victorian Wales: The Observers and the Observed* (Cardiff, 1992), pp. 103–65, 186–98.

Jones, Philip Henry and Eiluned Rees (eds), *A Nation and its Books: A History of the Book in Wales* (Aberystwyth, 1998).

Jones, R. Merfyn, 'The Liverpool Welsh', in idem and D. Ben Rees, *The Liverpool Welsh and their Religion* (Liverpool, 1984), pp. 20–43.

Jones, R. Tudur, *Yr Undeb: Hanes Undeb yr Annibynwyr Cymraeg, 1872–1972* (Swansea, 1975).

——, *Congregationalism in Wales*, ed. Robert Pope (Cardiff, 2004).

——, *Faith and the Crisis of a Nation: Wales, 1890–1914* (Cardiff, 2004).

Jones, Richard Wyn, *Rhoi Cymru'n Gyntaf: Syniadaeth Plaid Cymru*, vol. I (Cardiff, 2007).

Kadish, Alon, 'Toynbee, Arnold (1852–1883)', *ODNB*.

Kay, Elaine, 'Horton, Robert Forman (1855–1934)', *ODNB*.

Kendrick, T. D., *British Antiquity* (London, 1950).

Kidd, Colin, *British Identities before Nationalism: Ethnicity and Nationhood in the Atlantic World 1600–1800* (Cambridge, 1999).

Kjeldstadli, Knut, 'History as science', in William H. Hubbard et al. (eds), *Making a Historical Culture: Historiography in Norway* (Oslo, 1995), pp. 52–81.

Klausner, David N., 'Evans, John Gwenogvryn (1852–1930)', *ODNB*.

Knowles, David, *Great Historical Enterprises and Problems in Monastic History* (London, 1963).

Koninckx, Christian, 'Historiography and nationalism in Belgium', in Erik Lönnroth, Karl Molin and Ragnar Björk (eds), *Conceptions of National History: Proceedings of Nobel Symposium 78* (Berlin/New York, 1994), pp. 34–48.

Kretchmer, Richard, *Llanfyllin: Ei Hanes trwy Luniau* (Welshpool/Llanfyllin, 1992).

Kuper, Adam, 'The rise and fall of Maine's patriarchal society', in Alan Diamond (ed.), *The Victorian Achievement of Sir Henry Maine: A Centennial Appraisal* (Cambridge, 1991), pp. 99–110.

Lambert, Peter, 'The professionalization and institutionalization of history', in Stefan Berger, Heiko Feldner and Kevin Passmore (eds), *Writing History: Theory and Practice* (London, 2003), pp. 42–60.

Lambert, W. R., *Drink and Sobriety in Victorian Wales c.1820–c.1895* (Cardiff, 1983).

Leerssen, Joep, 'Englishness, ethnicity and Matthew Arnold', *European Journal of English Studies*, 10, 1 (2006), 63–79.

——, *National Thought in Europe: A Cultural History* (Amsterdam, 2006).

Lewis, Henry, 'Preface', in Elwyn Davies (ed.), *Celtic Studies in Wales: A Survey* (Cardiff, 1963), pp. v–xii.

Löffler, Marion, *The Literary and Historical Legacy of Iolo Morganwg, 1826–1926* (Cardiff, 2007).

Lönnroth, Erik, Karl Molin and Ragnar Björk (eds), *Conceptions of National History: Proceedings of Nobel Symposium 78* (Berlin/New York, 1994).

Lyon, Bryce, *Henri Pirenne: A Biographical and Intellectual Study* (Ghent, 1974).

MacDougall, Hugh A., *Racial Myth in English History: Trojans, Teutons, and Anglo-Saxons* (Montreal/Hanover, NH, 1982).

Macfarlane, Alan D. J., 'Some contributions of Maine to history and anthropology', in Alan Diamond (ed.), *The Victorian Achievement of Sir Henry Maine: A Centennial Appraisal* (Cambridge, 1991), pp. 111–42.

McKisack, May, *Medieval History in the Tudor Age* (Oxford, 1971).

Marten, C. H. K., revised Richard Symons, 'Fletcher, Charles Robert Leslie (1857–1934)', *ODNB*.

Martin, F. X., 'Appendix 3: The vacant chair at University College, Dublin, 24 May 1916–24 May 1918', in idem and F. J. Byrne (eds), *The Scholar Revolutionary: Eoin MacNeill, 1867–1945, and the Making of the New Ireland* (Shannon, 1973), pp. 385–90.

Mason, J. F. A., 'Edwards, Sir (John) Goronwy (1891–1976)', *ODNB*.

Mason, Rhiannon, *Museums, Nations, Identities: Wales and its National Museums* (Cardiff, 2007).

Masterman, Neville, *The Forerunner: The Dilemmas of Tom Ellis 1859–1899* (Swansea/Llandybïe, 1972).

Millward, E. G., '"Cenedl o bobl ddewrion": y rhamant hanesyddol yn Oes Victoria', in idem, *Cenedl o Bobl Ddewrion: Agweddau ar Lenyddiaeth Oes Victoria* (Llandysul, 1991), pp. 104–19.

——, *Yr Arwrgerdd Gymraeg: Ei Thwf a'i Thranc* (Cardiff, 1998).

Milne, Graeme J., *Trade and Traders in Mid-Victorian Liverpool: Mercantile Business and the Making of a World Port* (Liverpool, 2000).

Morgan, D. Densil, *Lewis Edwards* (Cardiff, 2009).

Morgan, Kenneth O., 'Welsh nationalism: the historical background', *Journal of Contemporary History*, 6, 1 (1971), 153–72.

——, *Rebirth of a Nation: Wales 1880–1980* (Oxford/Cardiff, 1981).

——, *Wales in British Politics, 1868–1922* (paperback edn, Cardiff, 1991).

——, 'Renaissance man', in Geraint H. Jenkins and Gareth Elwyn Jones (eds), *Degrees of Influence: A Memorial Volume for Glanmor Williams* (Cardiff, 2008), pp. 182–91.

Morgan, Prys, 'The creation of the National Museum and National Library', in John Osmond (ed.), *Myths, Memories and Futures: The National Library and National Museum in the Story of Wales* (Cardiff, 2007), pp. 13–22.

——, 'Lingen, Arnold a Palgrave: tri Sais a'u hagweddau at Gymru', in Tegwyn Jones and Huw Walters (eds), *Cawr i'w Genedl: Cyfrol i Gyfarch yr Athro Hywel Teifi Edwards* (Llandysul, 2008), pp. 87–106.

—— (ed.) *Brad y Llyfrau Gleision: Ysgrifau ar Hanes Cymru* (Llandysul, 1991)

National Library of Wales, *A List of Dissertations Submitted and Accepted for Higher Degrees in the University of Wales 1899–1949* (Aberystwyth, 1950).

Nicklas, Thomas, 'Gallier, Germanen, Trojaner. Zur Geschichtspolitik im Frankreich des 16. Jahrhunderts', *Francia*, 32, 2 (2005), 145–58.

Oldstone-Moore, Christopher, *Hugh Price Hughes: Founder of a New Methodism, Conscience of a New Nonconformity* (Cardiff, 1999).

O'Leary, Paul, 'Accommodation and resistance: a comparison of cultural identities in Ireland and Wales, *c.*1880–1914', in S. J. Connolly (ed.), *Kingdoms United? Great Britain and Ireland since 1500* (Dublin, 1999), pp. 123–34.

——, 'The languages of patriotism in Wales 1840–1880', in Geraint H. Jenkins (ed.), *The Welsh Language and its Social Domains 1801–1911* (Cardiff, 2000), pp. 533–60.

Parry, Graham, 'Edward Lhuyd: from formed stones to standing stones', *WHR*, 25, 1 (2010), 3–19.

Parry, Thomas, 'Daniel Silvan Evans, 1818–1903', *THSC*, 1981, 109–25.

Pooley, Colin G., 'The residential segregation of migrant communities in mid-Victorian Liverpool', *Transactions of the Institute of British Geographers*, new ser., 2 (1977), 364–82.

——, and John C. Doherty, 'The longitudinal study of migration: Welsh migration to English towns in the nineteenth century', in Colin G. Pooley and Ian D. Whyte (eds), *Migrants, Emigrants and Immigrants: A Social History of Migration* (London/New York, 1991), pp. 143–73.

Pryce, Huw, 'Cenedligrwydd a chymdeithas: dehongli oes y tywysogion', *TCHS*, 67 (2006), 12–29.

——, *Hynafiaid: Hil, Cenedl a Gwreiddiau'r Cymru. Darlith Goffa Syr Thomas Parry-Williams 2006* (Aberystwyth, 2007).

——, 'The Normans in Welsh history', in C. P. Lewis (ed.), *Anglo-Norman Studies XXX* (Woodbridge, 2008), pp. 1–18.

Pryce, W. T. R., 'Region or national territory? Regionalism and the idea of the country of Wales, *c.*1927–1998', *WHR*, 23, 2 (2006), 99–152.

Pugh, R. B., '*The Victoria County History*: its origin and progress', in idem (ed.), *The Victoria History of the Counties of England: General Introduction* (London, 1970), pp. 1–27.

Readman, Paul, 'The place of the past in English culture, *c.* 1890–1914', *Past & Present*, 186 (2005), 147–99.

Reynolds, Susan, 'Medieval *origines gentium* and the community of the realm', *History*, 68 (1983), 375–90.

Roach, John, *Public Examinations in England 1850–1900* (Cambridge, 1971).

Roberts, Brynley F., 'The *Historia Regum Britanniae* in Wales', in idem (ed.), *Brut y Brenhinedd: Llanstephan MS. 1 Version* (Dublin, 1971), pp. 55–74.

——, 'Scholarly publishing 1820–1922', in Philip Henry Jones and Eiluned Rees (eds), *A Nation and its Books: A History of the Book in Wales* ([Aberystwyth], 1998), pp. 221–35.

Roberts, Gwyneth Tyson, *The Language of the Blue Books: The Perfect Instrument of Empire* (Cardiff, 1998).

Roberts, Llion Pryderi, '"Y mae efe, wedi marw, yn llefaru eto": mawl a moes yng nghofiannau'r pregethwyr', *Y Traethodydd*, 161 (2006), 78–97.

Roberts, Peter, 'The "Act of Union" in Welsh history', *THSC*, 1972–3, 49–72.

Rowley-Conwy, Peter, *From Genesis to Prehistory: The Archaeological Three Age System and its Contested Reception in Denmark, Britain, and Ireland* (Oxford, 2007).

Shannon, Richard, *Gladstone and the Bulgarian Agitation 1876* (London, 1963).

Shaw, John, 'Land, people and nation: historicist voices in the Highland land campaign, *c.*1850–1883', in Eugenio F. Biagini (ed.), *Citizenship and Community: Liberals, Radicals and Collective Identitities in the British Isles, 1865–1932* (Cambridge, 1996), pp. 305–24.

Sims-Williams, Patrick, 'The visionary Celt: the construction of an ethnic preconception', *Cambridge Medieval Celtic Studies*, 11 (summer 1986), 71–96.

Slee, Peter R. H., *Learning and a Liberal Education: The Study of Modern History in the Universities of Oxford, Cambridge and Manchester, 1800–1914* (Manchester, 1986).

Smail, Daniel Lord, *On Deep History and the Brain* (Berkeley/Los Angeles/London, 2008).

Smith, J. Beverley and Llinos Beverley Smith, 'Wales: politics, government and law', in S. H. Rigby (ed.), *A Companion to Britain in the Later Middle Ages* (Malden, MA/Oxford, 2003), pp. 309–34.

Smith, Llinos Beverley, 'Llywelyn ap Gruffudd and the Welsh historical consciousness', *WHR*, 12 (1984–5), 1–28.

Smith, Robert, *Schools, Politics and Society: Elementary Education in Wales, 1870–1902* (Cardiff, 1999).

Soffer, Reba N., 'Nation, duty, character and confidence: history at Oxford, 1850–1914', *Historical Journal*, 30 (1987), 77–104.

——, *Discipline and Power: The University, History, and the Making of an English Elite, 1870–1930* (Stanford, CA, 1994).

——, 'Modern history', in M. G. Brock and M. C. Curthoys (eds), *The History of the University of Oxford. Volume VII: Nineteenth-Century Oxford, Part 2* (Oxford, 2000), pp. 361–84.

Stapleton, Julia, *Englishness and the Study of Politics: The Social and Political Thought of Ernest Barker* (Cambridge, 1994).

Stepan, Nancy, *The Idea of Race in Science: Great Britain 1800–1960* (London, 1982).

Stocking, George W., 'From chronology to ethnology: James Cowles Prichard and British anthropology 1800–1850', in idem (ed.), James Cowles Prichard, *Researches into the Physical History of Man* (Chicago, IL/London, 1973), pp. ix–cx.

——, *Victorian Anthropology* (New York, 1987).

Stone, Lawrence, 'The size and composition of the Oxford student body 1580–1909', in idem (ed.), *The University in Society*, vol. I (Princeton, NJ, 1974), pp. 3–110.

Taylor, M. A., 'Miller, Hugh (1802–1856)', *ODNB*.

Thomas, Ben Bowen, 'The Cambrians and the nineteenth-century crisis in Welsh studies, 1847–70', *Arch. Camb.*, 127 (1978), 1–15.

Tosh, John, *A Man's Place: Masculinity and the Middle-Class Home in Victorian England* (New Haven, CT/London, 1999).

Trigger, Bruce G., *A History of Archaeological Thought* (Cambridge, 1989).

Vardy, Steven Bela, *Modern Hungarian Historiography* (East European Monographs, 17, Boulder, CO, 1976).

Wakelin, Peter and Ralph A. Griffiths (eds), *Hidden Histories: Discovering the Heritage of Wales* (Aberystwyth, 2008).

Waller, P. J., *Democracy and Sectarianism: A Political and Social History of Liverpool 1868–1939* (Liverpool, 1981).

Walsh, W. H., 'The zenith of Greats', in M. G. Brock and M. C. Curthoys (eds), *The History of the University of Oxford. Volume VII: Nineteenth-Century Oxford, Part 2* (Oxford, 2000), pp. 311–26.

Walters, Huw, 'The periodical press to 1914', in Philip Henry Jones and Eiluned Rees (eds), *A Nation and its Books: A History of the Book in Wales* (Aberystwyth, 1998), pp. 197–208.

Webster, J. R., 'The Welsh Intermediate Education Act of 1889', in Owen E. Jones (ed.), *The Welsh Intermediate Education Act of 1889: A Centenary Appraisal* ([Cardiff] 1989), pp. 11–26.

White, Hayden, *Metahistory: The Historical Imagination in Nineteenth-Century Europe* (Baltimore, MD/London, 1973).

Williams, Christopher J., 'A. N. Palmer, historian of Wrexham', *Denbighshire Historical Society Transactions*, 46 (1997), 109–36.

Williams, Daniel G., *Ethnicity and Cultural Authority: From Arnold to Du Bois* (Edinburgh, 2006).

Williams, Emyr W., 'Liberalism in Wales and the politics of Welsh home rule 1886–1910', *Bulletin of the Board of Celtic Studies*, 37 (1990), 191–207.

Williams, Glanmor, 'Some protestant views of early British Church history', in idem, *Welsh Reformation Essays* (Cardiff, 1967), pp. 207–19.

——, 'Local and national history in Wales', in D. Huw Owen (ed.), *Settlement and Society in Wales* (Cardiff, 1989), pp. 7–26.

——, 'Haneswyr a'r Deddfau Uno', in Geraint H. Jenkins (ed.), *Cof Cenedl X* (Llandysul, 1995), pp. 31–60.

Williams, Gwyn A., 'Ambiguous hero: Hugh Owen and Liberal Wales', in idem, *The Welsh in their History* (London, 1982), pp. 151–70.

Williams, Ioan, 'Gwilym Hiraethog (William Rees, 1802–83)', in Hywel Teifi Edwards (ed.), *A Guide to Welsh Literature* c.*1800–1900* (Cardiff, 2000), pp. 48–68.

Williams, J. E. Caerwyn, 'Cenedlaetholdeb haneswyr Cymru gynnar Rhydychen', in Geraint H. Jenkins (ed.), *Cof Cenedl XIII: Ysgrifau ar Hanes Cymru* (Llandysul, 1998), pp. 1–32.

Williams, J. Gwynn, *The University College of North Wales: Foundations 1884–1927* (Cardiff, 1985).

——, *The University Movement in Wales* (Cardiff, 1993).

——, *The University of Wales 1893–1939* (Cardiff, 1997).

——, 'Owen, Sir Hugh (1804–1881)', *ODNB*.

Williams, John, *Digest of Welsh Historical Statistics*, vol. I ([Cardiff] 1985).

Woolf, Daniel, 'Of nations, nationalism, and national identity', in Q. Edward Wang and Franz L. Fillafer (eds), *The Many Faces of Clio: Cross-cultural Approaches to Historiography, Essays in Honor of Georg G. Iggers* (New York/Oxford, 2007), pp. 71–103.

Young, Robert J. C., *The Idea of English Ethnicity* (Malden, MA, 2008).

Unpublished theses

Easterling, Ruth Clarke, 'The friars in Wales' (unpublished MA thesis, University of Wales, 1913).

Hughes, Lowri Angharad, 'Writing the Welsh people: O. M. Edwards and the shaping of Welsh identity' (unpublished D.Phil. thesis, University of Oxford, 2007).

Jones, Manon, '"I godi'r hen wlad yn ei hôl": arolwg o weithiau O. M. Edwards ar hanes Cymru' (unpublished MA thesis, Cardiff University, 2006).

Llywelyn, Jen, '"The sun in splendour": George M. Ll. Davies (1880–1949), pacifist, conscientious objector and peace-maker, and the creation of a Nonconformist saint' (unpublished Ph.D. thesis, Aberystwyth University, 2010).

Ward, Dora, 'The mediaeval lordship of Montgomery' (unpublished MA thesis, University of Wales, 1924).

Website

Clwyd-Powys Archaeological Trust, 'Historic landscape characterisation: the Tanat Valley': *http://www.cpat.org.uk/projects/longer/histland/tanat/ tanat.htm* (last accessed 28 May 2010).

Index